The
Colour
of
Hope

The Colour of Hope

Poems of happiness in uncertain times

JEN FEROZE

Matador
9 Priory Business Park,
Wistow Road, Kibworth Beauchamp,
Leicestershire. LE8 0RX
Tel: 0116 279 2299
Email: books@troubador.co.uk
Web: www.troubador.co.uk/matador
Twitter: @matadorbooks

ISBN 978 1800461 864

British Library Cataloguing in Publication Data.
A catalogue record for this book is available from the British Library.

Printed by Printed and bound in Great Britain by 4edge Limited
Typeset in 11pt Garamond by Troubador Publishing Ltd, Leicester, UK

Matador is an imprint of Troubador Publishing Ltd

For Matt, Eleanor and Daniel – my happy thoughts.

Contents

FOREWORD

This project started out as a way to cheer up a friend. I asked her to name me three things that would be guaranteed to make her feel happy, without thinking too hard or agonising too long over it, and I combined them into a poem to lift her spirits.

That was in the middle of March... and then lockdown happened. It quickly became clear that 2020 was going to be a year in which crumbs of happiness would need to be gathered and stored in whatever way possible, and so *The Colour of Hope* was born.

Each of the poems in this collection is based on three 'happy thoughts' of its individual recipient, and all have been written while the world at large grapples with the effects of the Coronavirus pandemic and our own little worlds shrink down to the thresholds of our homes.

I received a wonderful range of briefs. From the beautifully universal – a longing for nature and freedom, time spent with family, the expanse of sea and sky, and summers spent in other lands; to the gloriously particular – snaffling a Toffee Crisp from the fridge late at night, Fleetwood Mac songs, baking scones, detective novels and Ceilidh dancing. I decided not to share the specific briefs that inspired each of the poems, preferring instead for you to draw your own conclusions, to find your own pieces of happiness within each one.

2020 will be one for the history books a year that has created emergencies on many fronts, not least the emotional. 60% of adults, and 68% of young people in the UK reported a decline in their mental health during lockdown. Mental health charities are working harder than ever to provide support to the vulnerable and in need, and every little helps. 20% from the sale of this book will be donated to Mind, to help provide a bit of light in these uncertain times.

I hope you enjoy this little museum of happiness that I've put together, and that you find comfort in these pages.

Here's to resilience. Here's to joy. Here's to hope.

Love,
Jen

For Kirsty

For a number of weeks,
I've held happiness curled tight
as a new leaf against my ribcage.
This morning there was music on the air,
so I tried a key and let it out.

Right now, happiness slinks across the lawn
like my mother's eldest cat,
chasing shadows in its own sweet time.
Fat, aloof and utterly secure
in its own beauty.

Happiness cascades
around the kitchen –
Stevie Nicks singing of velvet
and paper and lace –
notes rolling down the walls,
escaping like sweet smoke
around the window frames.

As I watch, happiness grows deeper, less fragile,
its colours strengthening. I'm nervous.
It's been a while.
But I keep my fluttering hands in my pockets.
I give it space to breathe.

When I look up, I see
happiness has placed flags
in each of the chimney pots,
the rooftops a sudden festival
calling to friends, neighbours,
passing blackbirds.

The garden smells of old rain and hyacinths.
Tomorrow I will paint my lips the colour of cherries.
So ripe they could burst.

For Faye

Up ahead, Stanley busies himself among the primroses.
Nose down, truffling out the scent of every rabbit
that's ever flashed across this laneway.

Along the path and into the trees, I can hear
my family's laughter. Banter in soprano and baritone
echoing off the branches like the satisfying thwack of tennis balls.

In my coat pocket, my phone glows with connections,
with the positivity of good people, in this together.
This virtual house that I have built has foundations lined with gold.

Look up.
The sky is the colour of hope.
There are new buds unfurling.

For Jennifer

The radio on the windowsill
dives between the seventies
and static crackle. I beat eggs,
add more butter to the foaming pan.

At the table, the boys are busy
with glue and shreds of paper,
a crazed, Gaudi-edged rainbow
emerging from beneath their sticky fingers.

There are whispers
bubbling between them –
heads glossy as conkers –
a brief, sharp geyser of silvery laughter.

Moments like these, our small world
slides into focus. The eggs cling to the spoon,
pale and creamy. A few more seconds.
There's suddenly music.

Swagger and feline slink,
the metallic velvet of Al Green.
I shoot the radio a grateful smile.
I think of the fall of confetti,
the heat of a dance floor years ago.
I hear your tread on the stairs.

For Catherine

The season is changing,
sliding from sepia into sudden colour.
Gardens are splashed with birdsong.
Despite everything,
everything,
there are pockets of real sunshine.
Looking out over fens and fields,
my mind spins months hence.

Take me to the other side of summer,
please. Take me to the time when freedom
tastes familiar again.
When the meadows towards Grantchester
are speckled with walkers,
and picnic hampers
packed with the last of the sweet strawberries
and hunks of warm bread from Market Square.

Show me Rocket
shooting ahead into crunching piles
of gold and russet, paws
sending up leaves like sparks.
And later, when it's colder,
when the house begins to doze,
let my summer-stunned ideas take flight,
matching the early thunder of colour
in the darkening sky.
An explosion of chrysanthemum and sparkle,
the smell of wood smoke and sugar on the air.

For Lindsay

These tiny, vivid rectangles of light
are our portals. In them, I see corners
of my sisters' houses: a square of wall
the colour of sea mist, the cushions we bought
together at the market;
hear my daughter's laugh
bounce through the screen before she appears.
I think of us all months ago,
salt striped, bedrizzled, together.
Half a Norfolk beach in our hair,
Moose loping ahead in impossibly long, damp strides,
our squawking tide of chatter
snatched by the wind and thrown to the gulls.

Still our talk is like water.
Words that flute and trickle, that run
over themselves in their urgency to be spoken,
the clear cold of a back garden stream.
There is always too much to say,
and I only spoke to you yesterday.
Afterwards, the house is quiet.
Richard is in the kitchen,
tucking doughy mounds in under tea towels
like chubby toddlers. I join him,
and time softens at the edges, butter
slowly melting. We work in comfortable silence –
no rush, no need. Sift and knead,
fold and stretch. We revel in tiny snowfalls of icing sugar,
the quiet triumph of licking the spoon.

For Sarah

Some people's hearts are forested,
jewelled with sunlight
and the whispered secrets of the trees.
Some feel salt air and seaspray
crash against their ribcages
with every deep exhale.
Some have threaded theirs with stars,
they wait quietly for the velvet fall
of evening, feel the soft glow of ages
move in their chests as they fall asleep.

Mine has four walls and a window,
where light the colour of lemons
patterns my writing table.
The words have spilled over.
They started as lithe floor puddles
but have begun to climb.
Tendrils of typography loop
and twist themselves around the walls –
the beginnings of so many stories.
They have folded themselves
into creatures of language. Cranes
flocking gently across the arched ceiling,
thousands of them,
a hive of black and white bees,
their honey shockingly, sweetly golden.
The warm winding of cats
like smoke around my ankles –
at once mine and not mine.

In the hazy blue distance,
the mountains rise. Cold and certain.
Full of their own stories.
They leave me breathless.

For Andri

This afternoon,
the sun has found the vase
on my office table,
and I can no longer ignore the peonies.

This one raspberry sorbet,
that one coy in frills
the colour of first love, there
a tight bud teasing a watermelon cascade,
tomorrow or perhaps the day after.

I sit with legs tucked up and sketch,
wrist loose, fingers dancing into stems,
and the fragile globes of petals that hold the light
like a child's cupped hands in a stream.

I don't know when it is that the music starts.

When I look up from my arcs
and swoops of colour, my garden studio
is bleached of shadows and sandy underfoot.
The London sky no longer
a pale imitation of summer, peppered with cloud
and doing its best.

It blazes cerulean, floods my body with heat,
makes my feet move the way
they only ever do on white isles,
when the rhythm wraps itself around me

like silk and sugar,
lime and jasmine and freedom.

I swirl more colour on the page,
to hell with the lines. To hell
with the propriety of peonies.
This is a howl for summer unfettered.
For ageless hot nights, rich beats,
for salted hair and perfumed sky
and the ballroom of the stars.
For us. For you.

For Gayle

The sky is stained with the soft pink of evening
and you ask me where I've been.
Look closely, and you'll see
waves cresting behind my eyes.
Let me paint you a picture with sea glass
and sand treasures. Gently gnarled driftwood,
a mosaic of mussel shell pieces,
the bluest blue there is.

Sit with me a while in the garden,
let me tell you a story of the ocean's music.
Of pale sunlight and salt air that raises
the hairs on my arms. Of the low cliffs
starred with daisies and sea thrift.
We'll sip lemon-scented tea,
while the bees play drowsy symphonies
among the young flowers,
and the sun slips away to other gardens,
other distant shorelines.

For Donna

It takes patience,
this many-hued awakening.
Down here
in the low fields, I'm poised
with trowel and with tea.
Soil scanning,
panning for green gold,
kneeling
while wing beats ripple
from the nearby trees.

I wish you wouldn't hide
your dances from me, each step
infinitesimal to my waiting eyes.
I'm ready for the gentle waves
of love in a mist,
the dizzying, creamy swirl
of the roses in their gowns.
Twisting skeins of scent
rising from the shy sweet peas
in the corner, a dahlia's sudden,
satisfying sunburst,
the tight clutch of gold
held in the bright fist of cosmos petals.
I'm ready.

And when I stand,
my face follows the sun,
eyelashes unfurling.
My veins hum, root deep.
With every step homeward,
I feel a slow, steadfast blossoming.

For Sarah

Your laughter is a release
of silver-skinned balloons
that float and fill any room. Every room.

Your laughter
streaks my hair with rainbows,
opens yellow petals on my skin.

It catches our settled daemons by surprise,
draws out a matching rumble from their furry chests –
a throaty ribbon of happiness.

Sunlight and birdsong
and padding through wet grass at dawn.

Your laughter is evening in Paris, a bridge
of initialled padlocks.
A hawthorn speckled with early flowers.

Your laughter is a crumb of madeleine
soaked in lime-blossom tea.
It's the Marches of years past, the Octobers
of years to come.

For Charlene

It's the heat,
the beach. The flavours of noontime –
salt-bite of squid, lemon tanged;
bread that drips golden with oil,
sun-warmed green olives
bigger than a thumb.
The turquoise roll of tide
and passing hours, hot chatter,
the distant splashing of my family.
Everything in this gilded afternoon holds me close,
sticky with dreams, drifting
somewhere between asleep and awake.
Here, on this drowsy isle, I can feel the ideas.
They float in tranquil clusters,
silent and fresh, each of them
shimmering with possibility.
I imagine you among them.
You who loved this place, who smiled
and looked as though you'd swallowed the sun.
If I were to reach out my hand,
my fingertips would graze new frontiers,
feel the flicker of new shapes and colours,
make me ache to pick up my paintbrush,
to write you a letter.

For Emma

As I sit here,
an ink stain is spreading across the sky.
It's late – the stars already jostling
at the edges of the stage like children,
craning to see faces they recognise.
The last thin shards of sunlight
jangle and chime above me, caught
in the gentle fingers of the topmost branches.

I have been coming here for years.
Have crowned myself
with young leaves, been quiet
amid summer storms, eyes wide,
heart open, the sky bruised
and crackling with things that needed to be said.
I have been here for the peridot, for the jade,
for tiger's eye, fire agate and blazing carnelian;
have shared this glorious shed skin
with the shy rustlings of tiny bodies.
I've collected fallen acorns –
burnished coins for barter. Here
I learned to wear stillness like a blanket.
Here my voice rose to meet the fledglings,
testing melody like new wings.

Now, the bats stake their claim on the deepening blue.
I could keep coming here for centuries.
This is the place I was grown.

For Kate

For us, there will be no tiers.
No edible gold, no sculpted birds.
I won't spend hours shaping petals,
building miniature sweetened gardens –
sugar paste blossoming under my fingers.

Instead, let's fill this kitchen
with the chink of cutlery,
the warm hum of happy chatter
on full stomachs. Pass the bread,
mop the sauce – every last glossy drop.

The oven is luminous in the corner,
and inside is the cake I made for us.
Simple, humble, delicious.
The scent of it rises
and fills this space of ours:

butter and vanilla,
comfort and safety. The smell of home.
This is what I make for us.
It is enough,
and so are we.

For Michelle

Eight miles, and the calm has settled over me,
clouds drifting between my ribs
with each breath, each footfall.

The rowboats rest their old bones, beached,
sun bleached. Content, as I am,
to be near the water,
to be among the tufts of wildflowers
that sprout like baby hair.

Next month, this quiet will be shot through
with a chaotic tangle of caramel fur
and over eager puppy limbs; with yips
that echo across the pond
and up to the Wedgwood sky,
sharp white teeth and new love, just as sharp.

Now, I step into the ghosts
of all who've walked these trails before me,
into the shimmer of their awe at this place,
the way the earth colours outside the lines,
or a skein of geese breaks the clouds
and spills a shaft of liquid sun onto the path.

These feelings – the deep exhales,
the unstoppable tug at the corners of mouths –
these have all been felt before, countless times,
by countless others. They are comfortable as old clothes.
I look at my watch, but already know what I'll see.

Four downward strokes
like the long shadows of silver birch.

When I move on,
I add the shape of my smile
for the next walker who rounds this corner,
who climbs this stile.

For Louise

Sometimes the skies will be bruised.
Sometimes, your skin will prickle
with the possibility of lightning,
your mind unable to settle on anything
for more than a few seconds. Sometimes,
the world will feel too tight – the skin of a peach
about to burst.

On days like these, you will know what to do.
Drive to the closest edge of the land you can find.
Stand barefoot and strong on the sand,
feet planted wide. Coax the sun
out from behind the clouds to add drops of blue
to the iron sea, add honeyed heat to your face and neck.
Let your hair tangle in the salt wind.

Remember the power that lives in your arms.
Enfold everyone under your heart's roof
in a hug the colour of Christmas clementines.
Bundle together in a chaos of flame
and flaxen hair and flailing limbs.
Knock the wind out of each other
with love and don't apologise for it.

Indulge your appetite.
Open the special occasion wine
and fill your glass with its berries and rubies,
feed yourself morsels of fat and salt
and everything that's good. Olives, prosciutto,

cheese that requires a silver spoon.
Fall into clean sheets with a single refrain in your head.

You are loved. You are loved. You are loved.

For Krysta

This time of night thrums with peaceful magic.
My daughters sprawl, hot like happy loaves in their beds,
their sleep-heavy breathing following me
through the house, where I pad on bare feet to the kitchen.

Small indulgences but important, hard won, mine alone:
steam curling from a mug of milky tea,
the guilty-pleasure crackle of the chocolate bar in its orange
wrapper –
crispy bits buried like nuggets of gold.

And outside in the thickening twilight,
the anemones curl themselves inwards.
A soft, velvet kiss of petals
before the quiet fireworks of the morning.

For Grania

I've been here for hours
or days. I don't remember.
I don't care to.
Here is where time stretches out
and up into the curves of the hot cloud.
This little strip of sand and salt
and white sky is mine –
the rest of the world
washes up and away from its edges.

It feels as though I can't be found.

Here I don't look at anything
too closely. I don't think about
each grain of sand,
the way hundreds of years can sift
and slip through my lazy fingers.
I don't think about this life
mapped out in ebbs and flows
and sudden flurries.
I don't think about the weight
of the water, its purr in my ears,
its capacity to smooth,
to wear away.
Instead, I breathe with it
as the seconds spool outwards
like silken ribbons in the wind.
Instead, I inhale the book that lies
warm and spread-eagled on my chest.

The scent of yellowed pages, old inks.
Of other worlds, of great loves
that taste like strawberry wine,
of battles yet to be won.

For Sophie

I used to think about making you a book.
Giving you pages that gleam
with the scales of mermaids,
where astronauts blast skyward
in trails of fire, stardust and courage.
Gardens you can safely get lost and found in.
Intricate spaces of paper and ink
and great big daydreams.

Now I think about making you a world
within each weekend.
Instinctively wrapping you in our arms
and our duvet when it's too early
for adult brains to be awake.
There being altogether
too many limbs in the bed, and twin blue stars
ignored on your alarm clocks.

Then pancakes, the hot drop
and sizzle of batter and bacon
in the pink heart of the kitchen.
Pools of syrup on the table.
No rush to be anywhere but here.
Perhaps jigsaws, perhaps strawberry picking –
a competitive tangle for the biggest, the juiciest –
perhaps the paddling pool or the beach.

Later we'll read somebody else's stories
of mermaids and astronauts,

and our daydreams will be just as big.
And my paintings will cover the walls.
Splashy abstracts in softly glowing navy and pink,
yellow and turquoise and teal.
In the past I've said they're seascapes.
I've said they're night-time arcade neon,
the stretch and sparkle of the pier. Right now,
bright against the gathering evening,
they look a lot like love.

For Kerri

Just for tonight,
you can keep your open skies,
the tickle of grass on bare ankles,
sparkles thrown across the water
like fistfuls of sequins
from a childish sun.
Tonight, I choose this place,
this gentle fortress. I choose you
(again and again, always and always).
I choose pizza crusts and greasy fingers,
I choose old love stories flickering
in black and white across the room.

Do you feel it?

The sofa lifting, taking us up
and away. From here,
the streets darken and disappear,
and if you listen closely, you can hear
the roar of waves below us.

Friends seeking peace
or a path through this fog,
look up.

The beam that shines
from our high windows is golden.
Solid and sure enough to share.
It will keep the clouds
and the shrieking gulls away until dawn.

For Justine

Last night we slept
with windows thrown wide,
and before the sun rose,
the rain came – long, soft fingers
tapping on the sills.

I wake to the many scents of green.
Moss, and droplet-spangled grass.
The first flush of new leaves, and something
deeper, darker.
The emerald stillness
at the heart of our piece of forest.

It takes me from the nest we've made
under these blankets. Down the stairs
and out towards the trees.
It's no surprise when, seconds later,
your arms encircle me. Footsteps,
heartbeats perfectly in sync.

The world has softened. Its edges
blurred to a watercolour painting.
While the city slumbers,
the ground out here is alive with song.
The skylarks weave their fluted enchantments
through the predawn quiet.

So lift me at the waist. I'm featherlight,
ready to take wing.

I'll clutch the birdsong in my fingers
like the tail of a silver kite. Feel my feet
leaving the ground. Soles brushing
the damp blades of grass,
the whispery tops of the trees.

As the lights flicker on
in our neighbours' houses,
I'll look down and wave.

For Olivia

We haven't seen each other for a while. You can tell
by the way our words spill across the table in a rich tide
like good red wine. I look around at our neighbours –
old friends, new friends, young love, could be love
if given half a chance, the mending of fences,
the pouring of hearts.

Give me an art gallery. High ceilings, blank walls,
an indrawn breath of a room.
Give me this café crowd. And watch.
Just watch us fill the space
with the colour of our conversation.
The woman with the voice like velvet
spangles the roof with stars. Gossip floats
in candy-coloured bubbles at ankle height,
daring you to pop. There's the neon strobe of
unexpected eye contact – not quite lightning bolt shaped.
A filthy laugh that starts lilac and drops with a stomach jolt
through to an indigo found only in the early hours.
Over in the far corner, a toast to a job well done bursts
into ripe fruit the colour of sunrise.
Behind you, the air is strung with the tiny jewels of secrets.
This clamour, this colour. The hum and bustle;
the great big glorious ordinariness of it all.

I push my chair back to leave, the afternoon
running to meet us. If you were to cut me open,
I would cast rainbow shadows on the last remaining white wall.

For Julie

From the day she was born,
Alice has been the flower.
She exists in a perpetual explosion
of petal and colour and wildness.
I look at her holding court in the garden,
spinning babble stories to the listening grass,
her bears lolling forwards towards her like bees
punch drunk on nectar and the promise of gold dust.

And I think I've always known that you, love,
you are the tree. Withstanding storms, surprising me
with sudden shocks of blossom,
your arms a warm nook
in which I would happily while away hours.
Retreat with a book. Let the world fall away.

I stack plates in the kitchen,
watch the two of you together,
feel the unstoppable spread of a smile.
Meanwhile, my inbox sings
with new steps forward, with tiny wins,
mistakes patched with gold,
firmer smiles, ideas that sprout
with the beginnings of wings. This is it.
This is everything. My little universe.

Standing on the threshold
in the shadows of the house, my eyes find yours.
I feel a tingling heat in the ends of my fingers.

A rush of liquid amber down my spine.
I think, perhaps, I have a piece of sun inside,
lodged in the hollow at my throat.
Brightening this garden of ours.
Helping it grow.

For Maddy

Bring me sunshine.
Bring me the kind of laughter that builds
in a rippling tide.
The kinds that tips your head back,
that blurs your mascara,
that clutches your stomach in a tight hug.

Bring me hugs, while you're at it –
the warm and unexpected,
those that linger, those that were almost
a handshake but suddenly got a promotion.
Bring me sequins that catch the light
and send it spinning across the room to you.

Bring me music with a beat
and lyrics that lodge in the curl of my smile.
Bring me tapping feet and shimmying hips.
Bring me colourful cocktails
and dark chocolate and ripe fruit.
Bring me long days and warm nights,
the certainty of the stars.

Bring me your brightest tomorrows.

For Vickie

If I could, I'd bottle this holiday
like perfume. Spritz it on my wrists,
the sides of my neck where my pulse quickens
and remember…

The wake-up blend of coffee and popcorn
amid the clang of trolleys on Main Street,
piped music that somehow bypasses your ears
and heads straight for your heartstrings.

In Animal Kingdom, grilled corn
and the sticky juice of watermelon slices
mingle over the stuccoed peaks of the Himalayas.
Hot pavements, and sudden rainstorms

and always the distant rumble-shriek
of wheels on downhill track.
Faster.
Faster.

Chlorine and coconut oil,
candyfloss and caricaturists.
An enveloping fizz of excitement –
all in different colours.

Bright neon for the little ones.
A bubbling hiss of molten gold and copper
barely contained in teens
who forgot they were too cool for this.

And for us, the grown ups
(who are never really grown)
it sparkles in subtler shades
of sage and sunrise.

This is our Neverland,
and we'll ride it straight on 'til morning.

For Ceri

And suddenly, it's evening again.
The hours have folded in on themselves,
chips of colour on a paint card. Shades darker,
shades calmer.
I step outside clutching tea,
called by the birds.
Their sundown serenades
filter through the latticework of branches.
In the early spring chill
the garden is a half-grown creature –
green shoots and vibrant earth and
lengthening shadows.

Upstairs, an afternoon well spent
rests on the spare room easel. Splashes
and spots in blues snatched
from Greek islands in summer
turn my knuckles into strange,
whirled dreamscapes.

You'll be home soon – the house
filled with light and the noise of dinner,
saucepans busy with steam and scent.
Our joyous volley of conversation
after these soft, quiet hours
holds my heart suspended
in perfect balance,
weightless and happy,
as the fat moon climbs into the night.

For Gabi

The breeze is picking up again,
lifting our hems and weaving
fallen cherry blossom through our hair.

I look back
towards the house.
Warm coats,
warm drinks,
warm hugs.

But Abigail hears music in the wind.
Her steps are light, arms lifted
face tilted skyward
smiling, untouched by the headlines
that keep us tethered here.

This is our own little world,
and I dance into it with her,
spinning and whirling until we fall
together under the trees.
She shows me
how to tell stories with the clouds.
How to find gold in the early sunlight.

For Emily

People are constantly in a rush
to leave this world beneath the world.
Always looking for the end, the 'out is through' –
seeking mackerel skies, feeling the full
span of the river and the way the evening air tastes.

I cut the engine and drift,
won't wish away this dank coolness, this place
where I can be hidden in plain sight.
I watch the water's flickering ballet
on the close roof, the way it catches
a corner of pale, fervent graffiti
and waves it like a prayer flag.
Tiny, greenish tongues lap the edge of the boat,
the edge of the stonework
with hollow, musical clangs. Flick-wristed,
I would tap on each dripping brick to hear it ring.
Bonang of the river, I would fill
this cylinder of London air and bring it alive
with stories from somewhere else;
with music thick enough to touch.
I would twirl the length of this boat
calling my own steps: Balancing The Star,
Kicking Up The Sawdust, Stripping The Willow –
my memories whirling, translucent dance partners.

The future waits for me outside,
but in this tunnel, in this moment,
I make my own light.

For Helen

Yesterday, the sky played me jazz.
It filled the garden with Benny and Toots,
Red and Fletcher and Jonny.
Sent the dog careening round the paddock
with every flashbang and sparkleburst
from across the valley.
I could feel their celebrations between my ribs,
would dance with you across the grass –
a sprawling, messy jive, dodging
the molehills and the fruit trees,
twirling through vines marked out by roses,
where the tight grapes wait for sweetness to arrive.

Now, it's quiet.
Wait… Almost quiet.
The waterfall of a nightingale begins
somewhere in the woods,
voice twining upwards
to mingle with the stars' lofty gossip.
The air smells of the minutes before midnight –
lavender, lemon verbena, the rain
that might fall on us tomorrow.
Our kitchen window burns
lighthouse golden,
and I would dance with you again.

For Ami

We keep pace,
Pearl and I,
her hooves the drum beat
I would set my life to.
Alongside us,
the light is playing tricks.
Patches of gold and dark scatter
and twist, into the curve of my mother's face,
the hair toss of an old friend
caught mid-laugh;
into long fingers
dancing over piano keys,
my grandmother's soft, birdlike tread.
And all the while,
the feeling of something brindled
and wild at our heels.
We're a strange sight –
the woman, the horse
and this joyously dappled army
of light and shadow.
We emerge blinking, into a sunlit future
at the end of the track.
Into plans for whisky and smoke
and Scottish coastlines.
The clink of glasses
and cackling over dinners,
the press of people and noise, and family,
and comfortable chaos.

The long squeeze of a hand when I need it most.

For Melissa

Someone has set the trees on fire with flowers,
the froth of blossom covering the pavements.

In the garden, there are sudden puddles of sunshine,
warm and syrupy. We stretch out in them like kittens.

You turn the hose on in a blast of rainbow droplets
and we're soaking, and we're shrieking with laughter

and it's not really warm enough for this.
But who cares?

Inside, there will be blankets; there will be old movies;
there will be enough milk for hot chocolates.

We're here.
We're together.
We're alright.

For Christine

The sun is impossibly large, swollen
and softened at the edges,
made tender by togetherness
and blushing into the evening sky.
We are one of several groups here tonight – clustered
like charms of birds among the reeds –
hooting the laughter our grandmother left us
out across the water as it laps molten gold over our hot feet.

The air tastes different here.
This morning as wheels hit tarmac
my tongue was eager to be flooded with it:
its dust and dry heat, old stories, older light;
the jacaranda's musky blue, my childhood
layered into the rock and hollow of this place,
catching the sun like shards of quartz.
Our arms have been linked since I arrived.

The sun is almost done now,
leaching the last of its papaya juice
into the dusk. My camera sleeps
but even silhouetted I can picture the shot.
Mum's head tipped back in an eruption of giggling,
and we three smoothed into children again,
faces wreathed with pride,
fingers interlaced.

For Cora

Yesterday, the rain came
and it felt like the earth was singing.
Droplets striking the ground –
hammers on a garden glockenspiel –
lifting up dust and tiredness, washing
the last calendar page clean.

This morning, it's as if the sun
is remembering favourite shades of gold.
The plates on the drying rack
are manuscript halos, the cheese plant
collects light in its green heart
like slow beads of syrup.

My cool hands have done this dance
many times: crumb, stir, dredge, fold, pat down,
press with silver into plump moons,
ready for the oven. Now they flutter
butter through flour almost of their own accord,
a small desert storm in the mixing bowl.

My mind is on you.
It settles first a few hours hence,
when the tea will be steeping
and the scones will be hot. We'll take a break
together, your arms encircling my waist
and pulling me into this honeyed afternoon.

It darts forward – catlike,
calendar pages underfoot,
to burnished leaves in Scotland,
when the sun after the rain makes the world new
all over again. And your gaze will hold mine
across a crowded room, comforting as a layer of cream.

For Becky

If someone were to place a lid over this garden,
a tight seal around this sky,
you would not see us seethe
against the glass like ants,
or bubble and scald like frantic milk.
The world would still be exactly wide enough.

We would have pizza with a perfect crust
from the oven the same shade as the twist of lime
on the edge of my fizzing glass –
herbs and juniper and tonic cooling my tongue.
The shrubs would hum with bees.
We would watch you conducting
elaborate tea ceremonies for dinosaurs
and rabbits, ready at any moment
for your run, launch and hug –
soft arms tight around my neck,
the smell of your hair another word for contentment.

And the air, the air would be singing out
with the sort of guitar that, in another lifetime,
would lift countless lighters skywards
like hedonistic fireflies. So go ahead.
Make this garden a summer snowglobe
and watch us dance and spin,
defiant in our glittering.

For Claire

The birds came back weeks ago
but now, as the trees remember
who they are – putting on green
and petalled coats – it's my turn to take wing.

I'm greedy for the light of other lands.
The way romance is painted into far horizons
with long, gilded brushstrokes.
Let me soar above and breathe it all in,
just for a little while.

Paris's antique gold,
its full-skirted lovers twirling
together like falling flowers
along the Boulevard Saint Germain.

The hot, unabashed blue
of the Maldives –
colour that soaks your skin;
that leaves you stunned
and smelling of salt and jasmine.

And, oh, Venice. The old city's jewelled slumber
under pale sorbet skies,
glinting blue ribbons threaded
through a patchwork of terracotta and church bells.

When my soul is quenched,
I'll return, as certain as any swallow.
To sunshine-warmed sheets
where Coco purrs. Freshly cut grass.
The sound of your laughter in the kitchen.

For Janet

This is where they keep the sky.
Vast chambers of cloud,
where raindrops wait
to be loosed like gentle arrows;
deepening the green below,
lifting the smells of the earth,
the flowers yet to be born, the memories
of being small, when the same damp grass was knee high.

Shadows play in the bracken with the dogs,
and there's a clicking in my chest,
too quiet for anyone to hear.
The turning of a key.
The untethering of something. I half expect
to see dewdrops lifting towards the heavens,
to feel my fingers floating skywards,
chin tilted towards the mountaintops, the crags
where eagles hover – silent, unseen.

I wheel around, arms outstretched,
my own glorious wingspan.
The basket with the broken handle
brims with shades of green. Wild sorrel,
a peppery clump of nettles, yarrow,
dandelion leaf. It foams with creamy meadowsweet,
is starred with a bounty of elderflower.

Tonight I will feed you
mouthfuls flavoured with this cold, wild air,
that leave the taste of freedom on your tongue.

For Sally Kate

We make our own rituals.
Every month, unspoken.
Same time, same place.
We talk with our eyes
among turquoise ripples
on the walls and ceilings,
unwilling to cause echoes.
Or sit, close and silent,
while hot coals spit. Sometimes
I breathe too deeply, and taste
raw heat and pine forest
on the inside of my throat.

Hours later, and we are lavender scented,
our muscles honeyed from practised hands.
Now our mouths are unstoppered, and we talk
around tea and scones slathered in cream
and jam the colour of new shoes
while the world turns outside.

The teapot is brown and crackle glazed.
Its round weight between my hands
takes me to its twin, warm
and fat in my parents' kitchen, decades old.
It leads me to Dad, to so many memories
and mornings I'd almost let slip.
Twirling on cold kitchen tile,
making our own breakfast soundtrack.
Fleetwood Mac and almost burnt toast
and the old kettle hissing along with us.

...

We link arms as we leave.
Crumbs on plates,
world put to rights. It's alright.
Outside, our chatter mingles
with countless other friends,
other tiny, vital rituals.
The clouds row softly across the sky,
and the branches are heavy with songbirds.

For Kelly

This wicker egg is my garden's dreaming space,
the place I can leave the plates
dancing on their sticks.
Can slow the turn of the world and shrink it,
sip crisp wine that pours fields of lavender
and peachy sunlight into each glass,
and marvel at the sky.

I think of the journeys the clouds have taken –
that one a breaching whale above my chimney,
then scudding away over the fields,
fluting into – perhaps –
the gilt-edged horn of a unicorn
as it reaches Polesden Lacey, as it crests the hill
near that golden house and its shawl of wisteria.

Remember, this light that touches my calves,
the bones of my wrists, is the same that falls like water
on the stained glass and stone of the château by the river,
the café with its red awning,
where words taste like velvet and warm bread.
I stay out after dark,
beckon you to come join me, coltish legs swinging.

I find solace in the stars,
those same glittering patterns being pointed out
in hundreds of gardens, courtyards
and open fields, on dozens of different angles.
Breathe deeply
at this collective joining of dots,
lean my head against your cheek.

For Sally

Late June and the sky
is languidly, lazily blue.
Today, we're hunters,
Lillyanna and I.
In sundresses and sandals,
our toes painted pink
as the heart of a seashell,
we head for the rose garden
for colours to catch.
This is my favourite place
to make rainbows.
Lillyanna is off like a sunbeam,
or a fairy tornado. Running
through the bowers and arches
in search of the searing hot pinks.
I take my time through creamy whites,
whispery blushes, deep, sensuous reds.
Breathing in the perfume of the flowers:
turkish delight and long baths
and daydreams of exotic markets,
where spices stand like bright mountains.
I find her transfixed by petals
the colour of melted butter.
When she holds them to her face,
it seems to glow.

For Valentina

For now, we have to settle
for slices of sky.
Our own patch of scrubby starlight:
peach-tinted, cloudy
and pock-marked
by the occasional unwise glitter
of a passing plane.

But tonight,
you spread a blanket feast
on the lawn. Pale moons
of salty cheese,
a terracotta dish of cherries
(you found cherries!)
small pots of honey
that look lit from within in the dusk.

We lie together, fit together,
my head under your chin.
And suddenly we're somewhere else.
The air feels sweeter,
heather scented.

These spinning satellites
become the Lyrids' breath-snatching star fall.
Clean, sudden, ice-bright.
There's no one but us for miles.
Beyond the horizon, tomorrow
is tightly wrapped,
beribboned,
an unopened present.

For Marianne

They say that the first year is paper.
Love notes and ink
the colour of fresh raspberries.
The second, cotton – new sheets,
the smell of apple blossom on our skin.
We're headed for the hills of ruby,
far-off shores lapped by tides of gold,
and we'll be singing Sondheim and Bernstein as we go.
But my favourite nights are those
without anniversary fanfare. Those like tonight,
when June skies darken too early with sudden,
urgent rain. The windows are lit with tiny diamonds,
and I am in the kitchen with you in my arms,
and 'what's for dinner?' on our lips.
Let's spin the old globe, shall we?
Turn this unremarkable Tuesday
into a silver platter of oysters –
all the moods of the sea in a mouthful –
make this kitchen a sunset piazza
where the clouds are Aperol orange.
Let's open the album of memories –
strands of saffron pinned to butter-splashed pages
like scented butterflies.
Grab Robin and Jackson,
tails swishing quizzically, and dance with me
through the market where we ate
watermelon slices and let the juice run
to our elbows, past the sizzle-spit of grills –
charred steak and garlic prawns

and skewers of blackened peppers,
to my mother's table
where mounds of ragù are heaped
on the plates I remember as a girl.
It still tastes like love.

For Jen

I wonder at what age
the smell of your child's head
stops being a direct line to your heart.
An intense inhale of motherhood,
sweetly raw.
No longer the newborn talc and milk,
downy fluff and the sheer,
glassy vastness of new love
that we attempt to understand,
to enfold in our arms,
remembering to breathe
as it swells in our chests.

Today, scrubbed pink in soft cotton,
with sleep beginning to bloom on their cheeks,
the girls' hair is a cacophony of ringlets.
Cuddled up for stories, I breathe in
scented bubbles, memories of shriek-laughter
ringing off the bathroom tile, the spark
of the day's tiny new discoveries,
the soft approach of dreams.
And underneath it all,
salt air, a rush of sky,
the wavelets of wildness
that live in them both.

Later, much later, I'll walk
down to the water's edge,
sit on the sea wall

and watch the lights dance.
Iced coffee in my flask.
Breath in my lungs. Uninterrupted
thoughts in my head.
Behind me, the town flickers
with bedtime conversation,
and tomorrow we'll do it all over again.

For Charlotte

Last night, I dreamed a forest
had sprung up around me.
The tomato plants huge and cascading
from the mantelpiece, spreading tendrils
that smelled of all things good:
of grandparents' glasshouses,
and damp soil,
and the throbbing heart of summer time.

Roses and dahlias covered the dining table
and crept across the floor
in a louche, perfumed sprawl.
Thick vines of bramble
pressed against the windows, desperate
to deposit their gifts in my lap,
to leave wine-dark stains on my dress.

Upstairs in the studio,
I could feel the pencils jostling
against the lid of the box,
greens thirsty with wanting.
From my small clearing
in this unexpected woodland, I sensed
the whispers of juniper, spruce and sap,
the spicy chuckle of cedar, the gossip
of olive and moss.

And through the thicket of stems and fronds,
I heard snippets and jigsaw pieces of conversation.

Laughter I recognised,
the echo of my name, a flash of sunlit wine
in a raised glass. I could have parted the leaves,
could have wandered through the creepers
in search of company. Instead I sat
in the sudden jungle of my living room,
eating squares of chocolate
dark enough to need tasting notes
 — *leather, tobacco, red berries* —
laughing at the wildness of the world.

For Rachel

The armchair in my bedroom
is the colour of Sunday clouds,
when the sky is clotted and wild.

It is the silence and the softness
that dwells in the corners of this house,
the early hours strung before me
like misshapen pearls.

This armchair is a cradle,
a time machine.
It's the sweet ache of let down,
flowing milk and the silk
of his blond hair.

It is a place for stories and heavy lids,
the turning of pages, the sipping of tea.
For the gathering of thoughts
like armfuls of warm laundry,
everything folded neatly,
finally in place.

Today I would carry it lashed to my back
to the top of the hill.
Would sit breathless and proud,
enthroned with the wind at my throat,
freckled with rain and the potential of thunder.
And the house, the whole town
would be laid out below me
like a quilt of light and shadows,
teeming with hundreds of tiny lives.

For Jo

I hope the new normal is malleable,
a future we can shape in our hands:
wet clay and moth-wing gold.

I hope that our tomorrows are salt-splashed,
echoing with whoops and the happy shock of cold,
wild swimming, when we bob like a family of gulls.

That we move forward craving
months of umami; no longer seek to spin truths
or half-truths from strands of sugar.

Give us a winter with the red bite of kimchi,
a January that stings our lips
with salt and chilli oil. I hope we pen

the last chapters of the novel,
leave the brooding detective open-mouthed
and stuttering. Leave no loose ends, no skeletons.

Not a thing with feathers,
but the loping velvet shadow of a greyhound,
and a sunset as ripe as a cider apple.

For Annabel

It's late. At this time of night,
the hands of the clock hold up
the day's perfumes to the stars
like an offering. The meadow's faint petals;
bitter sap from the trees that stand
clustered along the path –
drowsy sentinels in the dark;
drifts of woodsmoke;
the coconut tang of hot, freckled skin.

The moon is busy with her rebirth,
but my head torch and I,
we make our own moonbeams tonight.
My boots crunch miles underfoot. I conjure
tiny whirlwinds of moths for company –
spinning flakes of silver in the shaft of light.
Sleep salutes me as I pass.

At this time of night, my heart is quiet,
and my head is as still and full as a summer pond.
There are no echoes of half-finished
conversations among these dark lanes,
no missed connections, things left unsaid,
feelings unfelt. Everything is, in a strange way,
exactly as it should be.

The daylight hours bear sweet, well-tended fruit.
I'm starting to see them slowly ripening
on the lower branches.

As the clock hands turn,
I am mapless and unafraid.
Tomorrow, the sun will rise –
golden as a kept promise. And so will I.

ACKNOWLEDGEMENTS

Huge and heartfelt thanks to the fabulous women who so generously shared their happinesses with me, and really uplifted me in the process:

Kirsty Mackenzie | Faye Cornhill | Jennifer Daniels Curulli | Catherine Ledger | Lindsay Greenaway | Sarah Wayte | Andri Benson | Gayle Cheetham | Donna Bowen-Heath | Sarah Etrog | Charlene Russell | Emma Cullen | Kate Lieberman | Michelle Kelly | Louise Beukes | Krysta Smith | Grania O'Brien | Sophie Thomas | Kerri Awosile | Justine Chase Grey | Olivia De Santos | Julie Michaelsen | Maddy Shine Jones | Vickie Elliott | Ceri Olofson | Gabi Staniszewska | Emily Garland | Helen Wainwright | Ami Robertson | Melissa Booth | Christine Havill | Cora Moon | Becky Harley | Claire Graham | Janet Mactavish | Sally Kate Duboux | Kelly Chandler | Sally Bean | Valentina Ring | Marianne Moulder-McPhee | Jen Fuller | Charlotte Argyrou | Rachel Matthews | Jo Cranston | Annabel Beeforth.

ABOUT THE AUTHOR

(Author photograph: Ami Robertson – The Woman And The Wolf)

Jen has been in love with language for as long as she can remember. A former Foyle Young Poet of the Year, her poetry has appeared in regional and national journals and anthologies. This is her debut collection. Jen is a bookworm with a love of baking, conversation that makes your brain fizz with ideas, and really good cheese. She lives by the sea in Essex with her husband and two young children.

Matador

For exclusive discounts on Matador titles,
sign up to our occasional newsletter at
troubador.co.uk/bookshop

LONDON TRANSPORT

Restaurant
Guide

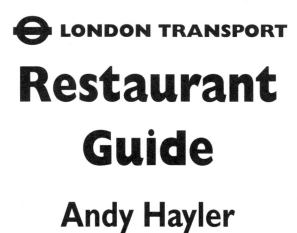

⊖ LONDON TRANSPORT

Restaurant Guide

Andy Hayler

BⒺXTREE

**Published in association with the
London Transport Museum**

To Stella

First published in Great Britain in 1995 by Boxtree Ltd, Broadwall House, 21 Broadwall, London, SE1 9PL

in association with the London Transport Museum
Text copyright © Andy Hayler 1995

1   3   5   7   9   10   8   6   4   2

ISBN 0 7522 1662 7

Designed by Robert Updegraff
Typeset in Palatino by SX Composing Ltd, Rayleigh, Essex
Printed and bound in Great Britain
by Cox & Wyman Ltd, Reading, Berks

A CIP catalogue entry for this book is available from the British Library

CONTENTS

About This Guide

The *London Transport Restaurant Guide* aims to provide a 'one-stop shop' guide to eating in London, covering restaurants and food shops, and giving a little background on the various cuisines and some information on wine buying. London has a remarkable variety of ethnic cuisines, representing a window on the world of cooking. This guide is a personal view, not the product of a company or committee, so is at least consistent.

The Reviews

All inspections of restaurants are strictly anonymous, so any mistakes are genuine rather than the product of avarice or advertiser pressure. The restaurant world changes rapidly, so while every effort has been made to ensure that information is up to date at the time of writing, chefs move on and prices change, so by the time you read this some information in the Guide may have become out of date. Neither the author nor publisher can be held responsible for any errors, omissions or changes in the details given.

At the back of this guide you will find a feedback form. Please take advantage of this to note any comments (positive or otherwise) about the Guide, or any suggestions for improvement, either in the style or layout or suggestions for new entries.

How To Use This Guide

When going out to eat, most people tend to base their choice of venue on type of cuisine, location, cooking quality, price and surroundings. In what follows, therefore, I have organised entries by cuisine and given a separate index by location. Each entry reflects the criteria:

- cooking

- ambience

- service

In this way I hope that you can easily home in on what you are seeking. There are various indexes at the back to help you find things.

Prices Quoted

This is always a thorny problem, since people have varying appetites and taste in wine. The figures quoted indicate a range of prices for one person for a typical three-course meal, including coffee, service and a half bottle of house wine (or equivalent). I have given separate prices for lunch and dinner where there are set lunches offered, as in some cases this can radically alter the likely overall price, and I have tried to err on the conservative side. I'd always prefer to be surprised by a bill being lower than expected rather than higher!

Value For Money?

The entries in this Guide highlight places which I believe represent good value for money; this does not mean they are all cheap. It is one thing to knock out a few bowls of pasta with some vegetables, quite another to aspire to the pinnacle of the great world cuisines. If you try cooking some of the recipes of dishes served at top French restaurants you will discover that the prices charged no longer appear quite so outrageous. It is simply not possible to make some of these dishes for less than £10 a portion, just for ingredients. Clearly different styles of cooking involve quite different levels of cost in terms of both ingredients and also preparation. A place charging £15 a head for some simple vegetarian food may actually be coining it in compared to somewhere charging £50 a head for elaborate cuisine involving expensive ingredients and lots of labour. This is not to say that all restaurant prices are fair, simply that you need to consider the context before assessing value for money. You shouldn't expect to sample a complex dish stuffed with truffles or foie gras for the same price as a pizza.

This is why you will find restaurants in this Guide where you can eat for £5 a head, and others which are more than ten times that. The intention is to reflect quality and value for money in each cuisine category.

But What About....?

Not all well-known London restaurants are in this Guide, since my emphasis throughout is on value for money rather than being completely comprehensive, though suffice it to say that virtually all places of any fame (and many without) have been sampled in the research, so omissions are generally conscious ones. Inevitably such choices are subjective, and you may not find your favourite place here, or disagree with choices I have made. That is what the feedback form is for, and your comments will be welcomed and taken into account for the next edition.

Wine In Restaurants

Wine drinkers effectively subsidise non wine-drinkers, since if most restaurants charged true prices for their food they (correctly) believe that few would pay. One or two noble attempts to charge for food and wine in correct proportion have been resounding failures, as people have become used to paying a certain amount for food, and are unwilling to pay much more even if the wine prices are cheaper. What is extremely irritating for wine drinkers is that the mark-up is not based on the real economics, i.e. a flat charge for each bottle based on storage costs (more expensive wines tie up more capital, but also generally increase in value as they get older) but a percentage mark-up. So a place with a usual mark-up of 100% will charge £10 for a £5 bottle, but £50 for a £25 bottle, which discriminates heavily against people who like better wines. There seems no likelihood that this practice will end, so unless you have very deep pockets (or find an unlicensed restaurant) the only solution for wine drinkers is to stick to basic wine when eating in restaurants and save the good stuff for drinking at home.

Acknowledgements

This publication could not have been completed without the invaluable assistance of many people, including those who selflessly volunteered to help me with my research.

Thanks to Margaret Harvey for her vast wine expertise; to Tiffany Hall for her research assistance and boundless enthusiasm, not to mention patient proof-reading; to Albert Roux for his kind support, to Geoffrey Ng for his encyclopaedic food knowledge and to Frania Weaver for her help on the publishing side. Thanks also to the many people who provided feedback and suggestions, including Clarissa Dickson-Wright, Philippa de Glanville, Janine Wallace, Annie Gammon, Huw Owen-Reece, Peter King, Chris Rodger, Claire Frost, Ian Brown, Amanda Johnson, Barbara Goodwin, Peter Jay and John Tidswell. Thanks to the staff at Boxtree for their professionalism and support, to Adam Sisman for introducing me to them, and to London Transport for their sponsorship.

Above all, thanks to my wife Stella, who has contributed much of the tasting expertise and gave me the support and encouragement that enabled me to complete this book.

A BAKER'S DOZEN

The following represent, in my own view, the most outstanding value-for-money places in London, places which I go back to time and time again. This does not mean that they are necessarily cheap; indeed a few are very expensive. It is just a list of personal favourites, my desert island dinners.

STOP PRESS

Recent exciting entries to the London restaurant scene, which were not in time for a full write-up, are as follows:

Interlude de Chavot 5 Charlotte Street, W1   0171 637 0222

Outstanding new French restaurant, serving extremely good food at very fair prices (a 3 course dinner is currently £26.50). Destined for stardom.

Tamarind   20 Queen Street, Mayfair, London W1   0171 629 3561

Classy Indian restaurant in the heart of Mayfair, elegant surroundings and delicately spiced curries of high quality, though with prices to match.

Union Café   96 Marylebone Lane, London W1   0171 486 4860

Excellent Modern British food in a casual atmosphere, not far from Oxford Street.

Restaurants

A Little History

Restaurants are a relatively recent development, a reflection of more widespread affluence and the development of a middle class. The rich have always had banquets; after all, the ancient Greeks, and especially the Romans, knew something about indulgence, but the rich could afford to have their own cooks. Inns and taverns had long served food to their guests, but did not provide a menu offering choice. The first 'restaurant' is generally recognised to have been opened in Paris in 1765 by a man called Boulanger. This establishment offered a menu of soups and broths, which were known as 'restoratives', the word restaurant coming from the verb *'restaurer'*. The hungry burghers of Paris had to wait just a few more years for restaurants which we might recognise today. The first was 'Le Grand Taverne de Londres', which opened in 1782, serving food in grand style. The crumbling of the age of kings heralded by the French Revolution had the indirect effect of spawning a boom in restaurants, as there were suddenly an awful lot of unemployed cooks whose previous employers had rather lost their heads. By 1789 there were 100 restaurants in Paris, and by 1804 over 500 establishments had opened. This growth in turn led to the very first restaurant guide, *'Almanche des Gourmandes'*, published in 1803.

Enough of history; where is it worth eating at today?

African

African cuisine offers a wide range of meats such as buffalo, zebra, antelope, etc. rarely seen in your local butcher. In the well-known Carnivore restaurant in Nairobi these meats and others are served in the style of a South American meat restaurant, with huge haunches of meat slowly grilled over a great pit of hot coals. The meat is then brought to the tables on long skewers, and slices are cut off as desired. Some of these meats are very interesting: harte-beest is very tender and tastes to me like an excellent, gamey ver-sion of beef, while impala, not surprisingly, is much like venison.

The local fish tilapia gets everywhere, and there is much use of spices such as pepper, ginger, garlic and nutmeg. Cassava is the staple in many countries, rice in others. Africa offers many spicy soups, e.g. the Nigerian pepper soup, and there is a lot of starchy food such as yams. Meat and vegetables are often cooked in stews. More original dishes include *zegeni* from Eritrea (mutton with pimento paste and vegetables, served with unleavened biscuits), and *vary amin* (stew of zebra with tomatoes and ginger) from Madagascar. Couscous is reasonably common but is usually based on millet rather than wheat. If you want to try African food then probably the best in the capital is at the Calabash. It is cheaper than flying to Africa, but you do miss out on the beautiful scenery, wildlife, corrupt customs officials, malaria, ...

Calabash

Price (lunch):	£10-£20
Price (dinner):	£10-£20

Address:	The Africa Centre, 38 King Street, Covent Garden, WC2 8JS
Phone:	0171 836 1976
Fax:	0171 836 7736
Reservations?	Yes
Nearest tube:	Covent Garden
Open lunch:	Monday - Friday 12:30 - 15:00
Open dinner:	Monday - Saturday 18:00 - 23:30
Closed:	Bank Holidays
Seats:	80
Private Room?	No
Credit cards:	Visa,Amex,Access, Diners
Disabled access?	No
Non-smoking?	No

The Calabash is a large basement restau-rant in Covent Garden. The advantage of the Calabash is that it plucks dishes from many parts of Africa, so that you can at least sample dishes from a wide range of areas. Examples of this are plantain-based dishes such as *aloco*, various chicken offerings, meat stews and a number of vegetarian options. The cook-ing would have to be described as com-petent rather than especially inspired. There are some African beers available (somewhat irregularly in my experience) such as Tusker from Kenya, and even some African wines. Zimbabwe, for one, does actually produce some competent wines, though the range at the Calabash is very limited.

Arabic

The best of Arabic cuisine is to be found in the Lebanon and Syria. Given the Mediterranean climate and the historical and trading connections, it is not surprising that there is a superficial resemblance between Arabic cuisine and Greek. Both have hummus, the chickpea-based dip, and baklava, the sweet filo pastry dessert. Arabic cuisine makes greater use of spices, uses borghul (cracked wheat) as a staple, while the main meat used is lamb. London has several Lebanese restaurants, the best of which is probably the Al Hamra.

Al Hamra

Price (lunch):	£30-£45
Price (dinner):	£30-£45

Address:	31-33 Shepherd Market, Mayfair, W1Y 7RJ
Phone:	0171 493 1954
	0171 493 6934
Fax:	None
Reservations?	Yes
Nearest tube:	Green Park
Open:	All week noon–midnight
Closed:	Christmas Day, New Year's Day
Seats:	75
Private Room?	No
Credit cards:	Visa,Amex,Access, Diners
Disabled access?	Yes (not to toilets)
Music played?	Yes
Non-smoking?	No
Chef:	Mahir Abboud

The Al Hamra is a smart establishment which has changed little over the years; it has a successful formula and is sticking to it. There is a wide range of dishes, and the easiest way to sample these is through the meze menus, which allow you to try a selection of hot and cold dishes. The usual set of dips (hummus, etc.) can be found, as well as stuffed vine leaves, falafel and many other dishes. Meats are mostly char-grilled and are handled competently, not drowned in olive oil as at so many Greek establishments. There are Mediterranean dishes such as baklava, or fresh fruit, to finish, and the coffee is Turkish. The somewhat high prices here are the main drawback.

Austrian/Hungarian

Austria and Hungary have a shared culinary tradition, derived from their common history under the Hapsburgs. Austrian cuisine resembles German in some ways; being a land-locked country there is little fish, so the emphasis is on meat. The national dish is breaded veal fillets (*wiener schnitzel*), served at almost every restaurant. There are also dishes such as *tapelspitz*, slices of beef with sautéed potatoes in a spicy sauce. The pinnacle of Austrian cuisine is undoubtedly the pastry, of which Austria is one of the world's greatest exponents. Hungarian food has a long tradition but, under communism, restaurant eating has declined so much that it now shares the foot of the Michelin league table with Greece, having not a single Michelin-starred restaurant. Hungarian cuisine that goes beyond goulash can be found in London, however, at the venerable Gay Hussar restaurant.

Gay Hussar

Price (lunch):	£23-£30
Price (dinner):	£25-£40

Address:	2 Greek Street, Soho, London W1V 6NB
Phone:	0171 437 0973
Fax:	0171 437 4631
Reservations?	Yes (advisable)
Nearest tube:	Leicester Square or Tottenham Court Rd
Set lunch:	£16
Open lunch:	Monday-Saturday 12:30 - 14:30
Open dinner:	Monday-Saturday 17:30 - 22:45
Closed:	Sundays & Bank Holidays
Seats:	72
Private Room?	Yes (12 people)
Credit cards:	Visa,Amex,Access, Diners
Disabled access?	Yes (not to toilets)
Music played?	No
Non-smoking?	No
Chef:	Leslie Holecz

Serving interesting Hungarian food in the heart of London since the 1950s, the Gay Hussar is a veteran of restaurants. Fashion impinges neither on the cooking, nor the red decor, here. The upholstery may be scruffy, but the portions are generous and the food interesting. Smoked goose with scholet, thick soups and spicy sausages are the sort of thing to be found on a long menu which might as well be carved out of stone tablets for all the changes which are likely to appear. Worth a visit for something a little different.

Belgian

People unfamiliar with Belgium may not realise that the Belgians are as obsessed with food as the French. The artistically inclined may recall Brueghel's scenes of gluttony, and Brussels is second only to Paris in the number of Michelin-starred restaurants (it even has two 3-star establishments). As well as the famous chocolates, the chips are wonderful, and there is a massive range of beers.

People in the Flemish north of Belgium cook a variety of stews, have interesting ways of cooking eels and are into waffles. The French-speaking Walloon south makes the most of the wonderful Belgian chocolate, and has many dishes using juniper berries. In general Belgians have what in less fitness-conscious times would have been described as healthy appetites, and you will rarely go hungry in a Belgian restaurant. Restaurants in Belgium serving minuscule but artistic portions of nouvelle cuisine tend to have the longevity of a mayfly.

Belgo

| Price (lunch): | **£15-£40** |
| Price (dinner): | **£15-£40** |

Address:	72 Chalk Farm Road, London NW1 8AN
Phone:	0171 267 0718
Fax:	None
Reservations?	Yes (essential)
Nearest tube:	Chalk Farm or Camden Town
Set lunches:	£5 - £10
Set dinners:	£10 (2 courses)
Open lunch:	All week 12:00 - 15:00
Open dinner:	All week 18:00 - 23:30
Saturday	12:00 - 23:30
Sunday	12:00 - 22:30
Closed:	Christmas Day, New Year's Day
Seats:	110
Private Room?	No
Credit cards:	Visa,Amex,Access, Diners
Disabled access?	Can be arranged
Music played?	No
Non-smoking?	No
Chef:	Philippe Blaise

Belgo aims for simple street food rather than haute cuisine: mussels and chips, wild boar sausage with mash and the like. This food is served in a fairly sparse setting, rather modern furniture with bare tables. The waiters are dressed as monks, which would normally be reason enough to avoid the place. However, these distractions should not detract from the food, which is very good indeed. Though most dishes are simple, the quality of the cooking can be seen in artichoke served en croute, artfully presented with a well-judged sauce. This would not embarrass a restaurant with a much greater reputation (and price). The chips are excellent and there is a selection of 30 Belgian beers. The price here is a little hard to gauge. Mussels with chips are around £8, but this is for a huge bowl with more mussels than you can shake a stick at. Salads (excellent) are around £4 and other meat dishes around £8-10, but the beers, served in small continental measures, are quite costly, and can bump up the bill. Around £25 per head should ensure plenty of food and beer. If you can ignore the spectacle of the waiter-monks, and actually obtain a reservation ahead of the hordes of trendy Camden residents who come here, then you will find Belgo a very refreshing addition to the London restaurant scene.

British

British cooking has a terrible reputation, thoroughly deserved in the 1940s to 1970s, and in general it is fair to say that as a nation the British have little interest in food. However, as with many generalisations, to describe the British as culinary Luddites would miss the mark. The ghastly grey food of the post-war years was not always the norm; indeed Britain was actually renowned for its cooking in the 17th and 18th centuries, particularly for its desserts (*creme brulée*, for example, originated in Britain, not France). Our cheese, and some of our meats, are as fine as any in the world. Many top French cooks use British beef, lamb, game and certain seafood, e.g. Dublin Bay prawns (langoustines), while the British use of herbs is considerably wider than that in traditional French cuisine. We even grow a wide range of excellent mushrooms, for those who can be bothered to find them, and there are unique things like the Welsh laverbread (boiled seaweed). British cooking has underwent a renaissance in the 1980s, with cooks such as Alistair Little, Gary Rhodes, John Burton-Race and Simon Hopkinson re-inventing British cooking by concentrating on high-quality ingredients served simply, and not being afraid to draw on oriental spices and flavours where appropriate. The establishments of young chefs like these are where to try British cooking at its best, rather than the oak-panelled rooms of traditional English dining rooms.

Alistair Little

Price (lunch):	£40-£70
Price (dinner):	£40-£70

Address:	49 Frith Street, Soho, London W1V 5TE
Phone:	0171 734 5183
Fax:	None
Reservations?	Yes
Nearest tube:	Leicester Square
Set lunch:	£10 (bar only) £25 (two courses)
Open lunch:	Monday - Friday 12:00 - 15:00
Open dinner:	Monday - Saturday 18:00 - 23:30
Closed:	Bank Holidays
Seats:	36 (18 in bar)
Private Room?	Yes (18 people)
Credit cards:	Visa,Amex,Access
Disabled access?	Partial (1 step, not to toilets)
Music played?	No
Non-smoking?	No
Chef:	Alistair Little

Alistair Little is one of the pioneers who has revitalised British cooking in recent years. His cooking reflects an obsession with the best ingredients, willingness to try dishes from other cuisines (e.g., spicy Thai sausages) and a relentless drive for improvement. This striving for perfection means that the menu changes much more rapidly than at many places, and even the way a particular dish is executed may vary from one week to the next. His first recipe book is called *Keep it Simple,* and this philosophy is reflected not just in the menu but the surroundings, which are very basic indeed. Such simplicity of style always has the drawback that flaws show up so much more starkly. This and the high prices make disappointment intense if errors occur. Nonetheless, there is no denying the talents of the chef, and at its best the food is very fine indeed. Summer is not the best time to eat here, as Mr Little teaches cookery in Italy then.

Atlantic Bar & Grill

Price (lunch):	£20-£25
Price (dinner):	£30-£40

Address:	20 Glasshouse Street
	Piccadilly
	London W1R 5RQ
Phone:	0171 734 4888
Fax:	0171 734 3609
Reservations?	Yes (essential)
Nearest tube:	Piccadilly Circus
Set lunch:	£11.90
Open lunch:	Monday-Saturday
	12:00-15:00
Open dinner:	Monday-Friday
	18:00 - 24:00
	Sunday
	19:30 - 23:30
Bar open:	12:00 - 03:00
Closed:	Bank Holidays,
	Christmas
Seats:	150
Private Room?	Yes (150 people)
Credit cards:	Visa,Amex,Access
Disabled access?	By prior arrangement
Music played?	Yes
Non-smoking?	No
Chef:	Richard Sawyer

The only restaurant I know with a bouncer on the door, protecting the basement premises against those lacking in sufficient glamour or money. A dinner reservation will enable you to glide past this hurdle, but if it is just a drink you are after then best don the Armani. The main room is a cavernous affair, the central bar packed with throngs of bright young things; you could cast a Hugo Boss advert here in seconds. The well-spaced dining tables are dwarfed by towering marble pillars. The food is altogether better than it might be reasonable to expect here, some classic French dishes mixed in with British, e.g. a baked onion tart with foie gras alongside a well-judged dish of freshly made linguini with cashew and pesto sauce. The wine list is also serious, with classy producers from around the world at tolerable prices.

Bibendum

Price (lunch):	£35-£40
Price (dinner):	£50-£75

Address:	Michelin House,
	81 Fulham Road
	South Kensington
	London SW3 6RD
Phone:	0171 581 5817
Fax:	0171 823 7925
Reservations?	Yes
Nearest tube:	South Kensington
Set lunch:	£27
Open lunch:	All week
	12:30 - 14:30
Open dinner:	All week
	19:00 - 11:30 (last
	orders at 11:15)
Closed:	24th-28th December
Seats:	72
Private Room?	No
Credit cards:	Visa,Amex,Access
Disabled access?	No
Music played?	No
Non-smoking?	No
Chef:	Simon Hopkinson

A delightful place for a Sunday lunch treat. The room was designed by Terence Conran and is wonderfully light and airy; the atmosphere is quite relaxed for a restaurant in this league (no ties needed). Simon Hopkinson concentrates on producing simple food well, so in addition to 'sole in truffle sauce' there is simply 'fish and chips' – though in a different league from your local chippie's. Ingredients are excellent, crucial when dishes are simply prepared, and the modern trends can be seen in a Mediterranean influence e.g. grilled rabbit with olive oil mash. Service is friendly, relaxed yet efficient. Bibendum's wine list is one of the best in London. There is a huge selection of wines from all over the world, with knowledgeable in-depth coverage of many countries. There is a fine selection of champagnes, and a wide selection of dessert wines, and the wine-buyer here is bang-up-to-date with the latest trends.

Boyd's

Price (lunch):	£20-£25
Price (dinner):	£40-£50

Address:	135 Kensington Church Street, Notting Hill, London W8 7LD
Phone:	0171 727 5452
Fax:	0171 221 0615
Reservations?	Yes
Nearest tube:	Notting Hill Gate
Set lunch:	£14
Set dinner:	No
Open lunch:	Monday - Saturday 12:30 - 14:30
Open dinner:	Monday - Saturday 19:00 - 23:00
Closed:	Christmas
Seats:	40
Private Room?	Yes (40 people)
Credit cards:	Visa,Amex,Access, Diners
Disabled access:	No
Music played?	No
Non-smoking?	No
Chef:	Boyd Gilmour

A tranquil refuge with understated but classy cooking. The dining room at Boyd's is long and narrow, with a calm and friendly atmosphere. An appealing menu has three fish options to add to the four or five meat dishes. One meal started with an excellent mini tomato pizza, and the high culinary standard continued with a dish of seared scallops in a red and green pepper sauce. The scallops were cooked perfectly, with the sauce deep and intense. A difficult dish to get right, warm goat's cheese with rocket, was also very balanced. A cep risotto was well handled, and the fish cooking is a high point. A 'quintet of lemon' dessert was original, with a lovely set of mini-dishes like lemon tart, a lemon creme brulée and lemon sorbet served in a little pastry tulipe. Coffee was strong, though if this was a double espresso then you would need specialist equipment to detect a single. The wine list is extensive with classy growers, though mark-ups are a little high, e.g. the excellent Vina Ardanza at a rather excessive £18.50.

Brackenbury

Price (lunch):	£20-£25
Price (dinner):	£20-£25

Address:	129-131 Brackenbury Road, Shepherds Bush, London W6 0BQ
Phone:	0181 748 0107
Fax:	0181 741 0905
Reservations?	Yes (necessary)
Nearest tube:	Hammersmith or Goldhawk Road
Open lunch:	Tuesday - Friday + Sunday 12:30 - 14:45
Open dinner:	Monday - Saturday 17:30 - 22:45
Closed:	Bank Holidays, 10 days at Christmas
Seats:	55 (+20 in summer)
Private Room?	No
Credit cards:	Visa,Amex,Access, Diners
Disabled access?	Yes (not to toilets)
Music played?	No
Non-smoking?	No
Chefs:	Adam Robinson and Toby Gush

If only all neighbourhood restaurants were like this one. There are two little dining rooms side by side, each facing the residential street. The menu changes daily, and has a short list of about half a dozen choices of starter and main course. A goat's cheese and haddock salad was delicious, served with the inevitable rocket. In an aubergine tart, the aubergines were delicately cooked and the pastry was of a very high standard. A seafood grill consisted of a very well-prepared fillet of sea bass, along with some squid (non-rubbery variety) and some moist and tender salmon. Adam Robinson's training at Alistair Little (see entry) has given him a keen appreciation of the importance of fresh seasonal ingredients, and his cooking is of a very high standard. A dessert of apple and blackberry crumble, served with a little freshly made custard on the side, was a delight. The wine list spans the world and has the nice feature of offering many choices (over half) by the glass, in a list of around 20 or 30 bottles.

Butlers Wharf Chop House

Price (lunch):	£30-£50
Price (dinner):	£35-£50

Address:	36E Shad Thames, Butlers Wharf London, SE1 2YE
Phone:	0171 403 3403
Fax:	0171 403 3414
Reservations?	Yes
Nearest tube:	Tower Hill or London Bridge
Set lunch:	£22.95
Open lunch:	All week 12:00 - 15:00
Open dinner:	All week 18:00 - 23:00
Closed:	Christmas
Seats:	115 (+40 at bar)
Private Room?	Yes (12 people)
Credit cards:	Visa, Amex, Access, Diners
Disabled access?	Yes
Music played?	No
Non-smoking?	No
Chef:	Rod Eggleston

I do love the view from the Conran gastrodome. The Chop House is just next to Pont de La Tour, though aimed slightly downmarket from its neighbour. The olives and breads are excellent, and the menu is no-nonsense British, with various old-fashioned dishes. Kedgeree is very good but extremely rich, while the duck and potato pie I tried was sublime. Not everything works so well, and the danger of such simple food is that fish and chips can taste like, well, fish and chips. Stalwarts like bread and butter pudding are well executed, and the coffee is strong. The wine list is just a subset of the excellent one at Pont de la Tour, though still extremely well chosen, e.g. the excellent Coldstream Hills Pinot Noir at a reasonable mark-up. The service is friendly and the only caveat would be that the bill for lunch, with a set menu for £22.95, can easily creep up to around £40 (coffee is extra, and service is 15%), which is a little high given the relatively straightforward food.

Le Caprice

Price (lunch):	£30-£50
Price (dinner):	£30-£50

Address:	Arlington House, Arlington Street, Piccadilly London SW1A 1RT
Phone:	0171 629 2239
Fax:	0171 493 9040
Reservations?	Yes
Nearest tube:	Green Park or Piccadilly Circus
Open lunch:	All week 12:00 - 15:00
Open dinner:	All week 18:00 - 24:00
Closed:	Christmas Eve after lunch to January 1st
Seats:	90
Private Room?	No
Credit cards:	Visa, Amex, Access
Disabled access?	Yes (not to toilets)
Music played?	Yes (evenings)
Non-smoking?	No
Executive Chef:	Mark Hix
Head chef:	Tim Hughes

Places known for their celebrity clientèle are generally well worth avoiding, but this is an exception. Le Caprice avoids the trap of seeming only to care about its seriously rich customers, and the service in my experience is consistently welcoming even if you don't turn up in a Ferrari. The cooking is bistro style, with superb tomato and basil tartelettes, risotto and salads. The decor is hi-tech modern, very smart yet managing to retain a relaxed air. Though the prices are hardly bargain basement the cooking is genuinely classy. The other customers will usually include some well-known faces.

The wines are well chosen, with markups less outrageous than one might imagine.

dell'Ugo

Price (lunch):	**£25-£40**
Price (dinner):	**£25-£40**

Address:	56 Frith Street, Soho London W1V 5TA
Phone:	0171 734 8300
Fax:	0171 734 8784
Reservations?	Yes
Nearest tube:	Leicester Square or Tottenham Court Rd
Open lunch:	Monday - Friday 12:00 - 15:00
Open dinner:	Monday - Saturday 17:30 - 00:15
Closed:	Bank Holidays
Seats:	180
Private Room?	Yes (14 people); also private catering for up to 60 people
Credit cards:	Visa,Amex,Diners
Disabled access?	Yes (not to toilets)
Music played?	No
Non-smoking?	No
Chef:	Mark Emberton

An interesting idea: three different restaurants within a restaurant, the surroundings moving from informal on the ground floor to moderately formal on the top floor. The food is fashionable modern British, with olive oil and Italian flavours much in evidence. Anthony Worrall-Thompson's gift is in spotting what the public like and delivering it, and here he has largely succeeded. A lively and fun atmosphere in the heart of Soho, with appealing and generally competent food. The simple things seem best: fish and chips, mini pizzas, etc. The wine list is short but well chosen. My concern is inconsistencies in the cooking, and a bill that is not unreasonable but can quickly add up to a sum which would obtain you classier food elsewhere. Still, a fun place.

Downstairs at 190

Price (lunch):	**n/a**
Price (dinner):	**£25-£40**

Address:	190 Queens' Gate, South Kensington, London SW7 5EU
Phone:	0171 581 5666
Fax:	0171 581 8172
Reservations?	Yes
Nearest tube:	South Kensington or Gloucester Road
Open lunch:	None
Open dinner:	Monday - Saturday 19:00 - 24:00
Closed:	Christmas Eve to beginning January, but open New Year's Eve
Seats:	65
Private Room?	Yes (25 people)
Credit cards:	Visa,Amex,Access, Diners
Disabled access?	No
Music played?	Yes
Non-smoking?	Separate section
Chef:	Carlo Corallini

Another Worrall-Thompson extravaganza, this basement restaurant specialises in seafood. There is certainly no lack of adventure here, as spices and techniques from around the world are drawn together, e.g. Creole style blackened fish, or grilled fish served with pesto sauce. The adventure generally seems to pay off, though some inconsistency slips in. The staff seem fairly harried, though manage to maintain a veneer of charm. Desserts see British goodies like bread-and-butter pudding, or cheesecake. The wine list is pleasingly up-to-date, with plenty of New World possibilities. Bistro 190 upstairs also has a lively atmosphere and fashionable cooking, but without the emphasis on seafood. I'm not sure that it is quite worth the money, but the crowds of customers indicate that many believe it is.

Eagle

Price (lunch):	£20-£30
Price (dinner):	£20-£30

Address:	159 Farringdon Road, Clerkenwell, London EC1R 3AL
Phone:	0171 837 1353
Fax:	None
Nearest tube:	Farringdon
Open lunch:	Monday - Friday 12:30 - 14:30
Open dinner:	Monday - Friday 18:30 - 22:30
Closed:	Bank Holidays, 2-3 weeks Christmas
Seats:	55
Private Room?	No
Credit cards:	None
Disabled access:	Partial (1 step)
Music played?	Yes
Non-smoking?	No
Chef:	David Eyre

Serving trendy Mediterranean food in an old pub in Clerkenwell may not seem an obviously inspired idea, but the formula is certainly successful. The pub premises are still very much in evidence, and you can just come for a drink. The daily specials which constitute the menu are chalked up on a blackboard, and you pay for each dish individually at the bar. The food is at its best when taking good basic ingredients and producing things like hearty vegetable soups, or a tomato and herb soup made with good tomatoes and very fresh herbs. The simple grilled dishes can disappoint, especially if you were expecting to pay pub rather than restaurant prices. Overall, the formula works well provided you have the correct expectations. There is a good selection of wines by the glass.

Fifth Floor

Price (lunch):	£30-£45
Price (dinner):	£30-£45

Address:	Harvey Nichols, 109-125 Knightsbridge, London SW1X 7RJ
Phone:	0171 235 5000
Fax:	0171 235 5020
Reservations?	Yes
Nearest tube:	Knightsbridge
Set lunch:	£17.50 (2 courses) £21.50 (3 courses)
Set dinner:	Same as lunch
Open lunch:	All week 12:00 - 15:00 (15:30 Saturday)
Open dinner:	Monday - Saturday 18:30 - 23:30
Closed:	25th, 26th December
Seats:	110
Private Room?	No
Credit cards:	Visa, Amex, Access, Diners
Disabled access?	Yes
Music played?	No
Non-smoking?	No
Chef:	Henry Harris

The showpiece of the new Harvey Nichols food hall (see entry), the Fifth Floor has two eating places: a café looking directly out on to the food market, and this restaurant to one side. It is impeccably designed other than the chairs, which were clearly intended to be admired rather than actually occupied. The designers have conjured up a bright, modern space that takes advantage of the fine views available from up here and it in no way feels like a typical department store eating place. The chef Henry Harris previously cooked at Bibendum, and is very capable. The menu is short (especially at lunch) but very appealing, with things like a ceviche of scallops and avocado, or grilled Dover sole with olive oil mash. There is a brief wine list displayed with the lunch menu, but there is also a much longer (and extremely well chosen) wine menu available on request. Moreover if you find a bottle you really like you can pop next door to the wine merchant and buy one afterwards. The atmosphere is lively and the service friendly and efficient. The bread is excellent.

Fulham Road

Price (lunch):	£20-£25
Price (dinner):	£35-£50

Address:	257-259 Fulham Road, Fulham, London, SW3 6HY
Phone:	0171 351 7823
Fax:	0171 490 3128
Reservations?	Yes
Nearest tube:	Gloucester Road or Fulham Broadway
Set lunch:	£14.50 or £17.50
Open lunch:	All week 12:00 - 14:00
Open dinner:	All week 18:30 - 23:00
Closed:	1 week at Christmas, Bank Holidays
Seats:	80
Private Room?	Yes (12 people)
Credit cards:	Visa,Amex,Access
Disabled access?	Yes (not to toilets)
Music played?	No
Non-smoking?	No
Chef:	Richard Corrigan

An exciting venture, Fulham Road is the latest of Stephen Bull's restaurants, and for me it is the best of the lot. The dining room is modern and well-lit, and service keeps its charm and efficiency even at the busiest times, or under provocation from the Sloaney clientèle. Chef Richard Corrigan, after an excursion at the fish restaurant Bentleys and the Irish Mulligan's, is in charge of the kitchen here, and his talent and experience shine through. Fish is especially well handled, sauces are spot-on and desserts are scrummy. There is close attention to detail, with the vegetables well-handled, fine bread and strong coffee (though paying for refills seems rather stingy). Prices can mount up a little unexpectedly, as the extras are added on, but for food of Michelin star quality the bill is not unreasonable.

Granita

Price (lunch):	£15-£20
Price (dinner):	£25-£30

Address:	127 Upper Street, Islington, London N1 1QP
Phone:	0171 226 3222
Fax:	None
Reservations?	Yes (essential)
Nearest tube:	Angel
Set lunch:	£11.50 (2 courses) £13.50 (3 courses)
Open lunch:	Wednesday - Sunday 12:30 - 14:30
Open dinner:	Tuesday - Sunday 18:30 - 22:30
Closed:	10 days Christmas, 2 weeks August, 1 week Easter
Seats:	62
Private Room?	Yes (55 people)
Credit cards:	Access,Visa
Disabled access:	Partial (1 step)
Music played?	No
Non-smoking?	No
Chef:	Ahmed Kharshoum

Finding restaurants in Islington is like being lost at sea – water, water everywhere, but not a drop to drink. Finally this situation has been rectified. Granita has fairly minimalist decor – bare wooden tables, basic chairs, and plain flooring. The menu is very short (just four main courses and four starters). A starter of scallops was cooked just right, served on a bed of tender lentils which had an element of spice to them, accompanied by a rocket salad with very good leaves. A tuna dish was superb, lightly grilled and served with perfect sauté potatoes and a few leaves of rocket salad. A linguini with wild mushrooms had excellent texture, and the seasoning was well judged. To round off, a chocolate cake with chocolate sauce, served with an ice cream of banana and walnuts and chocolate, and a creme brulée kept up the very high standards – a fine meal. Coffee is nice and strong. The wine list fits on a page but is intelligently chosen, e.g. Tim Adams, Coldstream Hills, at fair prices.

Greenhouse

Price (lunch):	**£30-£55**
Price (dinner):	**£30-£55**

Address:	27A Hays Mews, Mayfair, London, W1X 7RJ
Phone:	0171 499 3331
Fax:	None
Reservations?	Yes
Nearest tube:	Green Park
Set lunch:	No
Open lunch:	All week 12:00 - 14:30
Open dinner:	All week 19:00 - 23:00 (22:00 on Sundays)
Closed:	Christmas
Seats:	95
Private Room?	No
Credit cards:	Visa,Amex,Access, Diners
Disabled access?	No
Music played?	No
Non-smoking?	No
Chef:	Gary Rhodes

Nestling under a block of flats in a residential street, the designers have managed to conjure a leafy atmosphere: you enter through a covered walkway surrounded by plants. Inside the decor is very smart yet the atmosphere not too formal. The food ranges across English dishes such as fishcakes and faggots, through to the trendier dishes accompanied by mashed potato with olive oil. The quality of cooking throughout is very high, and the price shows a lot of variation to reflect the widely varying costs of ingredients; hence you can eat some very grand dishes, or stick to plain things and save some money. The wine list is short but well-chosen, ranging from easy drinking to seriously expensive.

Hilaire

Price (lunch):	**£20-£25**
Price (dinner):	**£30-£45**

Address:	68 Old Brompton Road, South Kensington, London SW7 3LQ
Phone:	0171 584 8993
Fax:	0171 581 2949
Reservations?	Yes
Nearest tube:	South Kensington
Set lunch:	£12.50 (2 courses)
Set dinner	£16 (supper) £25.50
Open lunch:	Monday-Friday 12:30-14:30
Open dinner:	Monday- Saturday 18:30-23:30
Closed:	Bank Holidays
Seats:	50
Private Room?	Yes (20 or 35 people)
Credit cards:	Visa,Amex,Access, Diners
Disabled access?	Yes (not to toilets)
Music played?	No
Non-smoking?	No
Chef:	Bryan Webb

Bryan Webb has fashioned a delightful little restaurant on the busy Old Brompton Road. The slightly cramped premises are soon to be expanded, and the service is always very friendly in my experience. The cooking is of a very high standard; a sea bass dish I had here was quite outstanding, and I have yet to have a disappointing meal here. There are some interesting touches, like laverbread (boiled seaweed) and Glamorgan sausage, as well as more conventional dishes. Desserts are excellent. There is a very cosy atmosphere, which helps overcome the slightly cramped feel of the restaurant. Wines are sensibly arranged by style rather than country and the care taken with selection is much better than at most places. Try to book one of the two tables on the ground floor by the window, where you can watch the world go by on the Old Brompton Road. For those working late there is a supper menu available.

Ivy

Price (lunch):	£15-£20
Price (dinner):	£25-£50

Address	1 West Street, London WC2H 9NE
Phone:	0171 836 4751
Fax:	0171 497 3644
Reservations?	Yes
Nearest tube:	Leicester Square or Covent Garden
Set lunch:	£12.50 (weekends only)
Open lunch:	All week 12:00 - 15:00
Open dinner:	All week 17:30 - 24:00
Closed:	Bank holidays, Monday lunch
Seats:	100
Private Room?	Yes (60 people)
Credit cards:	Visa,Amex,Access, Diners
Disabled access?	Yes (not to toilets)
Music played?	No
Non-smoking?	No
Chefs:	Mark Hix & Des McDonald

The Ivy is a bustling brasserie with bright lighting to match the bright young things who keep the place buzzing. It is a sibling to Le Caprice, and has a similarly well-heeled crowd. The food is as designer-conscious as the mirrored room, with dishes ranging from salmon fishcakes with sorrel to excellent risotto, to bangers and mash. There are also oriental touches, such as bang-bang chicken. The cooking is of a high standard, and the prices high but not outrageous given the level of the cooking. Service is friendly and competent in my experience, even to the few non-film stars eating here.

The wine list is unusually well thought-out, including the excellent Mas de Daumas Gassac. The growers are well selected whatever region is being covered, e.g. Marques de Murrietta from Spain or Penfolds from Australia.

Kensington Place

Price (lunch):	£20-£30
Price (dinner):	£25-£50

Address	201 Kensington Church Street, London W8 7LX
Phone:	0171 727 3184
Fax:	0171 229 2025
Reservations?	Yes
Nearest tube:	Notting Hill
Set lunch:	£13.50 (3 courses)
Open lunch:	All week 12:00 - 15:00
Open dinner:	All week 18:30 - 23:45
Closed:	Christmas Eve to Boxing Day + New Year's Day
Seats:	140
Private Room?	No
Credit cards:	Visa,Amex,Access, Diners
Disabled access?	Yes
Music played?	No
Non-smoking?	Separate section
Chef:	Rowley Leigh

Ultra-chic decor and clientèle Kensington Place continues to be immensely popular, crowded and noisy. The large dining room is bright and the atmosphere buzzing, especially later on in the evening when the fashionable eat (presumably few people in advertising have to be up at the crack of dawn). Not a venue for a romantic evening, but the kitchen turns out very fine food. The cooking is as voguish as the surroundings, with plenty of rocket salad and olive oil mash to accompany the superbly grilled meat and fish. The menu changes daily. The wine list is a model of its type, with very well-chosen growers from around the world and fair mark-ups. Despite the bustle, service is efficient and courteous.

Launceston Place

Price (lunch):	£30-£50
Price (dinner):	£30-£50

Address:	1A Launceston Place, Kensington, London W8 5RL
Phone:	0171 937 6912
Fax:	0171 938 2412
Reservations?	Yes
Nearest tube:	Gloucester Road or High Street Kensington
Set lunch:	£13.50 (2 courses) £16.50 (3 courses)
Set dinner	As lunch till 20:00 Supper menu available after 22:00
Open lunch:	Sunday - Friday 12:30 - 14:30 (15:00 Sunday)
Open dinner:	Monday - Saturday 19:00 - 23:30
Closed:	5 days at Christmas, Easter
Seats:	90
Private Room?	Yes (12 or 30)
Credit cards:	Visa,Amex,Access
Disabled access:	Yes (not to toilets)
Music played?	No
Non-smoking?	No
Chef:	Cathy Gradwell

A charming restaurant tucked away in Kensington, just by a quiet little green and near the Boltons, a set of beautiful houses for the seriously rich. The restaurant itself is fairly large, with a couple of big rooms, but the tables are well spaced out, so there is no sense of being crammed in. The service is exceptional, some of the most friendly I have had in London all year. The menu is an attractive selection of modern British. A starter of quail on a bed of spiced puy lentils in a simple jus was superb. A main course of wild salmon steak, served with some vegetables was good but did not quite maintain the standard, nor did a fairly ordinary black pudding. However things perked up again with dessert, a fine lemon tart, while coffee is also good. The wine list is excellent, with lots of New World wines together with some well chosen (mainly French) reds , e.g. a fine Fleury from Duboeuf. Most wines are under £25, and the mark-ups on the expensive bottles are also low, e.g. for those wishing to seriously indulge, Krug 1982 champagne at £85 is barely the retail price. Given the location the bill is fair.

Leith's

Price (lunch):	n/a
Price (dinner):	£40-£60

Address	92 Kensington Park Road, Notting Hill, London W11 2PN
Phone:	0171 229 4481
Fax:	None
Reservations?	Yes
Nearest tube:	Notting Hill Gate
Set dinner:	£25 (two courses)
Open dinner:	All week 19:30 - 23:30
Closed:	2 days at August Bank holiday, 4 days at Christmas
Seats:	70
Private Room?	Yes (40 or 55 people)
Credit cards:	Visa,Amex,Access, Diners
Disabled access?	Yes (not to toilets)
Music played?	No
Non-smoking?	On request
Chef:	Alex Floyd

Leith's trundles on, a cosy institution of rare reliability in the volatile restaurant world. Alex Floyd produces very fine food. To begin there is a trolley of starters, which is visually appealing and varies a lot. The main courses can be quite plain, e.g. roast duckling, but are none the worse for that, and there is a full vegetarian menu, still a rarity in top restaurants. Ingredients match the fine technique, with Leith's even running its own farm which supplies excellent produce to the restaurant. The wine list is particularly fine, with well-chosen growers, plenty of variety and a decent selection by the glass. Its coverage of many countries is strong, and with fair prices is one of the most attractive wine lists in London. Service has its ups and downs but is generally very good. The only real caveat would be that the food can seem a touch pricey for what it is.

Le Métro

Price (lunch):	£30-£35
Price (dinner):	£30-£35

Address:	The Capital Hotel, 22-24 Basil Street, Knightsbridge London SW3 1AT
Phone:	0171 589 6286
Fax:	0171 225 0011
Reservations?	Yes (parties of over 6 only)
Nearest tube:	Knightsbridge
Set lunch:	No
Set dinner:	No
Open:	Monday - Saturday 07:15 - 23:00 Sunday Breakfast only
Closed:	Christmas
Seats:	50
Private Room?	No
Credit cards:	Visa,Amex,Access, Diners
Disabled access?	Dining room only
Music played?	Yes, evenings only
Non-smoking?	No
Chef:	Philip Britten

This wine bar underneath the Capital Hotel is operated by the hotel itself, and the kitchen is supervised and guided by Philip Britten (see separate entry for the Capital). This is very much a haunt of the local Knightsbridge set, with much conversation about houses with prices like telephone numbers. The basement is a little cramped and has some rather awkward corners but the service is welcoming and efficient. A spinach pasta with wild mushrooms and pine kernels had authentic pasta, and the mushrooms were well prepared and seasoned. A dish of liver and bacon was pan-fried very well, the bacon of high quality, though the dish could have done with a sauce. An apple and almond tart had classy pastry, though using dessert apples rather than British cooking apples seems odd on a British menu, but shows the French influence from the main kitchen. The wine list shows care in its choice.

Museum Street Café

Price (lunch):	£15-£20
Price (dinner):	£25-£30

Address	47 Museum Street, London WC1A 1LY
Phone:	0171 405 3211 or 0171 405 3212
Fax:	None
Reservations?	Yes
Nearest tube:	Holborn or Tottenham Court Road
Set lunch:	£12 (two courses) £15 (three courses)
Set dinner	£17 (two courses) £21 (three courses)
Open lunch:	Monday - Friday 12:30 - 14:30
Open dinner:	Monday - Friday 18:30 - 23:00
Closed:	1 week in August, 1 week at Easter 1 week at Christmas
Seats:	35
Private Room?	No
Credit cards:	Visa,Access
Disabled access?	Yes
Music played?	No
Non-smoking?	Completely
Chefs:	Gail Koerber & Mark Nathan

This unusual restaurant has the rare distinction of serving high-quality food at reasonable prices. It feels more of a café than a restaurant, with an informal atmosphere in somewhat cramped surroundings. There is a very limited weekly menu with just a couple of dishes for each course. However the food is very well executed, particularly the chargrilled specialities. Salads are very good, with consistently fresh and succulent leaves. The style is simple, with good ingredients and careful preparation. Another strong point here is the quality of desserts, with some fine pastry skills in evidence. The restaurant is now licensed and has a short but cleverly chosen wine list, but you can still bring your own wine for a £4 corkage charge. Breads are home-made and coffee is good and strong. Vegetarian meals can be arranged if you ask when booking. The restaurant is completely non-smoking.

Nosh Brothers

Price (lunch):	n/a
Price (dinner):	£20-£30

Address:	773 Fulham Road, Fulham, London SW10 5HA
Phone:	0171 736 7311
Fax:	Same
Reservations?	Yes
Nearest tube:	Parsons Green
Open lunch:	None
Open dinner:	Monday - Saturday 19:30 - 23:00
Closed:	Sundays
Seats:	80
Private Room?	Yes (70 people)
Credit cards:	Visa, Amex, Access
Disabled access:	Yes (not to toilets)
Music played?	Yes
Non-smoking?	No
Chefs:	Chris Endeacott & Mick Nosh

Would you be tempted to eat somewhere with a name like this, especially when there is a large picture of the two chefs dressed up in Blues Brothers outfits adorning the dining room wall? Don't be put off – the cooking here is serious. The main basement dining room has a lively atmosphere, with minimalist black and white decor with bright lighting; many of the tables have benches rather than chairs. The menu changes daily; one day this offered an excellent gazpacho featuring very fresh tomatoes, onions, green peppers and herbs. Tortilla con pimento is not, as one might expect, a refugee from a Tex-Mex bar, but the Spanish for red pepper omelette. This was very good indeed, with potatoes, fresh peas and pimentos in a remarkably delicate omelette. A chocolate mousse was lovely, with good quality chocolate and a consistent, creamy texture. The wine list is short, with 17 bottles from around the world in the £8.50 to £24 range.

Noughts & Crosses

Price (lunch):	£20-£25
Price (dinner):	£25-£30

Address:	77 The Grove, Ealing, London W5 5LL
Phone:	0181 840 7568
Fax:	0181 840 1905
Reservations?	Yes
Nearest tube:	Ealing Broadway or Ealing Common
Set lunch:	£11.95 (2 courses) - £15.40 (3 courses)
Set dinner:	£15.60 (2 courses) - £19.50 (3 courses)
Open lunch:	Sunday only 12:00 - 14:00
Open dinner:	Tuesday - Saturday 19:00 - 22:00
Closed:	26th December - 5th January, August
Seats:	55
Private Room?	Yes (25 people)
Credit cards:	Visa,Amex,Access
Disabled access:	Yes (not to toilets)
Music played?	Yes
Non-smoking?	Separate section
Chef:	Anthony Ma

A good-quality neighbourhood restaurant in Ealing. The dining room itself is smart, while the menu is more adventurous than most 'local' places. There is attention to detail in the incidentals, for example a good selection of breads. The menu is strong on seafood, with an oriental influence showing in baked sea bass with spring onions and ginger in a black bean sauce. There are also more earthy dishes like cassoulet of green lentils and haricot beans with Italian sausage, which was excellent. There is a good choice of desserts, and a rich dark and white chocolate mousse flavoured with Cointreau was as nice as it sounds. The wine list has a broad range and is intelligently chosen with lots of choice between £10 and £15. Considering that plenty of places charge around £9 for a bottle of Liebfraumilch, this is a pleasant change. There are a few dessert wines by the glass, a nice touch. The cooking overall is competent rather than inspirational, but certainly very good for a local place.

Odette's

| Price (lunch): | £20-£25 |
| Price (dinner): | £35-£45 |

Address:	130 Regents Park Road, Primrose Hill, London NW1 8XL
Phone:	0171 586 5486
Fax:	None
Nearest tube:	Chalk Farm
Set lunch:	£10
Set dinner:	No
Open lunch:	Sunday - Friday 12:30 - 14:30
Open dinner:	Monday - Saturday 19:00 - 23:00
Closed:	1 week at Christmas
Seats:	60
Private Room?	Yes (8 or 30)
Credit cards:	Visa,Amex,Access, Diners
Disabled access:	No
Music played?	No
Non-smoking?	Separate section
Chef:	Paul Holmes

A lovely setting in the cosy, village-like atmosphere of Regents Park Road in Primrose Hill. The restaurant itself has lots of little rooms separated by short staircases, plenty of mirrors on the walls to give some illusion of space and greenery to give warmth. The menu is nothing if not experimental, with lots of exotic combinations. A slow roast fish soup with cardamom and orange had deep flavour, while a sweet onion tart had excellent pastry and was also of a high standard. The main courses did not match the starters, e.g. a mediocre red mullet, while vegetables were a disaster: green beans just warmed and semi-raw, mashed potato plain lumpy. Desserts also varied. The wine list is compensation for the erratic food, with an eclectic list with wildly varying mark-ups. The list is sensibly sorted by style rather than country and there is a wide selection by the glass and of half bottles. The prices are rather high for the standard of cooking, but the locals around here do not seem to mind.

O'Keefe's

| Price (lunch): | £15-£20 |
| Price (dinner): | £20-£25 |

Address:	18 Deering Street off Oxford Street, London W1R 9AA
Phone:	0171 495 0878
Fax:	0171 629 7082
Reservations?	Yes
Nearest tube:	Bond Street or Oxford Circus
Open lunch:	Monday - Saturday 12:30 - 15:30
Open dinner:	Monday - Friday 19:30 - 22:00
Closed:	Bank Holidays
Seats:	38
Private Room?	No
Credit cards:	Visa,Amex,Access, Diners
Disabled access?	Yes (not to toilets)
Music played?	Yes
Non-smoking?	No (except at bar)
Chef:	Beth Coventry

A reliable pit stop tucked away off Oxford Street. Fairly basic decor (plain walls, not all of the same colour!) and brown paper tablecloths, which makes you feel as if your lunch is about to be tied up with string and posted somewhere. There is a bar area on the left as you walk in, and the cooking is done in full view of the diners. A simple olive, mozzarella and basil tart was a pleasant starter, with competent rather than excellent pastry but benefiting from a genuinely good salad, with very fresh leaves and a simple walnut oil dressing. A mushroom risotto was very good indeed. The shitake mushrooms were well prepared, the arborio rice being mixed in with some more very good salad leaves. The only criticism that could be levelled was a slightly heavy hand with the salt cellar. White chocolate ice cream was definitely home-made with a hint of almonds, and had a rich texture. To round the meal off, coffee was welcomingly strong. Good value.

Le Pont de la Tour

| Price (lunch): | £40-£50 |
| Price (dinner): | £30-£70 |

Address	Butler's Wharf 36D Shad Thames, Bermondsey, London SE1 2YE
Phone:	0171 403 8403
Fax:	0171 403 0267
Reservations?	Yes (advisable)
Nearest tube:	London Bridge or Tower Hill
Set lunch:	£26.50
Open lunch:	Sunday - Friday 12:00 - 15:00
Open dinner:	All week 18:00 - 24:00
Closed:	Christmas Eve (dinner), Christmas Day, Boxing Day
Seats:	105 + 66 outside
Private Room?	Yes (20 people)
Credit cards:	Visa,Amex,Access, Diners
Disabled access?	Yes
Music played?	Yes
Non-smoking?	No
Chef:	David Burke

Le Pont de la Tour is blessed with perhaps the best view of any restaurant in London, nestling beside Tower Bridge. The sight of the bridge lit up in the evening is enchanting. The view certainly adds something to the price, which can seem rather high; however the food is of a matching standard. The cooking here is reminiscent of (though not as good as) Bibendum which, like this establishment, is also owned by Terence Conran. The menu is appealing, with the usual modern British repertoire. Seafood is treated well, and the wide range of breads is a lovely accompaniment. The wine list is one of the best in London, with an encyclopaedic coverage of wines from all over the world at mark-ups that are not outrageous. These include a set of selections under £20, and there is an unusually good set of dessert wines on offer. A delightful place for a romantic special occasion.

Quaglino's

| Price (lunch): | £30-£55 |
| Price (dinner): | £30-£55 |

Address	16 Bury Street, near Piccadilly, London, SW1Y 6AL
Phone:	0171 930 6767
Fax:	0171 839 2866
Reservations?	Yes (necessary)
Nearest tube:	Piccadilly Circus
Open lunch:	All week 12:00 - 15:00
Open dinner:	All week 17:30 - 24:00 (1:00 Fri, Sat, 23:00 Sun)
Closed:	Christmas
Seats:	338 (90 at bar)
Private Room?	Yes (40 people)
Credit cards:	Visa,Amex,Access, Diners
Disabled access?	Yes
Music played?	Yes
Non-smoking?	No
Chef:	Martin Webb

For fashion victims, Quaglino's is the only place to be seen at the moment, darlings. Terence Conran's most extravagant restaurant venture so far, Quaglino's is the ultimate in designer eating. The premises are magnificent, with a cavernous dining room and a higher-level bar area, beautifully decorated (even the pillars are each decorated by a separate artist). Every detail, down to the dress of the cigarette girl, is supposed to evoke memories of French bistros in the 1930s. The food however, is unashamedly modern: lots of pasta, unusual vegetables, and Mediterranean influence. After considerable inconsistency when it opened the cooking has now settled down somewhat, but dishes are still variable. There is no denying the success of the formula; despite its huge scale, the restaurant is often full even on weekdays. If you don't want to eat here than you can just pose at the bar.

Quality Chop House

Price (lunch):	£20-£25
Price (dinner):	£20-£25

Address:	94 Farringdon Road, Clerkenwell, London EC1R 3EA
Phone:	0171 837 5093
Fax:	None
Reservations?	Yes (advisable)
Nearest tube:	Farringdon
Open lunch:	Sunday - Friday 12:00 - 15:00
Open dinner:	All week 18:30 - 11:30
Closed:	Christmas period
Seats:	40
Private Room?	No
Credit cards:	Visa,Amex,Access, Diners
Disabled access?	Yes
Music played?	No
Non-smoking?	No
Chef:	Charles Fontaine

A quite remarkable place, styled in the manner of a working men's cafe. As you take your seat (in this case a famously uncomfortable bench) in the brightly lit room with bottles of ketchup on the table and other diners at your elbow, it is hard to believe that you are about to indulge in top class food. Yet disbelief melts away when the food arrives, with traditional dishes such as moist and delicious salmon fish cakes or fish and chips (excellent), venturing to some more Mediterranean touches (the menu changes slightly each day). Charles Fontaine used to cook at the Ivy (a bigger change of decor would be hard to imagine), and his skill shows through in his renditions of traditional English dishes like treacle tart. There is a short but competent wine list, and overall this represents excellent value, even if it is not the place for a lingering romantic evening.

Ransome's Dock Restaurant

Price (lunch):	£15-£20
Price (dinner):	£25-£35

Address:	35-37 Parkgate Road, Battersea, London SW11 4NP
Phone:	0171 223 1611 or 0171 924 2462
Fax:	0171 924 2614
Reservations?	Yes
Nearest tube:	None near
Set lunch:	£11.50 (2 courses)
Set dinner:	No
Open:	Monday-Friday 11:00-23:00 Saturday 11:00-24:00 Sunday 12:00-15:30
Closed:	Christmas
Seats:	70
Private Room?	No
Credit cards:	Visa,Amex,Access, Diners
Disabled access:	Yes
Music played?	Yes
Non-smoking?	No
Chef:	Martin Lam

Quite bright, attractive surroundings, though it does not overlook the river but rather a pond. The atmosphere is casual. Breads were excellent, especially the hazelnut variety. The menu is very appealing, though the execution is variable. A haddock and goat's cheese salad was very good, but Morecambe Bay potted shrimps with toast were rather ordinary. A John Dory was very well prepared, as was brill served with salad leaves and a simple buttery sauce. A sirloin steak was excellent and generous in size, with a simple jus that was quite good, though lacking in intensity, and the chips were only adequate. Desserts tried included a reasonable cherry tart and pleasant summer pudding. Service can be pretty flaky, with several things forgotten on an inspection visit. The wine list is good, with Mas de Daumas Gassac 1987 at £24 (very fair) and plenty of New World options. The concern is that food prices here are as high as some significantly better restaurants, though for the area this is good value.

Rules

Price (lunch):	**£25-£45**
Price (dinner):	**£25-£45**

Address	35 Maiden Lane
	London, WC2E 7LB
Phone:	0171 836 5314
Fax:	0171 379 0258
Reservations?	Yes
Nearest tube:	Covent Garden or
	Charing Cross
Set lunch:	£15.95
	(weekends only)
Set supper:	£12.95 for 2 courses
	(16:00-18:00)
Open lunch:	All week
Open dinner:	All week
Closed:	1 week at Christmas
Seats:	220
Private Room?	Yes (18- 46 people)
Credit cards:	Visa,Amex,Access,
Disabled access?	Yes (not to toilets)
Music played?	No
Non-smoking?	No
Chef:	Neil Pass

Generally speaking, grand old English dining rooms are to be avoided, so often serving gruesome school-dinner food at outrageous prices. Rules however, despite being the oldest restaurant in London (established in 1798), has moved with the times while keeping a traditional slant. The dining room itself is gorgeous, with dark wood and lots of interesting prints. The game is the thing, supplied from the restaurant's own estate. 'Furred' game includes three types of venison, while there is also guinea fowl, pheasant, and grouse (in season). Starters can be variable, but desserts are well-executed – lemon tart is excellent. The wine list is very short but carefully chosen, with Wolf Blass and Montana from the colonies among the choices.

The Square

Price (lunch):	**£35-£60**
Price (dinner):	**£35-£60**

Address	32 King Street,
	St James,
	London SW1Y 6RJ
Phone:	0171 839 8787
Fax:	0171 321 2124
Reservations?	Yes
Nearest tube:	Green Park
Open lunch:	Monday - Friday
	12:00 - 14:45
Open dinner:	All week
	18:00 - 23:45
	(19:00 - 22:00 Sun)
Closed:	Christmas period &
	Bank Holidays
Seats:	70
Private Room?	Yes (24)
Credit cards:	Visa,Amex,Access,
	Diners
Disabled access?	Partial (1 step)
Music played?	No
Non-smoking?	No
Chef:	Philip Howard

The Square certainly has a following amongst the well-heeled. It tries to be ultra-chic, with modern art littered about the place, chairs of varying colours, yellow cubes popping out of the walls for no apparent reason. To many it seems like the height of good taste, to the artistically challenged it may appear more like a bad LSD trip. The food can be very good indeed, but is also subject to inconsistency. The talented Philip Howard once cooked at Harveys, and has brought with him the virtue of experimentation with the vice of unreliability: while some dishes shine, others do not. For chocoholics, the desserts here involving this wondrous substance are sublime. The wine list is excellent, with a good choice at fairish prices. It is partly organised by style (much the most useful way of arranging a wine list) while the more expensive wines are still listed by region.

Stephen Bull

Price (lunch):	£30-£40
Price (dinner):	£30-£40

Address:	5-7 Blandford Street, Marylebone, London W1H 3AA
Phone:	0171 486 9696
Fax:	0171 490 3128
Reservations?	Yes
Nearest tube:	Bond Street
Set lunch:	£16, £19
Set dinner:	£19, £24
Open lunch:	Monday - Friday 12:00 - 14:15
Open dinner:	Monday - Saturday 18:30 - 22:00
Closed:	Bank Holidays, 1 week Christmas
Seats:	55
Private Room?	No
Credit cards:	Visa,Amex,Access,
Disabled access:	Partial (1 step, not to toilets)
Music played?	No
Non-smoking?	No
Chef:	S. Carter

A calm haven from the rigours of nearby Oxford Street, Stephen Bull's establishment has an attractive menu to match the minimalist decor. Ingredients are high quality, and there are rustic dishes such as Tuscan bean cassoulet to offset the trendier ones like roast sea bass with rocket, orange and thyme butter. In my experience the execution does not always fulfil the promise of the menu, which is a worry when the prices are quite high. The wine list is one of the most intelligently chosen in London, with very fine producers indeed at acceptable mark-ups. There is a decent selection of half bottles and wines by the glass, including the excellent Andrew Quady black Muscat dessert wine. The bill can creep up somewhat, but there is a loyal stream of regulars to testify to its perceived value. Also at:

Stephen Bull's Bistro & Bar 71 John Street, London EC1 (0171 490 3127)

Wilson's

Price (lunch):	£15-£20
Price (dinner):	£20-£30

Address:	236 Blythe Road, Shepherd's Bush, London W14 0HJ
Phone:	0171 603 7267
Fax:	None
Reservations?	Yes (necessary)
Nearest tube:	Hammersmith , Goldhawk Road or Shepherds Bush
Set lunch:	£10 (3 courses) £7.50 (2 courses)
Set dinner:	No
Open lunch:	All week 12:30 - 14:30
Open dinner:	All week 19:30 - 22:30
Closed:	Bank Holidays and Christmas
Seats:	48
Private Room?	No
Credit cards:	Visa,Access and Amex
Disabled access:	Yes (not to toilets)
Music played?	Yes
Non-smoking?	No
Chef:	Robert Hilton

A charming little place near Brook Green with homely decor: tablecloths are tartan, and there is bagpipe music. The staff are extremely welcoming. I thought for a moment that everyone else was a regular, as customers were greeted by name, until I realised that they also remembered my name from the booking, and used it throughout the evening without looking it up. Dishes included good haddock topped with Welsh rarebit on a bed of tomato salad, with a very good French dressing accompanying the rocket salad. Strips of beef fillet, served in a simple red wine sauce with mushrooms were perfectly competent but the fillet strips were cooked for too long and the red wine sauce needed greater reduction. Lemon posset, a lemon-flavoured custard, was very nice, while a chocolate mousse could have benefited from better chocolate but had an extremely smooth texture. A pleasant wine list, with careful selection of growers, e.g. Aotea and Cloudy Bay Sauvignon Blanc as the New Zealand choices.

Burmese

Burmese cuisine draws on influences from China, India and Thailand, yet has a unique identity of its own. Classic Burmese dishes include *panthe kaukswe*, a curried chicken noodle cooked with various spices. Another is *moo hing nga*, a thick fish soup with noodles. Most Burmese dishes contain onion, garlic, ginger, chillies and turmeric, and can be either quite mild or strikingly spicily hot. If you want to sample this interesting cuisine you have just one choice unless you want to venture to Myanmar or San Francisco, but fortunately it is a good one.

Maymyo

Price (lunch):	£15-£20
Price (dinner):	£20-£25

Address:	127 Dulwich Road, Herne Hill London SE24 ONG
Phone:	0171 326 4789
Fax:	None
Reservations?	Yes
Nearest tube:	None near - Herne Hill BR
Set lunch:	£10.50 (3 courses)
Open lunch:	Sunday 12:30 - 14:30
Open dinner:	Tuesday - Saturday 19:00 - 22:30
Closed:	Christmas
Seats:	32
Private Room?	Yes (22 people)
Credit cards:	None
Disabled access?	Yes (not to toilets)
Music played?	Yes
Non-smoking?	Separate section
Chef:	Gerald Andrews

The reincarnation of the old Mandalay in Greenwich, Maymyo is situated in an unpromising parade of shops near Herne Hill. The decor is a little too brown for my taste, with a sort of fake walnut panelling (resembling nothing if not lino) up to dado rail height, and then cream walls above this. There are some strip mirrors, and lots of framed photographs of Myanmar (née Burma). Sliced 'daul' cake is mixed with onion, oil, spring onions and lots of fresh coriander, together with chilli and garlic sauce. It is served warm; it has something of the texture of beancurd, and is very spicy indeed. The main courses were of a rather mixed standard on the inspection visit, the best being a simple one of fried cabbage and onion, cooked in a wok with garlic; this was judged perfectly, and had lovely texture. Prawns cooked with onions, garlic and tomatoes were rather lacklustre, lacking any of the spiciness which enlivened some of the other dishes. Burmese fishballs are cooked with garlic, ginger and onions, served with a simple sauce of tomatoes with coriander. This was quite good, and was complemented by some pickled cauliflower as a side dish, a pungent, slightly sour taste which was very good. Desserts also followed the up and down pattern, with almond cakes genuinely good, while the home-made mango ice-cream was very disappointing, with ice crystals, a crumbly texture and little trace of mangoes. Service is friendly but was rather harried on the evening of my visit, the owner running around the front of house before dashing back into the kitchen to do odd bits of cooking. Prices are rather high, though scarcely more so than in most Thai places.

Caribbean

Despite its appearance in one episode of Lenny Henry's TV series *Chef*, don't hold your breath for Caribbean food appearing in a serious restaurant. There are, sure enough, some interesting dishes: goat curry, sweet potatoes, plantain, but in order for you to enjoy them in most of the premises which serve these in London you need to have been smoking one of the Caribbean's better-known agricultural products.

The Plantation Inn

Price (lunch):	**n/a**
Price (dinner):	**£15-£20**

Address	337-339 High Road, Leytonstone, London E11 4TT
Phone:	0181 558 6210
Fax:	0181 556 5509
Reservations?	Yes
Nearest tube:	Leytonstone
Open lunch:	None
Open dinner:	Tuesday - Sunday 18:00- 24:00
Closed:	Christmas
Seats:	80
Private Room?	No
Credit cards:	Visa,Amex,Access, Diners
Disabled access?	Yes
Music played?	Yes
Non-smoking?	No
Chef:	Mayblin Hamilton

The Plantation Inn ambles on, serving reasonable Caribbean food to the denizens of Leytonstone. The cooking here is considerably better than at some other London Caribbean restaurants, though that is not necessarily a resounding recommendation. The menu offers specialities like goat curry, competently cooked, while sweet potatoes are well prepared here. There are spicy soups, and also simply grilled red snapper. Plantain dishes are also reliable. Service is sufficiently laid back as to be horizontal, but is pleasant enough if you are not in a hurry. Stick to Red Stripe beer to drink. There is also a takeaway service Monday to Saturday, from noon until midnight.

Chinese

Chinese food is complex and steeped in tradition, and it is a pity that in the popular imagination it is represented by a take-away serving cheap food awash with MSG. As explained in Yan-Kit So's excellent book *Classic Cuisine of China*, there are four major branches of Chinese cuisine:

- Peking (which includes Shandong)
- Cantonese (which includes Fujian and Guangdong)
- Shanghai (which includes Jiangsu, Zhejiang and Anhui)
- Sichuan (which includes Hunan)

Peking cuisine is noted for Peking duck, its use of white cabbage and its invention of sesame cakes. Shandong province was established as a centre of culinary excellence in 500 B.C., which rather puts European cooking into perspective. There are many seafood dishes, including abalone and sea cucumber, and shark's fin soup. Glass noodles also come from here, as does Tsing Tao beer. Peking cuisine also includes Mongolian influences like barbecued lamb and lamb hot pot (let's face it, if you are Mongolian, you had better like lamb). It has also created such delicacies as deep-fried beaver, deer penis and bear's paws, which are rarely seen down at your local take-away.

Cantonese cuisine is dominant in England since it is the main cuisine (and language) of Hong Kong, and most Chinese restaurants in London are run by Hong Kong Chinese. The Cantonese make the denizens of Peking look picky and fussy about their food; they eat just about anything that moves, and much that doesn't. Cantonese delicacies include snake soup (made from three different poisonous snakes and some civet cat) and rice worms, as well as the better known dim sum snacks eaten at lunch time. Generally, stir frying is the dominant cooking method, and it is the lightest of the styles in terms of its use of sauces.

Sichuan (there are almost as many spellings as people in the province) cuisine is noted for its use of peppercorns and red chillies, which in fact were only introduced to China from South America in the 17th Century. Heavy use is made of garlic and ginger, as well as extensive use of the 250 types of edible fungi which grow in this area. Delicacies include duck smoked in camphor wood.

Shanghai cuisine is infrequently seen in the West. It is richer and heavier than Cantonese cooking, involving a lot of slow cooking in dark soy sauce and Shaoxing wine. Dishes include drunken chicken and prawns, braised carp, freshwater crabs and deep-fried eel.

Vegetarianism might appear to have passed the Chinese by, but in fact there is a long tradition of it, mainly via the introduction of Buddhism from India in the first century. However, few Chinese restaurants in London cater well for strict vegetarians.

Dragon's Nest

| Price (lunch): | £15-£20 |
| Price (dinner): | £20-£25 |

Address:	58 Shaftesbury Avenue, Soho London W1V 7DE
Phone:	0171 437 3119
Fax:	None
Reservations?	Yes
Nearest tube:	Piccadilly Circus
Set lunch:	£10.50
Open lunch:	All week 12:00 - 15:00
Open dinner:	All week 17:00 - 23:30
Closed:	25th, 26th December
Seats:	150
Private Room?	Yes (40 people)
Credit cards:	Visa,Amex,Access, Diners
Disabled access:	Yes
Non-smoking?	No

The vibrant cooking at the Dragon's Nest caused quite a stir when it opened in 1988; though maddeningly inconsistent, the cooking at its best was really superb. The place seems to have slipped out of many restaurant guides, yet the cooking is still good, and while it lacks the sparkle of youth it has settled into a pleasing style that is better than most in the area. The decor is a cut above most of Chinatown, with clever use of mirrors and decently spaced tables. Service is also courteous. One good thing here is that they are not afraid to use chillies if the dish calls for it, which leaves some of the passing tourists wincing with surprise on occasion. Sichuan eggplant is a good example of this, while there are dishes to satisfy both those seeking the familiar as well as those wishing to explore. The spicier dishes have the most interest.

Fung Shing

| Price (lunch): | £20-£35 |
| Price (dinner): | £20-£35 |

Address:	15 Lisle Street, Soho, London WC2H 7BE
Phone:	0171 437 1539
Fax:	0171 734 0284
Reservations?	Yes
Nearest tube:	Leicester Square
Set dinner:	£11-12 (min two)
Open:	All week 12:00 - 23:30 (last orders at 23:15)
Closed:	Christmas Eve, Christmas Day & Boxing Day
Seats:	85
Private Room?	Yes (30 people)
Credit cards:	Visa,Amex,Access, Diners
Disabled access?	(yes) not to toilets
Music played?	Yes
Non-smoking?	No
Chef:	Kwun Fu

Keeping up with the machinations of Chinatown chefs and restaurants is a tricky business, but for some time the Fung Shing, while not offering the cheapest food around, has been consistently one of the very best Chinatown restaurants. There are plenty of unusual dishes, e.g. sizzling eel, on the Cantonese menu, and service is relatively civil for Chinatown (Hong Kong Chinese and Italians, at least in Florence, seem to have some sort of competition going to deliver the rudest service; personally my money is on the Italians). The noodles here are very good, as is anything with prawns. No dim sum dishes are served (see later section on 'Dim Sum').

Imperial City

Price (lunch):	£25-£30
Price (dinner):	£25-£30

Address:	Royal Exchange, Cornhill, London EC3V 3LL
Phone:	0171 626 3437
Fax:	0171 338 0125
Reservations?	Yes
Nearest tube:	Bank
Set lunch:	£13.90 - £24.80
Set dinner:	£13.90 - £24.80
Open:	Monday to Friday 11:30 - 20:30
Closed:	Bank Holidays
Seats:	180
Private Room?	Yes (18 people)
Credit cards:	Visa,Amex,Access, Diners
Disabled access:	Yes
Music played?	Yes
Non-smoking?	No
Chef:	Tan Kia Lian

There are surprisingly few decent places to eat in the City, given the amount of loose change sloshing about. Imperial City is aiming strictly for the business market, with a very fine location near the Bank of England, tucked away in a basement underneath the Royal Exchange. Of course this all adds up to quite high prices. These are certainly justified by the smart surroundings, with a long bar and various little alcoves where deals can be discussed. The food only partially lives up to expectations, as in the selection of starters, which can be rather ordinary. However some dishes show definite skill, and the quality of the basic ingredients is high. There is a surprisingly serious attempt to have a proper wine list, with the bottles organised by style and some decent producers on offer. Service is a world apart from Chinatown, courteous and efficient.

Mayflower

Price (lunch):	n/a
Price (dinner):	£20-£35

Address:	68-70 Shaftesbury Avenue, Soho, London W1V 7DF
Phone:	0171 734 9207
Fax:	None
Reservations?	Yes
Nearest tube:	Piccadilly Circus
Set dinner:	£12-13 (min 2)
Open lunch:	None
Open dinner:	All week 17:00 - 04:00
Closed:	Christmas
Seats:	124
Private Room?	Yes (40 people)
Credit cards:	Visa,Amex,Access, Diners
Disabled access?	Yes
Music played?	Yes
Non-smoking?	No
Chef:	Fook on Chung

The Mayflower is a long established Chinatown institution, perfectly placed for Theatreland. In the series of small rooms, on both the ground floor and basement, Cantonese food of a consistently high standard is served. As with many Chinatown places, it is worth trying the more exotic dishes on the list of specialities, such as the excellent hot pot dishes, though the long menu also has all the more familiar dishes for the squeamish. Seafood is good here, soups are competent, although sizzling meat dishes can be overcooked. Up until 11 p.m. (or as a take-away after this) you can indulge in a series of dishes which combine meat or seafood with either rice or noodles as an all-in-one meal. Service is, by the abysmal standards of Chinatown, not bad. The Mayflower is ideal for night owls: it only opens up at 5 p.m. but keeps going until 4 a.m.

Poons

Price (lunch):	£10-£25
Price (dinner):	£10-£25

Address:	4 Leicester Street, Soho, London WC2H 7BL
Phone:	0171 437 1528
Fax:	None
Reservations?	Yes
Nearest tube:	Leicester Square
Set lunch:	£7 to £17 (min 2)
Set dinner:	£7 to £17 (min 2)
Open:	All week 12:00 - 23:30
Closed:	4 days at Christmas
Seats:	130
Private Room?	Yes (24 - 35 people)
Credit cards:	None
Disabled access?	Yes (not to toilets)
Music played?	No
Non-smoking?	No
Chef:	K. Lam

One of the best-value places in Chinatown, serving good food at very fair prices. I hardly recognised the place after its recent smart facelift, but the cooking has not changed. As well as the usual Chinatown dishes, the wind-dried meats and hot-pot creations are excellent. Poons is cramped and this is not somewhere to linger, but the food is better than most in Chinatown. I have found this branch to be the most reliable, but Poons can also be found at:

27 Lisle Street WC2H 7BA (0171 437 4549)
Whiteleys, Queensway W2 4YN (0171 792 2884)
50 Woburn Place, Russell Square (0171 580 1188)
Minster Pavement, Minster Court, Mincing Lane, EC3R 7PP (0171 626 0126)

Vegetarian Cottage

Price (lunch):	£15-£20
Price (dinner):	£20-£25

Address:	91 Haverstock Hill, Belsize Park, London NW3 4RL
Phone:	0171 586 1257
Fax:	None
Reservations?	Yes
Nearest tube:	Belsize Park or Chalk Farm
Set lunch:	£8
Set dinner:	£11.80 - £13.50
Open lunch:	Sunday 12:00 - 15:00
Open dinner:	All week 18:00 - 23:15
Closed:	Christmas
Seats:	60
Private Room?	Yes (20 people)
Credit cards:	Visa, Access
Disabled access?	Partial (2 steps)
Music played?	Yes
Non-smoking?	Separate section
Chef:	C. Wong

The Vegetarian Cottage is on Haverstock Hill, between Camden and Hampstead. The smart premises have bright lighting, tall black chairs with crisp white tablecloths, and the service is friendly and competent. The menu is predominantly vegetarian, with some seafood dishes added. The many deep-fried starters can be rather samey, though a crab and sweetcorn soup was better and not cloying as it can be. 'Sichuan prawns' are in fact as bland as could be, though the prawns were cooked well, while mixed vegetables were served in a little basket made of a sort of potato crisp; the vegetables were competently prepared, and the basket itself pleasantly edible. Chinese mushrooms with black moss could have done with some balancing acidic flavour. At its best the cooking is very good, as shown by a beautifully tender scallop served on its shell in a ginger and black bean sauce. Jasmine tea is a refreshing drink to have, or try Tsing Tao beer.

Dim Sum

One of the joys of Chinatown is being able to sample the lunchtime snacks known collectively as dim sum. This type of cooking is quite different from the usual Chinese style, and involves trying lots of little dishes, which in some restaurants are wheeled round on large trolleys for you to choose from. At least that is the idea. The reality is often seeing your favourite snack either marooned at the other end of the restaurant or being whisked past you on a trolley propelled by a bored, deaf waitress intent on some destination in the middle distance. Hence ordering in this style is not for the faint-hearted (or faint-voiced). For those willing to take on the fearsome trolley waitresses, the best places are probably the huge Chuen Cheng Ku and New World. In all cases you can eat your fill of dim sum for no more than £10.

Chuen Cheng Ku

Price (lunch):	**£10-£15**
Price (dinner):	**£15-£30**

Address:	17 Wardour Street, Soho, London W1V 6HD
Phone:	0171 437 1398 and 0171 734 3281
Fax:	0171 434 0533
Reservations?	Yes
Nearest tube:	Leicester Square or Piccadilly Circus
Set dinner:	£9 - £30 (min two)
Set lunch:	£9 - £30 (min two)
Open:	All week 11:00 - 23:45
Closed:	24th, 25th December
Seats:	400
Private Room?	Yes (60-120 people)
Credit cards:	Visa,Amex,Access, Diners
Disabled access?	Partial (1 step)
Music played?	Yes
Non-smoking?	No
Chef:	Mr So

Multi-storey eating. A vast cavern of a place spread over several floors, Chuen Cheng Ku specialises in dim sum served on trolleys up to 6 p.m. On a weekend you may still have to queue, despite its 400 seats, as this is one of the places where Chinese people like to bring their families for lunch. The usual assortment of dumplings and nibbles are generally good here, but as with other places don't expect much help from the waitresses unless you speak Cantonese. It is best to approach the dishes with a sense of daring, though on one occasion when I pointed at some unidentifiable piece of dead animal which a Cantonese family were tucking into I was told 'you would not like that', which was probably correct. Food in the evening is adequate but uninspired, so it is best to stick to dim sum at lunchtime.

Harbour City

| Price (lunch): | **£8-£12** |
| Price (dinner): | **£15-£30** |

Address:	46 Gerrard Street, Soho, London W1V 7LP
Phone:	0171 429 7859 or 0171 287 1526
Fax:	0171 439 7859
Reservations?	Yes
Nearest tube:	Leicester Square or Piccadilly Circus
Set lunch:	No
Set dinner:	£10.50 to £25 per person (min two people)
Open:	All week 12:00 - 23:30 (23:00 Sunday)
Closed:	24th-25th December
Seats:	160
Private Room?	Yes (40 or 50 people)
Credit cards:	Visa,Amex,Access, Diners
Disabled access:	Yes (not to toilets)
Music played?	Yes
Non-smoking?	No
Chef:	Hing Lee

Really excellent dim sum can be found in this run-of-the-mill Gerrard Street location. Here you can order your dim sum calmly from a menu rather than watching it whizz by on a trolley. Prawn cheung fun is excellent, while Vietnamese spring rolls are also reliable. Scallop dumpling looks pretty and tastes great, while yam croquette is also of a high standard. The choice of dim sum is unusually wide, with things like fried taro paste and beef intestines in spicy bean sauce to tempt you away from the normal steamed dumplings. Away from the dim sum, Singapore noodles are also good. Of course if you wish to stray off the beaten track and try various animal innards in unusual combinations, there is plenty to suit here also, and there are hot pot dishes available. Service is quite civil and efficient, i.e. a miracle in Chinatown. To drink you can rely on good tea, or be daring and try a bottle of Tsing Tao Chardonnay Chinese wine.

New Loon Fung

| Price (lunch): | **£10-£15** |
| Price (dinner): | **£15-£30** |

Address:	42-44 Gerrard Street, Soho, London W1V 7LP
Phone:	0171 437 6232
Fax:	0171 437 3540
Reservations?	Yes
Nearest tube:	Leicester Square
Set lunch:	£9 (min two)
Set dinner:	£9 (min two)
Open:	Monday - Thursday 11:30 - 23:30, Friday & Saturday 11:30 - 24:00, Sunday 11:00 - 21:30
Closed:	2 days at Christmas
Seats:	400
Private Room?	Yes (30 people)
Credit cards:	Visa,Amex,Access, Diners
Disabled access?	No
Music played?	Yes
Non-smoking?	No
Chefs:	Mr Tsang, Mr Suen

Perched above the Loon Fung Chinese grocery store, this restaurant is another that is best at lunchtime. You have the luxury of ordering from a menu instead of rugby tackling a trolley waitress, so you have time to contemplate the dishes. Confusingly, there are two dim sum menus, one with pictures and a different one without, so a certain amount of trial and error is involved. However the food itself is very good indeed, the prawn cheung fung and separate spring rolls in particular being fine examples of the breed. Singapore noodles are excellent here, and these can be ordered as a lunch dish as well as in the evening. Service is also quite reasonable here.

New World

| Price (lunch): | **£10-£15** |
| Price (dinner): | **£15-£30** |

Address:	1 Gerrard Place, Soho, London W1V 7LL
Phone:	0171 434 2508
Fax:	0171 287 3994
Reservations?	Yes
Nearest tube:	Leicester Square
Set lunch:	£7.20 - £35
Set dinner:	£7.20 - £35
Open:	All week 11:00 - 24:00
Closed:	Christmas Day & Boxing Day
Seats:	650
Private Room?	Yes (300 people)
Credit cards:	Visa,Amex,Access, Diners
Disabled access?	Yes
Music played?	Yes
Non-smoking?	No
Chef:	Lap Diep

A huge establishment (it seats 650, spread over two enormous dining rooms), the New World specialises in dim sum served from trolleys. There is a wide range of the usual dumplings, but also less common dishes like meat and rice cooked in a lotus leaf, and some excellent Vietnamese spring rolls (when they are available). You can also order a huge bowl of noodle soup, which is cooked in front of you. The food in the evenings was never special but has really deteriorated recently, so stick to the dim sum. Despite the cavernous premises, you may still have to queue at weekends for lunch. Service is tolerable, but don't expect any translation of dishes from the trolley waitresses.

Royal China

| Price (lunch): | **£10-£15** |
| Price (dinner): | **£25-£45** |

Address:	13 Queensway, London W2 4QJ
Phone:	0171 221 2535
Fax:	None
Reservations:	Dinner only
Nearest tube:	Queensway or Bayswater
Open:	All week 12:00 - 23:15
Open dinner:	Monday - Saturday
Closed:	24th, 25th December
Seats:	100
Private Room?	Yes (15 people)
Credit cards:	Visa,Amex,Access, Diners
Disabled access?	Yes
Music played?	Yes
Non-smoking?	No
Chef:	Simon Man

Another place much better at lunch than in the evening, serving some of the best dim sum I have had in London. The black and chrome decor looks a little odd in the daylight, but even on a weekday lunch it was pretty busy here (my previous attempt go on a Sunday failed after being told it would be a two-hour wait). Prawn cheung fun is quite superb, lacking the rather greasy, slimy texture which normally detracts from this dish. The scallop dumplings were also very good, the baby scallops beautifully tender inside the dumpling. I think it is the quality of the dumplings and the very fresh ingredients which impressed me most, e.g. dumpling of prawn with coriander was bursting with flavour. Singapore noodles had good texture but needed a little extra spice for my taste. The only ordinary, somewhat mediocre, dish was the Vietnamese spring rolls. Overall this was very fine.

Fish & Chips

Despite being the quintessential British dish, we have become accustomed to fish and chips being ghastly, greasy things served from dubious premises, with plenty of salt and cheap vinegar to mask the lack of inherent taste. Fortunately there are some very fine fish and chip shops who take things seriously, use fresh fish with carefully prepared batter, and produce chips which do not groan with cheap fat. Curiously, many of the best fish and chip shops in London are run by Cypriots or even Chinese families.

Excellent fish and chips can also be eaten at some of the more up-market restaurants listed under British cooking; for example, Bibendum, though expensive, offers wonderful fish and chips, while there is also the cheaper downstairs oyster bar.

Brady's

Price (lunch):	£15-£20
Price (dinner):	£15-£20

Address:	513 Old York Road, Wandsworth, London SW18 1TF
Phone:	0181 877 9599
Fax:	None
Reservations?	Yes
Nearest tube:	None; Wandsworth Town BR
Open lunch:	Saturday only 12:00 - 14:30
Open dinner:	Monday to Saturday 19:00 - 22:45
Closed:	National Holidays
Seats:	38
Private Room?	No
Credit cards:	None
Disabled access:	Partial (1 step)
Music played?	Yes
Non-smoking?	No
Chef:	Luke Brady

A fish restaurant rather than fish and chip shop (there is no take-away) in Wandsworth village, though finding the place can resemble an excursion to Hampton Court maze if you do not know the road system. Service is friendly though occasionally forgetful. The basics are here, with haddock, plaice, cod, etc. available with chips and mushy peas, as well as some daily specials on a blackboard, and starters like potted shrimps. Haddock was certainly very fresh, with competent batter, and chips were in no way soggy or greasy. A home-made tartare sauce was a noble effort, but this one suffered from too much cream and not enough chives. Salmon fishcakes are excellent with generous amounts of moist salmon. It is best to stick to the fish dishes. I sampled a very ordinary apple crumble with custard that was not home-made. There is a modest wine list with just a few offerings. Brady's can also be found at: 696 Fulham Road (0171 736 3938)

Toff's

Price (lunch):	£10-£15
Price (dinner):	£10-£15

Address:	38 The Broadway
	Muswell Hill,
	London N10 3RT
Phone:	0181 883 8656
Fax:	None
Reservations?	No
Nearest tube:	Highgate is nearest
Set lunch:	£7.95
Set dinner:	No
Open:	Tuesday - Saturday
	11:30 - 22:00
Closed:	2 weeks at Christmas
Seats:	32
Private Room?	No
Credit cards:	Visa,Access
Disabled access?	Yes
Music played?	Yes
Non-smoking?	No
Chef:	A. Ttoffalli

This is what a real fish and chip shop should be like. The fish is bought fresh, the batter light and delicious, even the gherkins are wonderful. The take-away counter is at the front of the shop as you go in, and there are tables to sit at further back. Families wander in at lunchtime after a hard morning's shopping in the Broadway, and can revive themselves with a good cup of tea. Service is friendly and competent. Toff's has been voted best fish and chip shop in the UK, and it is not hard to see why. In my view it is better than many of its competitors which regularly crop up in other restaurant guides. Haddock in particular is marvellous, chips are good and the portions huge.

Two Brothers

Price (lunch):	£15-£20
Price (dinner):	£20-£25

Address:	297-303 Regents Park
	Road, Finchley
	London N3 1DP
Phone:	0181 346 0469
Fax:	None
Reservations?	Yes
Nearest tube:	Finchley Central
Open lunch:	Tuesday - Saturday
	12:00 - 14:30
Open dinner:	Tuesday - Saturday
	17:30 - 22:15
(Discount of 15% before 19:00)	
Closed:	Bank Holidays, last
	2 weeks August ,
	Christmas
Seats:	90
Private Room?	No
Credit cards:	Visa,Amex,Access
Disabled access?	No
Music played?	Yes
Non-smoking?	Separate section
Chefs:	Leon & Toni Manzi

A brightly lit, quite smart place in a parade of shops on the busy Regents Park Road. Although it is more like a café than a restaurant (no tablecloths), the service is in fact very welcoming and efficient. A fine meal can be had here provided you stick to the basics. If you stray then things can go badly wrong, as in a watery fish soup. Arbroath smokies (smoked haddock to you and me) were themselves very good, but served in a white sauce which was far too creamy. Fortunately the haddock and chips are great: no grease, very fresh fish, good batter. The chips are excellent, of really good consistency without a hint of grease. A grilled skate wing also showed the quality of the raw ingredients, with very fresh skate spoiled by being a touch overcooked. Avoid desserts. There is a surprisingly good wine list, with well-chosen New World wines, e.g. Rosemount Show Reserve Chardonnay at a fair price.

French

French cuisine hardly needs introduction, and since the eighteenth century has been acknowledged as probably the world's finest. Sadly, this reputation has often been used as an excuse for restaurateurs to rip off unsuspecting customers, preparing lousy food and charging exorbitant prices. Some well-known restaurant chains even buy in pre-prepared portions and just heat them up in a microwave, while pretending that they are serving fresh food.

As mentioned earlier, the first restaurants as we would know them today opened in Paris at the end of the 18th century. Interestingly, it was only in 1860 that dishes began to be served in sequence; this was called 'Russian service'. Previously, 'service a la française' involved serving all hot dishes together, from soups to roast, followed by cold meats and vegetables as a second course, then desserts. French cooking went from strength to strength in the nineteenth and twentieth centuries, with the landmark cookery encyclopaedia *Larousse Gastronomique* being published in 1938. George-Auguste Escoffier wrote some hugely influential cookery books from 1921-1934, and was responsible for organising restaurant kitchens in an efficient way, with areas of the kitchen, and staff, dedicated to specific roles. In the 1950s there was a reaction against Escoffier's rich *grande cuisine* by some young chefs, including Michel Guérard, Paul Bocuse, Alain Chapel and Jean and Pierre Troisgros, who invented a lighter style of cooking christened *nouvelle cuisine* by journalists Christian Millau and Henri Gault. Nouvelle cuisine aims at a lightness of touch, reducing sauces rather than thickening with flour, cream and butter, and increases the emphasis on presentation. Unfortunately imitators of this style have brought the name into disrepute, serving up ludicrously small, artfully arranged portions on almost empty white plates. This is a corruption of what nouvelle cuisine is intended to be about, and you can be assured that if you eat at one of the restaurants listed in this Guide you will not leave hungry, whether or not their style is nouvelle.

There are two relatively cheap ways of trying good quality French cuisine in London. One is to find a place where the dishes prepared are not haute cuisine but of more modest ambitions. The other is to sample one of the fixed-price lunches which some of the top places provide, virtually as a loss-leader, in the hope that at least some of the guests will return one evening. These lunches tend to offer a small range of dishes, usually less elaborate than those of the evening, but representing excellent value. For the genuine article, however, why not spoil yourself once on your birthday, and save up to eat at, say, Chez Nico at Ninety one evening, when you will be able to see why top-quality French cuisine truly is truly great, and could (just possibly?) be worth the money?

Associés

Price (lunch):	£20-£25
Price (dinner):	£35-£45

Address:	172 Park Road, Crouch End, London N8 8GT
Phone:	0181 348 8944
Fax:	None
Reservations?	Yes
Nearest tube:	Finsbury Park
Set lunch:	£15.95
Set dinner:	No
Open lunch:	Wednesday - Friday 12:30 - 14:00
Open dinner:	Tuesday - Saturday 19:30 - 22:00
Closed:	August, 1 week at Christmas, & Easter
Seats:	37
Private Room?	No
Credit cards:	Visa,Access,
Disabled access?	Yes
Music played?	Yes
Non-smoking?	No
Chef:	Gilles Charvet

An authentically French neighbourhood restaurant, the Associés is situated in the unlikely setting of a residential street in Crouch End. A cosy place, with anaglypta wallpaper with a pine-tree design, linen tablecloths and very friendly service. The cooking has some ability but is rather variable. One evening a John Dory and mango salad was delicious; the fish sautéed and crisp, yet the small plate of mixed vegetables with it was soggy and disappointing. It is also a pity that the chicken was sad British fare, rather than the wonderful French version from Bresse. The meal was then lifted by a good selection of French cheese in prime condition. Desserts also suffer inconsistency, with a delicate and delicious strawberry mousse offset by some chewy pastry in an otherwise good tarte tatin. Coffee is good and strong. The wine list is very Gallic, somewhat obscured through the authentic haze of cigarette smoke, with the list updated each August with wines from France.

Aubergine

Price (lunch):	£25-£30
Price (dinner):	£35-£45

Address:	11 Park Walk, Chelsea, London SW10 0AJ
Phone:	0171 352 3449
Fax:	0171 351 1770
Reservations?	Yes (essential)
Nearest tube:	South Kensington, or Sloane Square
Set lunch:	£18 (3 courses)
Set dinner:	£28 (3 courses) £36 (6 courses)
Open lunch:	Monday - Friday 12:00 - 14:30
Open dinner:	Monday - Saturday 19:00 - 23:00
Closed:	10 days at Christmas 1 week at Easter 2 weeks in August
Seats:	45-50
Private Room?	No
Credit cards:	Visa,Amex,Access, Diners
Disabled access?	No
Music played?	No
Non-smoking?	Separate section
Chef:	Gordon Ramsey

A dazzling new entry to the London food scene, the Aubergine produces outstanding French food at very fair prices. Another ex-Harveys chef cooks here, and unfortunately the Harveys heritage of mediocre service has also been inherited. This is not a place for a rushed meal before the cinema – things here happen s..l..o..w..l..y. As long as this is not a problem you can sit back and enjoy some fabulous food, the sauces in particular exhibiting great intensity and accuracy. Even the bread is superb, supplied from the same source as the Canteen. Now that his reputation is secure it would be nice to see Gordon Ramsey's talents blossom through greater experimentation, delightful though it is to have such fine renditions of classic dishes, e.g. the sea bass with vanilla is a variant on a lobster with vanilla dish from the 3-star Michelin Lucas Carton in Paris. The wine list at the Aubergine is reasonable, with mark-ups variable but generally not excessive. There is a good selection in a sensible price range, and New World offerings to supplement the cleverly selected French ones.

Bistro Bruno

Price (lunch):	£25-£40
Price (dinner):	£25-£40

Address:	63 Frith Street, Soho, London W1V 5TA
Phone:	0171 734 4545
Fax:	0171 287 1027
Reservations?	Yes
Nearest tube:	Tottenham Court Road or Leicester Square
Open lunch:	Monday - Friday 12:15 - 14:30
Open dinner:	Monday - Saturday 18:15 - 23:30
Closed:	24th December to New Year
Seats:	40
Private Room?	No
Credit cards:	Visa,Amex,Access, Diners
Disabled access?	No
Music played?	Yes
Non-smoking?	No
Chef:	Bruno Loubet

Bruno Loubet was chef at the Inn on the Park, where he deservedly earned a Michelin star for his efforts at the Four Seasons restaurant. He has now struck out on his own in much less grand premises in Soho. Once he took over at the stoves full-time, some of the skill demonstrated at the Four Seasons can be seen: a sea bass on a bed of vegetables was outstanding. The menu is quite adventurous and is not afraid to deal with offal: tripe and oxtail appear alongside more conventional dishes involving scallops and oysters. Not all the dishes emerge to the same high standard, but overall this is very good value. The wine selection is varied and includes the Argentinian Weinart, reckoned by Robert Parker to be South America's best wine. Loubert has just opened a new dining club, but this is members-only

Canteen

Price (lunch):	£30-£45
Price (dinner):	£30-£45

Address:	Unit G4, Harbour Yard, Chelsea Harbour, London SW10 0XD
Phone:	0171 351 7330
Fax:	None
Reservations?	Yes (essential)
Nearest tube:	Sloane Square (but no Tube nearby)
Open lunch:	All week 12:00 - 15:00
Open dinner:	All week 18:30 - 23:45
Closed:	Christmas
Seats:	150
Private Room?	No
Credit cards:	Visa,Amex,Access, Diners
Disabled access?	Partial (3 steps)
Music played?	No
Non-smoking?	No
Chefs:	Tim Payne and Peter Reffel

Set up by Marco Pierre White, the Canteen is situated in the Chelsea Harbour development. The high culinary standards were initially set by Steve Terry, who after a row with Marco Pierre White left for Paris, but the cooking has not suffered. The atmosphere is lively and the surroundings elegant. On offer is a mix of French with some modern British touches. Instead of experimenting, the kitchen maintains a very constant menu, but the consequence of this is highly consistent cooking. Many dishes are superb, for example the sublime lemon tart. The wine list is short but well chosen. Prices are not excessive for cooking of this quality, and service is slick. Though it seats well over 100, it is very popular and advance booking is essential. When booking, ask for one of the seats in the conservatory area, which have a pretty view over the marina – these are much in demand, so the further ahead you book, the better your chances.

Capital

Price (lunch):	**£30-£40**
Price (dinner):	**£40-£70**

Address:	22-24 Basil Street, Knightsbridge, London SW3 1AT
Phone:	0171 589 5171
Fax:	0171 225 0011
Reservations?	Yes
Nearest tube:	Knightsbridge
Set lunch:	£22 and £25
Set dinner: ·	£40
Open lunch:	All week 12:00 - 14:30
Open dinner:	All week 18:30 - 23:30
Closed:	never
Seats:	35
Private Room?	Yes (24 people)
Credit cards:	Visa,Amex,Access, Diners
Disabled access?	Yes
Music played?	No
Non-smoking?	No
Chef:	Philip Britten

Hotel dining rooms usually leave much to be desired, but this is an exception. The Capital is a small, though exclusive hotel, with a cosy dining room seating just 35. The furnishings are rich but tasteful, and the atmosphere elegant but not stuffy. It manages to conjure up a welcoming ambience missing from most hotel dining rooms. Philip Britten is a fine cook, and he has an excellent command of classic French cooking. The technique here is not flashy, but everything is in balance: meat is cooked very well, seafood handled even better, and the sauces are of a uniformly high standard. Service is discreet and excellent, and the set meals represent very good value. The wine list, though it has some very fine choices, is set at Knightsbridge prices.As we went to press, the dining room was about to have a facelift.

Chez Max

Price (lunch):	**£20-£25**
Price (dinner):	**£35-£40**

Address:	166 Ifield Road, Fulham, London SW10 9AF
Phone:	0171 835 0874
Fax:	None
Reservations?	Yes (essential)
Nearest tube:	West Brompton or Earls Court
Set lunch:	£15.50
Set dinner:	£23.50
Open lunch:	Tuesday - Friday 12:30 - 14:30
Open dinner:	Monday to Saturday 19:00 - 23:00
Closed:	Christmas, Easter, Bank Holidays
Seats:	85
Private Room?	Yes (15 people)
Credit cards:	Access, Visa
Disabled access:	No
Music played?	No
Non-smoking?	No
Chef:	Redmond Hayward

Chez Max is a delight. The basement dining room is rather cramped (soon to be refurbished), but the warmth of the welcome compensates for this. The menus from famous French restaurants on the walls indicate the serious culinary intent here, and though chef Bruce Poole has now moved on, the cooking maintains its high standards. A chilled tomato and basil soup was deep and intense, and a crab and saffron tart delicate and full of flavour. The Turkish dish imam bayildi, frequently a tasteless mush, is here a revelation: the combination of aubergine with cinnamon, cumin and coriander working remarkably well. Simple dishes are perfectly executed here, say a succulent poached salmon, served with an excellent salad. Desserts are also a treat, e.g. a ravishing cherry tart or a gorgeous lemon tart. The short French wine list is very well chosen indeed, and wines are priced just a few pounds above shop prices. Alternatively for £5 corkage you can bring your own wine.

Chez Moi

| Price (lunch): | £20-£25 |
| Price (dinner): | £35-£50 |

Address:	1 Addison Avenue, Holland Park, London W11 4QS
Phone:	0171 603 8267
Fax:	None
Reservations?	Yes
Nearest tube:	Holland Park
Set lunch:	£14
Open lunch:	Monday to Friday 12:30 - 14:00
Open dinner:	Monday to Saturday 19:00 - 23:00
Closed:	Bank Holidays
Seats:	45
Private Room?	No
Credit cards:	Visa,Amex,Access, Diners
Disabled access:	Yes (not to toilets)
Music played?	No
Non-smoking?	Separate section
Chef:	Richard Walton

Only in Holland Park could this pretty little place be classified as a 'neighbourhood' restaurant. Very French, with charming French waiters offering genuinely superb service. There is a 'traditional' menu to satisfy long-standing regulars and also a modern menu, so as well as tender fillet steak with béarnaise sauce there is also seared tuna with Japanese wasabe mustard. Cooked goat's cheese on a garlic crouton was served with fine salad leaves, which was followed by succulent quenelles of salmon in a lobster sauce. Vegetables, so often the Achilles' heel of restaurants, are good here. The selection of French cheeses is kept in good condition. Lemon tart was served warm and was gorgeous, though it did not need both a fluffy crème anglaise and a strawberry coulis. Coffee ice cream was deep and intense. Wines are mostly French with a handful of New World, the sommelier is helpful and knowledgeable, and there is a whole page of half bottles.

Chez Nico At Ninety

| Price (lunch): | £35-£45 |
| Price (dinner): | £70-£90 |

Address:	90 Park Lane, Mayfair London W1A 3AA
Phone:	0171 409 1290
Fax:	0171 355 4877
Reservations?	Yes
Nearest tube:	Marble Arch
Set lunch:	£25 (three courses)
Set dinner:	£57 (three courses)
Open lunch:	Monday - Friday 12:00 - 14:00
Open dinner:	Monday - Saturday 19:00 - 23:00 (last orders 22:45)
Closed:	3 weeks at Christmas
Seats:	90
Private Room?	Yes (20 people)
Credit cards:	Visa,Amex,Access, Diners
Disabled access?	Yes
Music played?	No
Non-smoking?	No
Chef:	Nico Ladenis

Nico Ladenis is a chef from central casting; huge, bearded, temperamental, brilliant. After several previous ventures he has settled in the premises of the Grosvenor House hotel in Park Lane, which provides a luxurious frame for his talents. Over the last couple of years he seems to me to have achieved greater consistency (no one ever doubted Nico's cooking ability, but running a great kitchen requires more than just creative genius). If I had to select one restaurant in London now at which to eat, and money was no object, this is where I would come. Some of the dishes I have eaten here recently have been simply sublime. A simple grilled sole with beurre blanc sauce was remarkable, while the fillet of beef was extraordinarily tender. A langoustine soup tried here is the best I have ever had. Service is efficient and not stuffy. Some of the mark-ups on the wine list are ridiculously high, but the house Bergerac is very drinkable. Prices here are significantly lower than at other restaurants in this league.

L'Escargot

Price (lunch):	£30-£45
Price (dinner):	£30-£65

Address:	48 Greek Street, Soho, London W1V 5LQ
Phone:	0171 437 2679
Fax:	0171 437 0790
Reservations?	Yes (essential)
Nearest tube:	Leicester Square or Tottenham Court Rd
Set lunch:	£20
Set dinner:	£20
Pre-theatre	£14 (2 courses)
Open lunch:	Monday - Friday 12:15 - 14:15
Open dinner:	Monday - Saturday 18:00 - 23:15
Closed:	4 days at Christmas
Seats:	Brasserie 90 1st Floor 50
Private Room?	Yes (34 & 50 people)
Credit cards:	Visa,Amex,Access, Diners
Disabled access?	No
Music played?	Yes
Non-smoking?	No
Chefs:	Garry Hollihead & David Cavalier

The culinary credentials here are impeccable: David Cavalier and Garry Hollihead are two of Britain's rising stars in the culinary firmament. The cooking style is firmly French, with dishes like cassoulet and classically prepared fillet of beef with a delicious rich jus. The surroundings vary by floor, with a brasserie on the ground floor, and a more formal setting (with significantly higher prices) on the upper two floors. Modern art litters the walls. The wine list does few favours for bargain-hunters, and the prices in the restaurant can seem excessive when compared to what can be obtained in London in the same range; fortunately the brasserie prices are less rapacious. Service, especially in the brasserie, does not always match the food, with potentially long waits and some amusing asides. One waitress's English was somewhat limited: the not unreasonable question 'What is the haddock Monte Carlo?' received the immortal reply: 'Eeez a fish.'

L'Esprit de l'Escalier

Price (lunch):	£30-£35
Price (dinner):	£40-£50

Address:	34 Brook Street, Mayfair, London W1Y 1DH
Phone:	0171 629 2471
Fax:	0171 499 4377
Reservations?	Yes
Nearest tube:	Green Park
Set lunch:	£16.50 (2 courses) £19.50 (3 courses)
Set dinner:	£24.50 (2 courses) £29.50 (3 courses)
Open lunch:	Monday - Saturday 12:00 - 14:30
Open dinner:	Monday - Saturday 18:00 - 23:00
Closed:	Bank Holidays
Seats:	65
Private Room?	Yes (20 people)
Credit cards:	Visa, Amex, Access
Disabled access?	No
Music played?	No
Non-smoking?	No
Chef:	Anand Sastry

CLOSED

A very promising new venture in a smart Mayfair basement. The cooking at present is of a remarkably high standard, surpassing Anand Sastry's considerable achievements at his previous restaurant, the Argyll. Medallions of salmon were wrapped in leeks with caramelised cloves of garlic, field mushrooms and a fondant potato with a hint of rosemary. Tender and moist breast of guinea fowl was served off the bone on top of a perfect thyme potato rosti, all in a rich, dark sauce of the cooking juices. An assiette of chocolate had no fewer than five separate chocolate dishes, e.g. white chocolate sorbet served in a dark chocolate cup and chocolate cage. The cooking technique here is impeccable. Service complements the smart modern surroundings, discreet but welcoming. The wine list is good e.g. the superb Maximin Grünhauser Riesling, though mark-ups are quite steep. Despite the hefty bill, it is good value for cooking of such a high standard.

Le Gavroche

Price (lunch):	£40-£55
Price (dinner):	£90-£120

Address	43 Upper Brook Street, Mayfair, London W1Y 1PF
Phone:	0171 408 0881 or 0171 499 1826
Fax:	0171 491 4387
Reservations?	Yes (recommended)
Nearest tube:	Marble Arch
Set lunch:	£37 (3 courses, coffee + half bottle of wine)
Set dinner:	£5 (3 courses)
Open lunch:	Monday - Friday 12:00 -14:00
Open dinner:	Monday - Friday 19:00 - 23:00
Closed:	Bank Holidays
Seats:	70
Private Room?	Yes (8 - 20 people)
Credit cards:	Visa,Amex,Access, Diners
Disabled access?	No
Music played?	No
Non-smoking?	No
Chef:	Michel Roux

Le Gavroche was where Albert Roux made his reputation, and it was the first British restaurant to receive three Michelin stars. Albert has now retired from active cooking, and his son, Michel, now heads up the kitchen. The handover seems to have worked well, and Le Gavroche is producing very fine dishes. The incredibly rich, heavy sauces have been toned down, and the cooking now seems to have more balance. Le Gavroche is very formal, but service is excellent, and the classics of French cuisine are faultlessly executed. It is very expensive in the evening, but has a much cheaper set lunch. Service is impeccable, but the habit of giving only one menu with prices to the 'host', automatically assumed to be male whoever is actually paying, is something that is authentically French, but can be irritating nonetheless. Cooking like this never comes cheap, but the set lunch is much less stingy with rich ingredients than some of its competitors.

The Heights

Price (lunch):	£25-£30
Price (dinner):	£35-£45

Address:	St George's Hotel, Langham Place, Marylebone London, W1N 8QS
Phone:	0171 636 1939
Fax:	0171 753 0259
Reservations?	Yes
Nearest tube:	Oxford Circus
Set lunch:	£14 (2 courses) £18 (3 courses)
Set dinner:	No
Open lunch:	Monday - Friday 12:00 - 14:30
Open dinner:	Monday - Saturday 19:00 - 22:30
Closed:	2 weeks August
Seats:	80
Private Room?	Yes (10 people)
Credit cards:	Visa, Amex, Access, Diners
Disabled access?	Yes
Music played?	Yes
Non-smoking?	No
Chef:	Adam Newell

On the 15th floor of the unprepossessing St George's Hotel is a serious new venture, combining experienced staff with the inventive cooking of Adam Newell, who has long experience with the Roux Brothers. From the smart, modern dining room you gaze across London rooftops while sampling some innovative cooking combined with solid technique and a flair for artful presentation. A wild mushroom tart I sampled had excellent pastry and was served with beautifully judged red onion marmalade. A salmon and spinach lasagne was prettily presented with a ring of baby vegetables surrounding the perfectly cooked pasta. Perhaps the chef is trying a little too hard for effect at present, but there is no denying his skill. The waiting staff seem to have genuine concern for you without being too fussy, and are led by a very experienced maitre d'. The wine list at the time of writing is reasonable, but a major revamp is planned. Prices are very fair for cooking of this calibre.

Le Meridien Hotel, Oak Room

Price (lunch):	**£35-£40**
Price (dinner):	**£55-£70**

Address	21 Piccadilly, London W1V 0BH
Phone:	0171 465 1640
Fax:	0171 437 3574
Reservations?	Yes
Nearest tube:	Piccadilly Circus
Set lunch:	£24.50 (3 courses)
Set dinner	£28 (3 courses, wine) £46 (7 courses)
Open lunch:	Monday - Friday 12:00 - 14:30
Open dinner:	Monday - Saturday 19:00 - 22:30
Closed:	August
Seats:	50
Private Room?	No
Credit cards:	Visa,Amex,Access, Diners
Disabled access?	Yes
Music played?	Yes
Non-smoking?	No
Chef:	Alain Marechal
N.B. Children are not encouraged	

This offers excellent food for a very fair price at lunchtime. The Oak Room serves extremely well prepared French food, served in wonderful surroundings. The room is beautiful, with high oak-panelled walls, magnificent chandeliers and perfectly presented tables. David Chambers set very high standards of cooking over his eight years here, which are being maintained now that he has moved to the Hilton. For £24.50 the lunch here is a real bargain. As well as classic dishes, there is a sense of adventure in the cooking here, the menu being prepared in consultation with three-Michelin-starred chef Michel Lorian. Service is impeccable. The wine list offers some relief from the usual epic of unaffordable clarets and burgundies, with a few well chosen Spanish and New World wines.

Mijanou

Price (lunch):	**£25-£30**
Price (dinner):	**£45-£60**

Address:	143 Ebury Street, Victoria, London SW1W 9QN
Phone:	0171 730 4099
Fax:	0171 823 6402
Reservations?	Yes
Nearest tube:	Sloane Square, or Victoria
Set lunch:	£13.50 (2 courses)
Set dinner:	£38.50 (6 courses)
Open lunch:	Monday - Friday 12:00 - 14:00
Open dinner:	Monday - Friday 19:00 - 23:00
Closed:	Christmas
Seats:	34
Private Room?	Yes (20 people)
Credit cards:	Visa,Amex,Access, Diners
Disabled access?	No
Music played?	No
Non-smoking?	Separate section
Chef:	Sonia Blech

The Mijanou is a small, friendly restaurant serving classic French cuisine. The ground floor is more appealing than the basement, and the tables are rather cramped, but this is made up for by the warm welcome. Sonia Blech's cooking here emphasises high-quality ingredients and attention to detail, and the excellent presentation makes the dishes all the more appealing. The wine list is one of the best in the country, organised by type rather than country, with intelligent suggestions as to which wines would complement which dishes; mark-ups are very fair. There is a complete and imaginative vegetarian menu, though you need to ask for this. The prices are rather high in the evening, but the lunch offers good value.

Nico Central

Price (lunch):	£30-£50
Price (dinner):	£30-£50

Address:	35 Great Portland Street, Marylebone, London W1N 5DD
Phone:	0171 436 8846
Fax:	0171 355 4877
Reservations?	Yes
Nearest tube:	Oxford Circus
Open lunch:	Monday - Friday 12:00 - 14:00
Open dinner:	Monday - Saturday 19:00 - 23:00
Closed:	Christmas & Easter
Seats:	55
Private Room?	Yes (10 people)
Credit cards:	Visa,Amex,Access, Diners
Disabled access?	Partial (1 step)
Music played?	No
Non-smoking?	No
Chef:	Andrew Jeffs

Nico Ladenis is a footloose chef. Starting in Dulwich, he moved to Battersea and, less wisely, Reading (how many foodies do you know in Reading?) before returning to Victoria. Since then he has moved twice more, on each occasion leaving behind a trusted sous chef to run things. Nico Central does not aspire to the heights of Chez Nico at Ninety, where Nico now cooks, but instead offers simpler fare at much lower prices. The dining room is tastefully decorated, the service friendly and competent. I think it is exceptionally good value for money here, producing superb French food at a price no higher than many rip-off joints. The menu offers a wider choice than at many places, with a sure hand being shown whether with meat, seafood or vegetables. Desserts are lovely, pastry in particular being very good.

Petit Max

Price (lunch):	n/a
Price (dinner):	£30-£35

Address:	97A High Street, Hampton Wick, Kingston upon Thames KT2 5NB
Phone:	0181 977 0236
Fax:	None
Reservations?	Yes
Nearest tube:	None (Hampton Wick BR)
Set lunch:	n/a
Set dinner:	£23.50 (3 courses)
Open lunch:	late Sunday only 15:30 onwards
Open dinner:	Tuesday - Sunday 19:00 - 22:30
Closed:	1 week at Christmas 2 weeks in summer
Seats:	34
Private Room?	Yes (30 people)
Credit cards:	None
Disabled access?	Yes (not to toilets)
Music played?	No
Non-smoking?	No
Chef:	Max Renzland

Sister restaurant to Chez Max in Fulham (see entry), Petit Max offers the same high standards of cooking, but in rather more basic surroundings. So basic in fact, that during the day Petit Max becomes Bonzo's cafe, a greasy spoon. The framed menus of some of the world's best restaurants on the walls must provide an odd setting in which to scoff your egg and chips. Max Renzland is an enthusiastic provider of high quality provincial French cooking. There is nothing fancy here, just extremely high quality ingredients, a lack of fussiness and supreme technique. Everything, from a thick wild mushroom soup, to perfect strips of sirloin steak in a rich sauce on a bed of spinach, through to faultless pear tarte tatin, is a delight to eat. Even the olives are wonderful, marinated in garlic, thyme and rosemary. You can bring your own wine for just £2 corkage (Petit Max is unlicensed), which helps to keep the bill down. It is often said that England lacks high the quality restaurants which can be found in the French provinces - not any more.

Pied A Terre

Price (lunch):	£30-£50
Price (dinner):	£50-£65

Address	34 Charlotte Street London W1P 1HJ
Phone:	0171 636 1178
Fax:	0171 916 1171
Reservations?	Yes
Nearest tube:	Goodge Street
Set lunch:	£19.50
Set dinner:	£39.50
Open lunch:	Monday - Friday 12:15 - 14:00
Open dinner:	Monday - Saturday 19:15 - 22:00
Closed:	Sundays, last week December to first week January, last two weeks August
Seats:	40
Private Room?	Yes (12 people)
Credit cards:	Visa,Amex,Access, Diners
Disabled access?	Yes (not to toilets)
Music played?	No
Non-smoking?	No
Chef:	Richard Neat

The Pied à Terre achieved the unusual distinction of a Michelin star in its first year, but time has shown that this was well deserved. Richard Neat used to cook under Raymond Blanc at Le Manoir Aux Quat' Saisons (in Great Milton), and more recently refined his skills at Jamin in Paris, the restaurant of Joel Robuchon. Since M. Robuchon is commonly regarded as the finest cook in the world at present, this is a pretty good place to learn. The cooking here is of the highest standard, comparing well with more famous places. The cooking of fish, which so often falls down even in otherwise excellent restaurants, is here confident and assured. The only criticism might be a limited cheeseboard and a lack of possibilities for vegetarians. Here is a rising star, at present offering a relative bargain in London for truly outstanding French food. The wine list shuns non-French offerings, which seems a pity, but there are at least some affordable bottles.

P'tit Normande

Price (lunch):	£15-£20
Price (dinner):	£25-£40

Address:	185 Merton Road, Wandsworth, London SW18 5EF
Phone:	0181 871 0233
Fax:	None
Reservations?	Yes
Nearest tube:	Southfields
Set lunch:	£9.95 (3 courses), £11.95 Sundays
Open lunch:	Sunday - Friday 12:00 - 14:30
Open dinner:	All week 19:00 - 22:00
Closed:	Never
Seats:	40
Private Room?	Yes (20 people)
Credit cards:	Visa,Amex,Access, Diners
Disabled access?	Yes
Music played?	Yes
Non-smoking?	No
Chef:	Philippe Chevis

Very Gallic local bistro in Southfields. Old-fashioned, with red and white check tablecloths, and a menu of traditional French favourites: fish soup, entrecote steak, etc. Daily specials are put up on a blackboard, though non-meat eaters should note that there may only be one fish dish available. Stalwarts like mussels cooked in white wine and cream sauce with bacon and herbs are competently handled, though a selection of turbot, monkfish and red mullet in cream sauce was rather ordinary. The weakest feature is the vegetables, fresh but overcooked. By contrast the cheese is wonderful. Imported regularly from France direct (from Normandy, but not from Philippe Olivier), there is a lovely selection, e.g. epoisses, camembert with calvados, all in excellent condition and served attractively on a wooden board. Dessert was crème brulée, quite good, and peach tart, again reasonable. The main caveat is the somewhat high food prices. The wine list is all French, fairly limited in its ambitions, with most wines under £20.

Les Saveurs

Price (lunch):	£25-£40
Price (dinner):	£40-£60

Address	37A Curzon Street, Mayfair, London, W1Y 8EY
Phone:	0171 491 8919
Fax:	0171 491 3658
Reservations?	Yes
Nearest tube:	Green Park
Set lunch:	£22.50 (3 courses)
Set dinner:	£38 (3 courses)
Open lunch:	Monday - Friday 12:00 - 14:30
Open dinner:	Monday - Friday 19:00 - 23:00
Closed:	2 weeks in August, 2 weeks at Christmas
Seats:	65
Private Room?	Yes (10 people)
Credit cards:	Visa,Amex,Access, Diners
Disabled access?	No
Music played?	No
Non-smoking?	No
Chef:	Joël Antunès

No expense has been spared in decking out this basement restaurant in the heart of Mayfair. The Japanese backers (Fujikoshi Ltd) have hired Joël Antunès, a talented French chef who has trained with the very best (the Troisgros brothers, Joel Robuchon) and who has recently returned from cooking at the exclusive Oriental Hotel in Bangkok. The food here is highly rated, and there is some truly inventive cooking here, some dishes drawing on Oriental spices in a way more usually seen in modern British or Californian cuisine than French. Yet, in this striving for new ground, errors can creep into the simpler dishes, and even the set menu can lack balance. The set lunch represents the best-value way of trying things out; prices in the evening are steeper. The wine list has a few gems, e.g. the house Bergerac, though leaning heavily towards France rather than the New World.

Simply Nico

Price (lunch):	£30-£40
Price (dinner):	£30-£40

Address	48A Rochester Row Victoria, London SW1P 1JU
Phone:	0171 630 8061
Fax:	None
Reservations?	Yes
Nearest tube:	Victoria
Set lunch:	£23.50
Set dinner:	£25
Open lunch:	Monday - Friday 12:00 - 14:00
Open dinner:	Monday - Saturday 19:00 - 23:00
Closed:	10 days at Christmas
Seats:	50
Private Room?	No
Credit cards:	Visa,Amex,Access, Diners
Disabled access?	Yes
Music played?	No
Non-smoking?	No
Chef:	Darran Bunn

This is very similar to Nico Central in style, offering simple French cooking of an extremely high standard at very fair prices. Simply Nico has a set menu, which makes the bill more predictable, but has some dishes in common with Nico Central. Fish is cooked well here, and dishes like confit of duck with lentils and herb dumpling have been very good in my experience. Bread is good and desserts are excellent. The premises are a little cramped so this is not the place for a romantic dinner, but service is friendly and competent.

Both Nico Central and Simply Nico offer a good selection of wines by the glass at reasonable prices, including the excellent Cloudy Bay Sauvignon Blanc.

La Tante Claire

| Price (lunch): | £35-£45 |
| Price (dinner): | £65-£90 |

Address:	68 Royal Hospital Road, London SW3 4HP
Phone:	0171 352 6045
Fax:	0171 352 3257
Reservations?	Yes (essential)
Nearest tube:	Sloane Square
Set lunch:	£24.50
Open lunch:	Monday - Friday 12:30 - 14:00
Open dinner:	Monday - Friday 19:00 - 23:00
Closed:	Christmas & New Year, 3 weeks in August, Bank Holidays, weekends
Seats:	43
Private Room?	No
Credit cards:	Visa,Amex,Access, Diners
Disabled access?	Partial (1 step)
Music played?	No
Non-smoking?	No
Chef:	Pierre Koffmann

A treat to save up for. For years one of the best two or three restaurants in the UK, La Tante Claire still offers an excellent value lunch at just £24.50 for three courses. The food is of the same standard as that in the evening, though the dishes are simpler and there is less choice. Pierre Koffmann is a great and innovative cook, and this price for food of such quality is a real bargain. If you've never understood how a meal can possibly be worth more than £50 a head (which it is in the evening), why not try the lunch here and find out? The dining room is bright and the service very good. Koffmann has now been awarded his third Michelin star (long overdue). He has continually challenged himself to strive for greater heights, and has never rested on his laurels.

Turner's

| Price (lunch): | £20-£30 |
| Price (dinner): | £35-£55 |

Address:	87-89 Walton Street Chelsea, London SW3 2HP
Phone:	0171 584 6711
Fax:	0171 584 4441
Reservations?	Yes
Nearest tube:	Knightsbridge or South Kensington
Set lunch:	£9.95 (2 courses) £13.50 (3 courses)
Set dinner:	£23.50 (2 courses) £26.50 (3 courses) £29.50 (4 courses)
Open lunch:	All week except Saturday 12:30 - 14:00
Open dinner:	Monday - Sunday 19:30 - 23:15
Closed:	Christmas period + Bank Holidays
Seats:	52
Private Room?	No
Credit cards:	Visa,Amex,Access, Diners
Disabled access:	Yes (not to toilets)
Music played?	Yes
Non-smoking?	No
Chef:	Brian Turner

Turner's is a very understated place, never flashy, just reliable and comfortable. The decor is attractive and the atmosphere serene, the staff unobtrusive but there when needed. There is a menu of the day with a very limited choice, or an attractive à la carte selection. The dishes are often deceptively simple, e.g. salmon with a mushroom stuffing in a little pastry case, or rack of lamb with a herb crust, but there is always very fine balance and careful seasoning. The degree of subtlety can sometimes contribute to a sense of 'so what', but this would be unfair; few places can turn out such consistently good food. Another thing in Turner's favour is that the set meals have no nasty sting in the tail: everything, including service, is included. This makes the set lunch menus even more of a bargain than they might appear. The wine list is extensive but is almost entirely French, with just a token page of New World wines. Moreover mark-ups are steep, with most of the wines being above £30 a bottle.

Greek

When it comes to Michelin-starred restaurants, Greece, as they say in cricket, doesn't trouble the scorers, with a grand total of zero (even Finland manages one). Dishes like moussaka, stuffed vine leaves and baklava are popular enough to make it to supermarket frozen food sections, and there are some pleasant Greek restaurants where a night of meze and plate smashing can be had, but this hardly qualifies as fine cuisine. Greek cooking is not redeemed by its wine, for despite several thousand years of viniculture they still can't get it right. Acceptable Greek food can be eaten in London at the Kalamaras.

Kalamaras

Price (lunch):	n/a
Price (dinner):	£20-£35

Address:	76-78 Inverness Mews, Bayswater London W2 3JQ
Phone:	0171 727 9122
Fax:	None
Reservations?	Yes
Nearest tube:	Bayswater or Queensway
Set dinner:	£15.50
Open lunch:	None
Open dinner:	Monday - Saturday 18:30 - 24:00
Closed:	Sundays and Bank Holidays
Seats:	96
Private Room?	Yes (26 people)
Credit cards:	Visa,Amex,Access, Diners
Disabled access?	Yes (not to toilets)
Music played?	Not usually
Non-smoking?	No
Chef:	Stelios Platonos

Despite its appearance, with red table-cloths, and an occasional bouzouki player, the Kalamaras (aka Mega Kalamaras) is definitely not one of the plate-smashing brigade of restaurants. Hardly a stag night, hen night or strip-a-gram in sight, but there is genuine Greek food. Yes, you can have moussaka, but you can also stray into less familiar terri-tory: baked crab with lemon juice, for example. The truly adventurous can even try some of the Greek wines. Try baklava, Greek pastry or fresh fruit to fin-ish. There is another branch called Micro Kalamaras a few doors down (at 66 Inverness Mews, 0171 727 5082) which is of a similar standard, though the premises are smaller and there is a little less choice on the menu.

Indian

You can be sure that Indian food has entered deep into the British psyche now that you can buy chicken tikka flavoured crisps. However, while even small villages in England usually have an 'Indian' restaurant, most of these seem to serve exactly the same dishes, and there is a sameness about the flavours. There is a reason for this. No less than 85% of the 5,000 (!) 'Indian' restaurants in London (8,500 in the UK) are actually run by Bangladeshis. There are some interesting Bangladeshi dishes, but the cooking style is less varied than that of India, and most high street tandooris just serve a limited range of dishes which it is assumed the customers will want. At the start of each day from one to five basic sauces are prepared, and everything is based around these. This accounts for why so many of the dishes you get at the high street tandoori taste alike, which is a pity since real Indian cuisine is far more varied than the general experience would suggest.

India has fifteen major languages and is home to a billion people. Its culinary traditions reflect its scale and its long and varied history, with a wide range of styles in the different Indian provinces. In general, in North India bread is the staple, in the South rice, though sometimes both are eaten. Many Hindus are vegetarian, which accounts for the richness of the vegetarian cuisine in India - indeed it is hard to think of another of the world's cuisines which offers so much to vegetarians. The cow is sacred to Hindus, so beef is not eaten; indeed the most common meat is goat. A flavour of the different regional variations is given below, though of course there is much regional cross-over, so a dish which may have originated in Kashmir may be eaten all over India.

Bombay	The capital of Maharashtra province has given us the *bhel poori* snacks (see entries later for Diwana Bhel Poori and Chetna's).
Delhi	Home to the moghuls, Muslims who ruled India until the English removed them. The moghuls ate in style, and some restaurants in England offer an interpretation of moghul food. The region also offers snacks like *aloo-ki-tikhas* (a potato snack), stuffed okra and *shami kabab* (minced lamb patties).
Goa	For some time colonised by the Portuguese, there is a significant Catholic influence here. Goa is famous for its many fish dishes.
Gujerat	Bombay used to be in Gujerat, and so the cuisines have similarities. As well as the many vegetarian snacks, Gujerat has dishes such as fish in coriander chutney cooked in a banana leaf.
Kashmir	This region gave us the famous lamb dish *rogan josh*, so common in restaurants in England. Saffron is grown here, and an unusual type of bread called kulcha is made.

Kerala   This part of India has many Christians, and has developed
                        slightly different culinary traditions. Coconut sauce is
                        much used in the curries, and there are many fish dishes,
                        as well as *appams* (rice pancakes).

Punjab   This region makes heavy use of the tandoor, which has
                        swept Indian restaurants in England throughout the last
                        couple of decades.   Dishes familiar in England, like
                        chicken tikka and naan bread, are eaten here. There is no
                        history of restaurants in the Western sense in India until
                        after 1947, but the early ones were mainly run by Punjabis.

South India   Here we find dosas (rice pancakes, often stuffed with a
                        vegetable filling) and the Indian 'pizza' uthappam.

Uttar Pradesh   This region is home to the thali, where a complete meal is
                        served in several little dishes on a tray. This came about
                        since the ruling Marwari Hindus were exceptionally fussy
                        about who touched their food. Only Brahmins (the high-
                        est caste) were allowed to prepare their food, and no serv-
                        ing dishes were used so that the purity could be seen to
                        pass directly from the kitchen to the diner. Also from here
                        are dishes like achar gosht (lamb braised with green chill-
                        ies and pickling spices) and pooris (deep-fried whole-
                        wheat bread).

London offers genuine Indian cuisine, from Gujerat to Goa, as follows.

Bodali

| Price (lunch): | **n/a** |
| Price (dinner): | **£10-£15** |

Address:	78 Highbury Park, Highbury, London N5 2XE
Phone:	0171 359 3444 or 0171 704 0741
Fax:	None
Reservations?	Yes
Nearest tube:	Arsenal or Finsbury Park
Open lunch:	None
Open dinner:	Monday - Saturday 18:00 - 22:00
Closed:	Bank Holidays, August
Seats:	26
Private Room?	No
Credit cards:	None
Disabled access:	Yes (not to toilets)
Music played?	Yes
Non-smoking?	No
Chef:	Jayanti Patel
N.B. No young children	

Bodali makes a refreshing attempt to
reproduce something like Indian home
cooking in a restaurant setting.   The
premises are unprepossessing, a con-
verted take-away in a parade of shops. It
is a husband and wife team, an Indian
chef of Gujerati origin (though with a
strong North London accent) and his
wife, who runs the front of house. Decor
is a little eccentric, and service can be a
little scatty to match, but this should not
detract from the food, which is a cut
above the norm. For example vegetable
samosas had good texture and spices
fresh enough to retain their distinct
tastes. A curry of chickpeas and potato
was also good, both main constituents
being cooked well, the chickpeas very
tender and the potatoes cooked just right.
Some dishes slip into normality, like the
breads and a rather ordinary rogan josh,
but generally the standards are kept up.
Bodali is unlicensed, and you can bring
your own alcohol without charge.

Bombay Brasserie

Price (lunch):	£20
Price (dinner):	£30-£45

Address:	Courtfield Close, Courtfield Road, Gloucester Road London SW7 4UH
Phone:	0171 370 4040
Fax:	0171 835 1669
Reservations?	Yes
Nearest tube:	Gloucester Road
Set lunch:	£14.95
Set dinner:	£28.50 + 10% service for groups only
Open lunch:	All week 12:00 - 15:00
Open dinner:	All week 19:30 - 24:00
Closed:	25th, 26th December
Seats:	180
Private Room?	Yes (80-100 people)
Credit cards:	Visa,Amex,Access, Diners
Disabled access?	Yes
Music played?	Yes (evenings)
Non-smoking?	No
N.B.	No children under 10
Chef:	Udit Sarkhel

At one time the Bombay Brasserie was perhaps the best Indian restaurant in London, and I used to go very frequently (over 100 times in all). Sadly the last few years have seen the prices go up and the food become patchy. Nonetheless, if you order carefully you can still taste some interesting and well prepared food, e.g. fish with mint chutney wrapped in a banana leaf or the excellent rogan josh. All main dishes come with three vegetable dishes brought separately. Lunch is a buffet with a selection of dishes served at the imposing central table; the range of dishes is narrower than in the evening, but it is much cheaper. Service is usually competent but can have lapses. The surroundings are very grand, decorated in a colonial style with plenty of space, high ceilings and fans. When booking ask for the conservatory, which has the best seats and is also a safe distance away from the pianist, who sometimes ventures into vocals.

Bombay Palace

Price (lunch):	£15
Price (dinner):	£15-£25

Address:	50 Connaught Street Bayswater, London W2 2AA
Phone:	0171 258 3507
Fax:	0171 706 8072
Reservations?	Yes
Nearest tube:	Marble Arch or Edgware Road
Open lunch:	All week 12:00 - 15:00
Open dinner:	All week 18:00 - 23:30 (23:00 Sunday)
Closed:	Never
Seats:	100
Private Room?	Yes (40 people)
Credit cards:	Visa,Amex,Access, Diners
Disabled access?	Yes
Music played?	Yes
Non-smoking?	On request
Chef:	Mr Sandosh

This is one of an international chain of restaurants (other branches are in the US and Canada, as well as India) run by the colourful Sant Singh Chatwal, an ex-pilot expelled from Ethiopia in less enlightened times. The dining room is spacious, set out over the a large floor area, and decor is very smart. Service is polite and discreet. This may make you wonder whether this is a tourist trap (there are, sadly, quite a few such in London, presenting mediocre food in smart surroundings at high prices), but Indian friends testify to the authenticity of the food here. The high-quality Punjabi cooking relies on very good ingredients and subtle but accurate use of spices. Breads are very well made and the menu has a few variations from the predictable. As usual in Indian restaurants, it is best to stick to beer rather than venture into wine.

Brilliant

Price (lunch):	£10-£15
Price (dinner):	£10-£15

Address:	72-74 Western Road, Southall, Middlesex UB2 5DZ
Phone:	0181 574 1928
Fax:	0181 574 0276
Reservations?	Yes
Nearest tube:	None (Southall BR)
Open lunch:	Tuesday - Sunday 12:00 - 15:00
Open dinner:	Tuesday - Sunday 18:00 - 23:30 (last orders 23:15)
Set lunch/dinner:	£10/head for groups of 30 or over
Closed:	3 weeks in August
Seats:	120
Private Room?	Yes (40 people)
Credit cards:	Visa,Amex,Access, Diners
Disabled access?	Yes
Music played?	Yes
Non-smoking?	Separate section
Chef:	D.K. Anand

This Southall institution serves food in the style of Indian home cooking rather than the standard high street offerings. In my view it offers, along with Madhu's Brilliant, the best Indian food to be found in England. Run by the Anand brothers for over two decades now, the Brilliant is popular with local Asian families. The distinguishing feature of the cooking is the attention to detail given to the spicing, while the short menu means that only tried and tested dishes are on offer. The mixed bhaji starter is remarkable, the aloo tikki vegetarian starter delicious, as are the methi chicken and chilli chicken. In my experience you can't really go wrong. Service is above average for an Indian restaurant, portions huge (they will wrap up whatever is left for you) and prices extremely fair. The surroundings look rather dated, but the food is magnificent, and a fraction of the price of more swish establishments.

Chetna's

Price (lunch):	£5-£10
Price (dinner):	£5-£10

Address:	420 High Road, Wembley, Middlesex HA9 6AH
Phone:	0181 900 1466 0181 903 5989
Fax:	None
Reservations?	No
Nearest tube:	Wembley Central
Open lunch:	Tuesday - Friday 12:00 - 15:00 Saturday & Sunday 13:00 - 22:30
Open dinner:	Tuesday - Friday 18:00 - 22:30 Saturday & Sunday 13:00 - 22:30
Closed:	Bank Holidays
Seats:	75
Private Room?	No
Credit cards:	None
Disabled access?	Yes (not to toilets)
Music played?	Yes
Non-smoking?	Separate section
Chefs:	M.M. & J.G. Patel

This bustling Wembley establishment is reminiscent of the Diwana Bhel Poori (see later), since it serves a very similar menu, though without the curries. Things get seriously hectic here, with seating for over 75 people and frequently a queue out of the door. Oddly, there is a take-away pizza operation going on in one part of the restaurant, but don't let that put you off. Chetna's does not cater to the lager and vindaloo crowd; this is a place where Asian families go out to eat. The food is of a very high standard, the dosas being excellent and the snacks (bhel poori, etc.) superb. It would be easy to eat here for under £5, and hard to spend £10. Chetna's is unlicensed, and the (Muslim) management seem to frown on you bringing alcohol in.

Chutney Mary

| Price (lunch): | £15-£20 |
| Price (dinner): | £30-£45 |

Address:	Plaza 535,
	535 King's Road,
	Fulham,
	London SW10 0SZ
Phone:	0171 351 3113
Fax:	0171 351 7694
Reservations?	Yes
Nearest tube:	Fulham Broadway
Set lunch:	£10.00, buffet on
	Sunday £13.95
Set dinner:	£10 only after 22:00
Open lunch:	All week
	12:30 - 14:30
Open dinner:	All week
	19:00 - 23:30
	(22:30 on Sunday)
Closed:	Christmas dinner
Seats:	110
Private Room?	No
Credit cards:	Visa,Amex,Access,
	Diners
Disabled access?	No
Music played?	Yes
Non-smoking?	Separate section
Chef:	Hardev Singh Bhatty

When Chutney Mary opened it got some dazzling reviews, yet I found it inconsistent and overpriced. Things have settled down somewhat now, but this entry is in recognition of the lunch, where the buffet usually has interesting dishes and is quite good value. Going in the evening is a gamble: the food can either be very good or very ordinary, the only consistency being in the steep prices. The menu is certainly interesting, being 'Anglo Indian' to reflect the cooking associated with the long British presence in India. So there are dishes like 'Bangalore bangers and mash', and some interesting regional specialities, e.g. Goan green chicken curry. A sea bream curry I had was delicious, and the breads and chutneys are very good. There is a charming conservatory, and the surroundings are fairly classy in a colonial sort of way.

Curry Craze

| Price (lunch): | £8-£15 |
| Price (dinner): | £8-£15 |

Address:	8-9 Neeld Parade,
	Wembley Hill Road,
	The Triangle,
	Wembley
	Middlesex HA9 6QU
Phone:	0181 902 9720
Fax:	None
Reservations?	Yes
Nearest tube:	Wembley Park or
	Wembley Central
Open lunch:	Daily except Tuesday
	12:00-14:30
Open dinner:	Daily except Tuesday
	18:00 - 23:00
Closed:	Tuesdays only
Seats:	100
Private Room?	No
Credit cards:	Visa,Amex,Access
Disabled access:	Yes
Music played?	Yes
Non-smoking?	No
Chef:	Mrs Malhotra

It is a pity that most 'Indian' restaurants make no attempt at producing the excellent food that is made in most Indian homes; only in Southall and Wembley are there places catering primarily to Asians and prepared to offer choices beyond chicken tikka massala. The Curry Craze offers a mixture of fairly standard dishes along with more interesting Punjabi fare. Vegetarian starters like aloo tikki and various poori dishes are offered, while there are also meat specialities like butter chicken and chilli chicken. The cooking seems to me below the standard of the best places in Southall, but still well above that of most Indian restaurants. Portions are designed for families, so although prices seem to be only a bit lower than a high-street tandoori, if you order normally, you will end up with a meal that is at least twice as big as you were expecting. I don't know why Indian restaurants feel obliged to offer ghastly wines, but the tradition is faithfully followed here, so stick to beer.

Diwana Bhel Poori

Price (lunch):	£6-£10
Price (dinner):	£7-£12

Address:	121 Drummond Street, Euston, London NW1 2HL
Phone:	0171 387 5556
Fax:	0171 383 0560
Reservations?	Yes
Nearest tube:	Euston
Set lunch:	£4.95
Open:	All week 12:00 - 23:45
Closed:	Christmas Day
Seats:	100
Private Room?	Yes (36 people)
Credit cards:	Visa,Amex,Access, Diners
Disabled access?	Yes (not to toilets)
Music played?	Yes
Non-smoking?	No
Chef:	A. Qadir

Where else in London (or England) can you eat genuinely classy food for around £7? This café does not take bookings and has fairly basic decor (no tablecloths) but the service is efficient and you can buy alcohol from the shop two doors down (Diwana's is unlicensed). The South Indian vegetarian food is superb. Personally I think Diwana is best at the starter snacks, so I normally order two or three of these per person, and then just skip to the wonderful home-made kulfi (Indian ice cream). In particular you should try the bhel poori, samosas and aloo papri chat, which are outstanding. Also the de-luxe dosa (basically a big crisp pancake stuffed with a spicy potato and onion filling) is excellent, though some of the curries are quite ordinary. Feeling that their prices were too high for lunchtime trade, they offer an 'eat as much as you want' lunch for £4.95; this is excellent value, but does not usually include the snacks at which they are best.

Also at: 50 Westbourne Grove, London W2 (0171 221 0721)

Geetanjali

Price (lunch):	£15-£20
Price (dinner):	£20-£25

Address:	16 Court Parade, Watford Road, Wembley, Middlesex HA0 3HU
Phone:	0181 904 5353
Fax:	None
Reservations?	Yes
Nearest tube:	Wembley Central
Open lunch:	All week 12:00 - 15:00
Open dinner:	All week 18:30 - 23:30
Closed:	Christmas
Disabled access?	Yes
Music played?	Yes
Non-smoking?	No

My heart sank when I walked in here, on an Indian friend's recommendation. This looks just like another formula tandoori, with a few potted plants and light brown hessian wallpaper. There were an encouraging number of Indians dining, but I was still sceptical. Vegetable samosas were a little over-crisp, but had a lively filling, with lots of fresh spices sparkling on the tongue. Aloo chat was also good, with big chunks of potato and lots of fresh coriander. But things really got into their stride with the main course: butter chicken was excellent, with a spicy and well judged sauce, though the chicken itself could have been of higher quality. Chana was excellent, the chickpeas tender but not in a mush, while a vegetable curry managed to keep its vegetables with a recognisable texture. Rice and the breads were good. Service was good throughout, and portions are huge – enough leftovers for another complete meal as a takeaway.

Gopal's

Price (lunch):	£15-£35
Price (dinner):	£15-£35

Address:	12 Bateman Street, Soho, London W1V 5TD
Phone:	0171 434 0840
Fax:	0171 434 1621
Reservations?	Yes
Nearest tube:	Tottenham Court Rd or Leicester Square
Open lunch:	All week 12:00 - 15:00
Open dinner:	All week 18:00 - 23:30
Closed:	Christmas & Boxing Day
Seats:	50
Private Room?	No
Credit cards:	Visa,Amex,Access
Disabled access?	Yes (not to toilets)
Music played?	Yes
Non-smoking?	No
Chef:	Mr N.P. Pittal

This restaurant is the best of the pink tablecloth brigade of up-market Indian restaurants, many of which actually serve very poor food indeed. Gopal's, while having some faults (the vegetable starters are rather disappointing) is particularly good at the main course meat-based curries, which are delicate and nicely judged. The rogan josh, for example, is excellent. The vegetable side dishes are also above average. Service is efficient and prices higher than for a high street tandoori but not outrageous given the standard of food. Gopal's is one of the few Indian restaurants to have taken the trouble to get in a wine consultant to advise on the list, and the result is a very respectable selection, ordered by style, with bottles suitable for this style of food. If only more Indian restaurants could do the same.

Kastoori

Price (lunch):	£10-£20
Price (dinner):	£10-£20

Address:	188 Upper Tooting Road, Tooting, London SW17 7EJ
Phone:	0181 767 7027
Fax:	None
Reservations?	Yes
Nearest tube:	Tooting Bec
Set lunch:	£7.25-£11.25
Open lunch:	Wednesday - Sunday 12:30 - 14:30
Open dinner:	All week 18:00 - 22:30
Closed:	Christmas
Seats:	84
Private Room?	No
Credit cards:	Visa,Amex,Access, Diners
Disabled access?	Yes (but not to men's toilet)
Music played?	Yes
Non-smoking?	No
Chef:	Dinesh Thanki

Tooting is not renowned as a culinary centre, but the Kastoori is an excellent Gujerati-run restaurant. Tucked away in an unpromising parade of shops, it offers quite a wide range of Indian vegetarian cooking. There are common dishes such as sev poori and dosas, but there are also Gujerati specialities, and even some 'family specials', drawing on East African ingredients. Breads are particularly good, with varieties like bhatura as well as the usual chapati, and chutneys are home-made rather than emanating from a jar. There is a Gujerati thali if you want to try a variety of dishes. Service is very friendly, even to the extent that you are occasionally offered an extra complimentary dish to sample. There is even some attempt at choosing some reasonably suitable wines, though sweet lassi is a refreshing alternative.

Lahore Kebab House

Price (lunch):	£5-£10
Price (dinner):	£5-£10

Address:	4 Umberston Street, Whitechapel London E1 1PY
Phone:	0171 481 9738
Fax:	None
Reservations?	No
Nearest tube:	Aldgate East
Open:	All week 12:00 - 24:00
Closed:	Never
Seats:	80
Private Room?	No
Credit cards:	None
Disabled access?	Yes
Music played?	No
Non-smoking?	No
Chef:	M. Din

A sort of Indian greasy spoon, the Lahore Kebab House (not to be confused with at least two other restaurants of the same name in the vicinity, so check your street signs carefully!) is an odd place. Despite some recent attempts at smartening up, it still looks very tatty, the upstairs a little less so than the ground floor. Service is usually brusque, and you will be hustled out of your cramped table (which you will probably have to share with others) if you hesitate for a moment. If you can put up with all this, then you will be able to eat some of the best tandoori dishes in London. The turnover is very fast, the meat fresh and extremely well prepared. There some unusual dishes like brain massala, but the tandoori dishes are the specialities. It also has the great virtue of being very cheap. Bring your own beer.

Madhu's Brilliant

Price (lunch):	£10-£15
Price (dinner):	£12-£18

Address:	39 South Road, Southall, Middlesex UB1 1SW
Phone:	0181 574 1897
Fax:	0181 813 8639
Reservations?	Yes
Nearest tube:	No tube (near Southall BR)
Set lunch:	£8-£12.50
Set dinner:	£10 to £15
Open lunch:	Monday and Wednesday - Friday 12:30 - 15:00
Open dinner:	Wednesday - Monday 18:00 - 23:30
Closed:	Christmas
Seats:	104
Private Room?	Yes (60 people)
Credit cards:	Visa,Amex,Access, Diners
Disabled access?	Yes (not to toilets)
Music played?	Yes
Non-smoking?	No
Chef:	Sanjeev Anand

My joint-favourite Indian restaurant (along with the Brilliant — see page 56). The dishes are mainly Punjabi, and are like Indian home cooking served in a restaurant. The judgement of spices is superb, and the garam massala is ground specially to an old family recipe. Madhu's specialises in catering for Indian weddings, and this is now much bigger business than the restaurant itself. You must try the wonderful 'aloo tikki', a roadside snack of vegetables, chickpeas, spicy chutney and yoghurt that is rarely seen outside Southall (and India). The chicken tikka massala is completely different from the usual bland high-street variety (if they are not busy ask for the 'special' version, not on the menu) and the vegetable dishes in particular are outstanding. Service is friendly and portions large. The pilau rice is magnificent, bursting with flavour and fragrance, and the kulfi is home-made. The only criticism that can be levelled at the food is that the sauces can be a little oily, but this is a minor point. Sanjay Anand runs the front of house with an efficiency and care for customers rare in Indian restaurants. This really is worth the trip.

Namaste

Price (lunch):	£10-£13
Price (dinner):	£15-£20

Address:	30 Alie Street, Whitechapel, London E1 8DA
Phone:	0171 488 9242
Fax:	0171 488 9339
Reservations?	Yes
Nearest tube:	Aldgate East
Open lunch:	Monday - Friday 12:00 - 15:00
Open dinner:	Monday - Saturday 19:00 - 22:00
Closed:	Christmas week, Bank Holidays
Seats:	72 (80 in summer)
Private Room?	Yes (35 people)
Credit cards:	Visa,Amex,Access, Diners
Disabled access?	No
Music played?	Yes
Non-smoking?	No
Chef:	Cyrus Todwila

The Namaste is a fine addition to the London Indian restaurant scene. Rather more up-market than most East London Indian places, it has a very talented chef and offers an interesting range of dishes. For example 'chicken piri piri' is an authentic dish of marinated chicken with a sharp chilli element – no watering down to perceived Western tastes here. Unfortunately I have experienced some inconsistency, but the cooking here is generally excellent, a world apart from most high-street places. Vegetable dishes are excellent, as is the kulfi. You could try sweet lassi (the yoghurt–based drink rather than the cute collie dog), which is very good. If you are feeling hungry then the thali, rather than being a fixed selection of dishes, allows you to roam far and wide through the menu and choose exactly what you want, all delivered in miniature (though still generous) portions.

Ragam

Price (lunch):	£10-£15
Price (dinner):	£10-£15

Address:	57 Cleveland Street, London W1 5PQ
Phone:	0171 636 9098
Fax:	None
Reservations?	Yes
Nearest tube:	Goodge Street
Open lunch:	All week 12:00 - 15:00
Open dinner:	All week 18:00 - 23:30 (last orders 23:15)
Closed:	Christmas Day & Boxing Day
Seats:	54
Private Room?	Yes (20 people)
Credit cards:	Visa,Amex,Access, Diners
Disabled access?	Yes
Music played?	No
Non-smoking?	No
Chef:	G. Nair

There are some places that I hope remain undiscovered by the masses in case I can't get a table any more. This is how I feel about the Ragam, an unashamedly old-fashioned Indian restaurant tucked away behind the Middlesex hospital. It only seats 36, but if there is a wait for your table the owner will park you in the King & Queen a few doors down, and come and fetch you when your table is ready. This is not flashy cooking, but it is consistently good and it is possible to eat well for a tenner each. How many places within easy walking distance of Oxford Street can this be said of? The speciality is South Indian (Kerala) vegetarian food, with dosas and snacks. There is also a standard menu of meat dishes, competent though not exceptional. The staff are friendly if usually overstretched, but above all this is excellent value. When you compare the food here with the endless high-street tandooris serving the same oily food you will see its appeal.

Rani

Price (lunch):	£20-£30
Price (dinner):	£20-£30

Address:	7 Long Lane, Finchley, London N3 2PR
Phone:	0181 349 4386
Fax:	0181 349 4386
Reservations?	Yes
Nearest tube:	Finchley Central
Set lunch:	£8 buffet
Set dinner:	£10 buffet (Monday only)
Open lunch:	Tuesday - Friday 12:15 - 14:15 Sunday 12:15 - 15:00
Open dinner:	All week 18:00 - 24:00
Closed:	Christmas Day
Seats:	90
Private Room?	Yes (23 - 60 people)
Credit cards:	Visa,Amex,Access
Disabled access:	Partial (1 step)
Music played?	Yes
Non-smoking?	Monday & Saturday
Chef:	Mrs Kundan Pattni

North London (as distinct from North West London) is desperately lacking in decent Indian restaurants, so the Rani is a welcome haven of good cooking. This is no formula curry house, instead there is a wide selection of mainly Gujerati vegetarian dishes. The place is quite bright and well-decorated by Indian restaurant standards, though the mainly Western clientele are prepared to pay higher prices than their Asian counterparts in Wembley, and this shows when the bill arrives. Things are definitely home-made here: chutneys sparkle on the tongue with flavour and have not emerged from a pickle jar. The menu offers a wide choice, so as well as the usual pooris and samosas, there are various vegetable curries and unusual desserts like shrikand (a yoghurt dessert flavoured with cardamom and saffron), rarely seen outside Asian areas. There are also various daily dishes, e.g. aloo tikki on Thursday. The restaurant offers a discount scheme for regulars, and there

is even a Braille menu.

Sabras

Price (lunch):	£5-£10
Price (dinner):	£15-£20

Address:	263 Willesden High Road, London NW10 2RX
Phone:	0181 459 0340
Fax:	Fax
Reservations?	Yes
Nearest tube:	Dollis Hill or Willesden Green
Set lunch:	£5.95 - £7.95
Set dinner:	£8 - £12
Open lunch:	Tuesday - Friday 12:00 - 15:00
Open dinner:	Tuesday - Sunday 18:30 - 22:30
Closed:	Christmas
Seats:	32
Private Room?	No
Credit cards:	None
Disabled access?	Yes
Music played?	Yes
Non-smoking?	Separate section
Chef:	Hemant Desai

Although not the sort of area to take your granny, Willesden does boast some good Indian food. The Sabras is quite the best exponent, a café serving superb Gujerati vegetarian dishes. It only has a few tables but the menu is extensive and the owner, Hemant Desai, is both helpful and very knowledgeable. As well as the more familiar pooris there is a wide selection of unusual dishes (how often do you see violet yams on a menu?). The Hyderabad dosa is particularly delicious, but in fact it is hard to go wrong on this menu. Ingredients are of high quality, but it is the complexity of the spicing which shows the true class of the kitchen. Breads are very good, kulfi is home-made, as are the chutneys used here. There is also a range of over twenty beers from around the world. Well worth an excursion, as I would rate this as the best vegetarian Indian restaurant in London.

Shree Krishna

Price (lunch):	£8-£12
Price (dinner):	£8-£12

Address:	192-194 Tooting High Street, Tooting, London SW17 0SF
Phone:	0181 672 4250 or 0181 672 6903
Fax:	None
Reservations?	Yes
Nearest tube:	Tooting Broadway
Set lunch:	No
Set dinner:	No
Open lunch:	Sunday - Thursday 12:00 - 15:00
Open dinner:	All week 18:00 - 23:00 (24:00 Saturday)
Closed:	Christmas
Seats:	120
Private Room?	Yes (60 people)
Credit cards:	Visa, Amex, Access, Diners
Disabled access:	Yes
Music played?	Yes
Non-smoking?	No
Chef:	Mullath Vijayan

The Shree Krishna is a sister restaurant to the excellent Ragam (see entry), and this also specialises in the cooking of the Kerala Coast of India, though there is also a wide selection of more familiar dishes offered. It is best to stick to the Kerala vegetarian dishes – why come somewhere like this in order to have a lamb vindaloo? Dosai, the crispy pancakes stuffed with various fillings, are excellent here, with consistently good texture, the filling bursting with fresh flavours. There is also uthappam, the Kerala pizza-like pancake made with rice and lentil flour and topped with onions, green chillies and tomatoes. There are also exotic dishes like avial, a vegetable dish cooked with coconut and curry leaves, options which are not common on Indian menus in South London. Breads, such as paratha are fair. There is the usual chamber of horrors in the wine list, so stick to lassi or beer. Prices are very fair, e.g. a basic dosa is a remarkable £2, while even the main course meat dishes are only £3.50.

Indonesian

Indonesia is big: it consists of several thousand islands and has a population of 190 million people. It has a varied cuisine to match, with Malaysian and Chinese influences, but a distinctive style of its own. Arabian merchants introduced Islam around 1300, and the country is today predominantly Muslim (though Bali, for example, still practises a form of Hindusim). The Dutch invaded in 1596, and so there is a long colonial link between these countries, which is why there are so many Indonesian restaurants in the Netherlands (just as there are so many Indian ones in England). In Indonesia it is customary to serve everything together and, when guests are invited, to put out more than can be eaten, to assure them that there is plenty to eat. This tradition led to the development of the *rijstafel* banquet, where a great many dishes may be served all at once.

Melati

| Price (lunch): | £15-£25 |
| Price (dinner): | £15-£25 |

Address	21 Great Windmill Street, Soho, London W1 7PH
Phone:	0171 734 6964
Fax:	0171 434 4196
Reservations?	Yes
Nearest tube:	Piccadilly Circus
Set lunch:	£5.50
Set dinner:	£21.25 (minimum 2)
Open:	All week 12:00 - 24:00 (last orders 23:30)
Closed:	Christmas Day only
Seats:	120
Private Room?	Yes (40 people)
Credit cards:	Visa,Amex,Access, Diners
Disabled access?	Yes (not to toilets)
Music played?	Yes
Non-smoking?	No
Chef:	S. Alamsjah

Don't be put off by the dubious Soho location. For years this informal little café has been producing excellent Indonesian food at fair prices, completely outclassing the more fashionably located (and decorated) rivals. The *beef rendang* is delicious, as is the classic noodle dish *mee goreng*, while satay is very well handled. There are also some more exotic dishes. The point about this place is the sheer quality of the cooking. It is always packed here, but the waiter will come and fetch you from the pub next door if there is a long wait for a table. The Minang, just up the road at 11 Greek Street, is owned by the same people and serves similar food.

Italian

Italian cuisine has given us pizza and pasta, and has had a significant influence on cooking elsewhere. Indeed it is difficult to go into a fashionable bistro these days without being served ciabatta bread, or something with sun-dried tomatoes and balsamic vinegar. Cooking in Italy has a long tradition, with cookery books dating back to the fifteenth century (quite apart from the Roman tradition), and this is the area where the fork was invented. Refined Italian cooking was widely introduced to the rest of Europe when Catherine de Medici married the second son of Francis I of France, and brought with her a retinue of Italian cooks. This led to Italian cooking becoming fashionable in the courts of Europe.

Italian cuisine has several distinct regional styles. In the north, rice is the staple and butter is much used for cooking; in the south, pasta is the staple, and olive oil is used more than butter.

North-east	In Trentino-Alto Adige there is something of an Austrian influence, with many dishes of veal (e.g. *crauti*, which is similar to the Austrian schnitzel) and smoked meats, though there are imaginative uses of wild mushrooms and shellfish as well. Polenta dishes dominate closer to the sea, with many seafood dishes emanating from the area around Venice.
North-west	This area has many dishes based on polenta (cornmeal) and also rice. This is where short-grain arborio rice, ideal for risotto, comes from. In the far west is the region of Piedmont, where the famous white truffles come from (see the section 'Luxuries: Truffles and Foie Gras' for more on these). There is a lot of game, so there are dishes involving wild boar and venison cooked in rich sauces, as well as hearty soups and stews. From Genoa in the far west comes the basil-based sauce pesto. In Lombardy veal is the speciality, such as the stewed veal *ossobuco; polenta e osei* involves serving fowl roasted on a spit on a bed of polenta.
North	The Emilia-Romagna region, and especially Bologna, is the best-known area of the north for food. This area has very fertile soil, and there is a great variety of sausages and smoked meats. This part of Italy is where Parma ham comes from, and Parmesan cheese. Pasta dishes include *lasagna al forno, tagliatelli* and *tortellini*. In Tuscany meat is often roasted or charcoal grilled, but since this region has the best olive oil in Italy, it may also be fried. Another speciality is dishes using the famous Tuscan beans, e.g. bean soups, or beans cooked with garlic, tomatoes and herbs. In Umbria we find *bruschetta*, toasted country bread rubbed with garlic and sprinkled with salt and olive oil. There are also black truffles.
Central	With Rome at its heart, it is not surprising that the Lazio region has drawn on a wide range of culinary experiences from around the world. Many dishes are cooked in *battutu*, a mixture of butter, pork fat and oil.

Artichokes are a favourite food here in many forms, while lamb is the most common meat. The many pasta specialities include cannelloni and spaghetti dishes, as well as dishes like potato dumplings, e.g. *gnocchi alla romana*. The Abruzzi and Molise regions to the east of Lazio have many local sausages and cheeses.

South

The south of Italy has given the world pizza (from Naples) and is commonly regarded as the home of pasta. Again olive oil is used extensively, and there are fish stews and many dishes based on seafood such as clams. The Campania area still has buffaloes: hence buffalo mozzarella cheese, though most of this famous cheese is made from cow's milk these days. In Calabria mushroom dishes are specialities, as well as hearty soups and grilled swordfish.

Sicily and Sardinia

Remarkable for the fact that saffron grows here (probably introduced by Phoenician traders), Sicily makes little use of rice despite its Arab trading traditions. Sicilian cooking revolves around fish and vegetables, mussels are very common also. Sicilians make good sweets, e.g. *cassata alla siciliana*, the layered ice-cream Sardinia is known for its spit-roasting of meats, as well as making good use of its fish and seafood; lobsters, mussels and clams are plentiful here.

With all this heritage to draw upon, London is a mixed bag as far as Italian restaurants go. I am particularly ambivalent about up-market Italian restaurants. I love good pasta and pizzas, but when the cooking gets more ambitious the prices seem to head towards the stratosphere. I am simply unconvinced that the cuisine can compete at the top end with the best French food, and yet the prices are just as high. My ultimate disappointment came at one of only three restaurants in Italy to have three Michelin stars (the Enoteca Pinchiorri in Florence) paying over £90 a head several years ago for a pleasant, but completely uninspiring meal. What is strange is how the best aspects of Italian cooking have been picked up by top French chefs, and enhanced well beyond the original roots. The best pasta I have ever eaten has been at French rather than Italian restaurants.

So, what is the Italian food lover to do in London? If you like pasta there are some simple places otherwise you venture into the trendy territory of the River Café and its inferior imitators. Technical errors show up all the more when food is prepared in a very plain way. I am all for simple dishes, but if someone is merely grilling a piece of fish then I expect simple prices to match. Apart from using better ingredients (e.g. olive oil from Lucca rather than Sainsbury's) I cannot for the life of me see what in the cooking justifies the high prices at most of these establishments other than the smart surroundings. Perhaps the best Italian food I have had in London is at the Osteria Antica Bologna (see entry). The food here, in my limited experience, has been at least as good as the more famous establishments, and at a fraction of the price.

N.B. Pizza places have their own separate section.

L'Altro

Price (lunch):	£15-£20
Price (dinner):	£35-£45

Address:	210 Kensington Park Road, Notting Hill, London W11 1NR
Phone:	0171 792 1066
Fax:	None
Reservations?	Yes
Nearest tube:	Ladbroke Grove or Notting Hill Gate
Open lunch:	All week 12:00 - 15:00
Open dinner:	Monday - Saturday 19:00 - 23:00 (23:30 Friday & Saturday)
Closed:	4 days at Christmas
Seats:	45
Private Room?	Yes (45 people)
Credit cards:	Visa,Amex,Access, Diners
Disabled access?	Yes
Music played?	Yes
Non-smoking?	No
Chef:	Massimo Bianchi

L'Altro attracts the roving fashion victims of Notting Hill in search of something a little different, together with actors discussing their careers with their agents. The decor is almost a parody of itself, with the plate-glass frontage beckoning towards stone-effect plaster walls and the odd classical statue more in keeping in a grand Italian palace than in a small restaurant. The recommendation here is primarily for the lunch, where a sort of Italian version of tapas is served. Here you can choose from a selection of vegetarian and seafood dishes, with the odd meat offering thrown in for confirmed carnivores. The simply prepared dishes rely on very fresh ingredients and a delicate touch, which is evident here more than at most places serving this style of food. Naturally, rocket and balsamic vinegar are liberally strewn across the menu, but there are some interesting dishes on offer. There is a sensible wine list. In the evening the price soars and consequently it is harder to feel a sense of good value.

Del Buongustaio

Price (lunch):	£15-£20
Price (dinner):	£25-£35

Address:	283 Putney Bridge Road, Putney, London SW15 2PT
Phone:	0181 780 9361
Fax:	0181 789 9659
Reservations?	Yes
Nearest tube:	East Putney or Putney Bridge
Set lunch:	£9.50
Set dinner:	No
Open lunch:	Sunday - Friday 12:00 - 15:00
Open dinner:	Monday - Saturday 18:30 - 23:30
Closed:	2 weeks Christmas
Seats:	60
Private Room?	No
Credit cards:	Visa,Amex,Access
Disabled access:	Partial (1 step)
Music played?	Yes
Non-smoking?	No
Chefs:	Aurelio Spagnuolo & Antonio Strillozzi

The cooking here is pleasingly down to earth. The menu is based on dishes from North Italy, and it changes weekly, while there are some daily specials as well. Examples of the dishes tried are a flan *di carciofi vecchio piedmonte*, served simply with a bed of leaves garnished with olive oil. The artichokes were puréed and had been cooked with *porcini* (cep) mushrooms prior to being puréed together, the *porcini* lending a lovely flavour to the artichokes. Not all dishes work as well, but the standard overall is high. The wine list is a mixture of Italian and Australian and has some fine choices, though set out in a most peculiar way. Instead of listing by country or grape variety, there are instead sections like 'serious but worthwhile', and 'wines for the good times'. Wines from top Australian growers like Wolf Blass and David Wynn are represented at quite fair mark-ups, while the Italian wines are also well chosen. There is even a selection of eight dessert wines at £3.50 a glass.

Florians

Price (lunch):	£15-£25
Price (dinner):	£20-£25

Address:	4 Topsfield Parade, Middle Lane, Crouch End London N8 8PR
Phone:	0171 348 8348
Fax:	None
Reservations?	Yes
Nearest tube:	None near (Finsbury Park or Highgate)
Set lunch:	£5.50 at bar
Bar open:	All day from 12:00
Open lunch:	All week 12:00 - 15:00
Open dinner:	All week 19:00 - 23:00
Closed:	Christmas
Seats:	70 (+40 in bar)
Private Room?	Yes (24 people)
Credit cards:	Visa,Access
Disabled access?	Yes
Music played?	No
Non-smoking?	No
Chefs:	Ricardo Isolini and Francesco Scelsi

There are two rooms at Florians, a bar at the front and a dining room at the back. The menus are different, the bar menu simpler and cheaper. The walls are plain and painted white; the bar has café style wooden chairs, with a little middle room with a skylight and tablecloths. The main back room has plain-painted walls with oils and pastel paintings for sale, with a large mirror on one wall and attractive plants. A blackboard has specials of the day. The Italian dishes on offer include such things as risotto with beef ragu, an odd-sounding dish which was actually very good indeed. Sadly, not all the cooking is to the same standard, with one dish turning up with slightly different ingredients to the ones claimed, and a salad with gritty salad leaves. Still, overall this a pretty good local place, and the bar menu in particular is very fair value. The wine list is Italian, with a reasonable selection at normal mark-ups.

Orso

Price (lunch):	£15-£25
Price (dinner):	£15-£25

Address	27 Wellington Street, Covent Garden, London WC2H 9BD
Phone:	0171 240 5269
Fax:	0171 497 2148
Reservations?	Yes
Nearest tube:	Covent Garden
Open:	All week 12:00 - 24:00
Closed:	24th, 25th December
Seats:	100
Private Room?	No
Credit cards:	None
Disabled access?	No
Music played?	No
Non-smoking?	Separate section
Chef:	Martin Wilson

Tucked away in a basement near the Royal Opera House, Orso serves good quality Italian food at fair prices. The basement can be a little gloomy, and the tables are too tightly packed, but the decor is pleasant and the service friendly. The menu tends to the modern, with delicious little mini-pizzas, and good risotto. There are reliable salads and plenty of changing selections based on available ingredients. The Orso is not unbearably pretentious, nor does it fleece its customers. This in itself gives it an edge over many of its contemporaries. The Italian wine list is very well-chosen, and mark-ups are by no means outrageous.

Osteria Antica Bologna

Price (lunch):	£10-£20
Price (dinner):	£15-£30

Address:	23 Northcote Road, Battersea London SW11 1NG
Phone:	0171 978 4771
Fax:	None
Reservations?	Yes
Nearest tube:	Tooting Bec, or Clapham Junction BR
Set lunch:	£7.50 (2 courses), not on Sunday
Open lunch:	All week 12:00 - 15:00
Open dinner:	All week 18:00 - 23:00 (22:30 Sunday)
Closed:	Christmas
Seats:	70 (82 summer)
Private Room?	No
Credit cards:	Visa, Amex, Access
Disabled access?	Yes (not to toilets)
Music played?	Yes
Non-smoking:	Separate section
Chef:	Aurelio Spagnuolo

If only more Italian restaurants were like this one. The regional variation is accounted for by the cook, Aurelio Spagnuolo, born in Sicily and raised in Bologna. Here you can have a range of Bolognese starters (*assagi*) such as raw swordfish marinated in lemon, and brown lentils with sun-dried tomatoes and chillies. The pasta is excellent, and there are unusual dishes such as goat (which is delicious) and cuttlefish with artichokes as well as classics like risotto. Booking is essential and conditions are rather cramped, but the service is friendly. Prices are very fair, especially when compared with the up-market places cooking much the same food.

Quercia d'Oro

Price (lunch):	£10-£15
Price (dinner):	£10-£15

Address	16 Endell Street, Covent Garden London WC2H 9BD
Phone:	0171 379 5108
Fax:	Same
Reservations?	Yes
Nearest tube:	Covent Garden
Open lunch:	Monday - Friday 12:00 - 15:00
Open dinner:	Monday - Saturday 18:00 - 23:30
Closed:	Christmas Day & Boxing Day
Seats:	90
Private Room?	Yes (60 people)
Credit cards:	Visa, Amex, Access,
Disabled access?	Yes (not to toilets)
Music played?	Yes
Non-smoking?	On request
Chef:	Luis Goncalves

NEW OWNER AND CHEF

Something of a caricature of an Italian restaurant, with checked red and white tablecloths, lighting that is dark to the point of macabre, and somewhat inept and sexist service. However the pasta is truly wonderful served in huge portions at very fair prices. The spaghetti al pesto is quite superb, and would grace the table of a much grander place. Beyond the pasta the cooking becomes less sure of itself, though mussels are usually good here. The wine list is fairly cursory. Whatever its faults, this is a haven from the tourist traps masquerading as restaurants which are the general fare around Covent Garden.

Regent - The Dining Room

Price (lunch):	£15-£20
Price (dinner):	£20-£25

Address:	222 Marylebone Rd Marylebone , London NW1 6JQ
Phone:	0171 631 8000
Fax:	0171 631 8080
Reservations?	Yes
Nearest tube:	Marylebone, Baker Street
Set lunch:	£21.50 (Monday to Friday) £28 (Sunday) Set dinner: £29
Open lunch:	Monday - Friday 12:00 - 15:00 Sunday 12:30-15:00
Open dinner:	Monday - Sunday 19:00 - 23:00
Closed :	Never
Seats:	120
Private Room?	Yes (4 to 360)
Credit cards:	Visa,Amex,Access, Diners
Disabled access?	Yes
Music played?	Yes
Non-smoking?	Separate section
Chef:	Paolo Simioni

The bar in the Regent hotel must be one of the most spectacular anywhere in the world. As you climb the wide staircase past the reception, you are presented with a breathtaking six-storey atrium lined with palm trees, the hotel rooms designed to look like the exterior of London town houses. It is fair to say that food critics are divided on the quality of the cooking; but my inspection visit here was generally impressive. The Italian menu has a very wide choice for vegetarians and lovers of seafood. A deep-fried goat's cheese with rocket salad was excellent, with very fresh salad leaves and a perfectly judged balsamic vinaigrette. Desserts come on a trolley, but are rather better than they appeared: a chocolate cake, which can so often be so horrid, was a rich, moist affair with deep chocolate flavour. Service struggled to match up to the surroundings; though it was at all times friendly and courteous. The wine list is costly but well put together and is sensibly arranged (mainly) by style.

River Café

Price (lunch):	£35-£50
Price (dinner):	£35-£50

Address	Thames Wharf Studios, Rainville Road, Hammersmith, London W6 9HA
Phone:	0171 381 8824
Fax:	0171 381 6217
Reservations?	Yes
Nearest tube:	Hammersmith
Open lunch:	All week 12:30 -15:00 except Sat 13:00 - 15:00
Open dinner:	Monday - Saturday 19:30 - 22:00
Closed:	Bank Holidays
Seats:	100 (+40 in summer)
Private Room?	No
Credit cards:	Visa,Amex,Access
Disabled access?	Yes
Music played?	No
Non-smoking?	No
Chefs:	Rose Gray & Ruthie Rogers

One of the pioneers of the modern Italian cooking that has become so fashionable in London, the River Café is still the best of its class. The lovely river setting is great in the summer, and the place is trendy to the point of trying too hard, though the decor is quite simple. There is valet parking, which I have always found rather disconcerting, ever since reading about a man in Manchester who gave away the keys of his new Lotus to be parked only to be informed later 'we don't have valet parking here'. The food itself is simple and emphasises use of the very best ingredients. This approach results in lovely food if it works well (as it usually does here) but also exposes any faults mercilessly. Seafood is generally char-grilled simply, letting the quality of the ingredients speak for themselves. There is a long and well-chosen Italian wine list, but with the notes describing the wines not linked to the wines themselves. The main drawback is the price, which is high and seems especially so if any faults creep in.

Japanese

Japanese cuisine is perhaps the only one that could seriously challenge French at the pinnacle of culinary excellence. There are many different styles of Japanese cooking, ranging from simple to elaborate. Japan was almost entirely vegetarian (though seafood was allowed) from 1600 to 1868 following the introduction of Buddhism. After the re-opening of the country to the outside world in 1868, all things foreign gained appeal, and the Japanese took to meat-eating in style. Perhaps the best beef in the world is from Kobe, where the cows are fed only the finest food and beer, and are massaged while alive to ensure tenderness. Kobe beef is fabulous, but also fabulously expensive. The Japanese also like to eat dangerously, and a prized delicacy is fugu, or blowfish. This remarkably hazardous delicacy can only be served in restaurants where the chef is specially licensed, for the very good reason that fugu is extremely toxic, and can result in considerably more than indigestion if not prepared properly. Though it is safe to eat in licensed premises, every year dozens of people die from eating fugu which has been prepared at home. Apparently a fugu diner experiences a slight numbing sensation as the first mouthful of food passes the lips, since the poison is also present in small quantities in the skin. A frisson indeed. The poison affects the nervous system, and one of the first symptoms is impairment of motor function, so one practical joke played in fugu restaurants is for a diner to drop his chopsticks suddenly, look distressed and wait for the reaction of the other diners. All this really makes me wonder how anyone discovered that this thing was (just) edible. Picture the scene. Fred-san sits around in mediaeval Japan and tries cooking fugu, drops his chopsticks and promptly dies. His friends all immediately reckon that if only he had prepared it a little more carefully it would be delicious, so start to eliminate the various organs of the fish (and themselves) one by one until they discover that the liver is the dangerous bit. Does this sound plausible? Still, I guess people had to make their own entertainment in the days before television.

As explained by Shizuo Tsuji in his excellent book *Japanese Cooking: A Simple Art*, a full Japanese banquet would have a sequence of dishes shown below.

Beginning	Appetiser	Zensai	
	Clear soup	Suimono	
	Fresh, raw fish	Sashimi	
Middle	Grilled food	Yakimono (includes sukiyaki, and teriyaki)	
	Steamed food	Mushimono	
	Simmered food	Nimono	
	Deep fried food	Agemono (which includes tempura)	
	Salad	Sonomono	
End	Boiled rice	Gohan	⎫
	Miso soup	Miso-shiru	⎬ served together
	Pickles	Tsukemono	⎭
	Green tea	Ryokucha	
	Fresh fruit		

While few meals would have as many courses or dishes as this, they are likely to respect the same sequence of dishes.

In practice, many Japanese restaurants specialise in just one of the styles above, for example tempura or sashimi. In addition, there are some other important styles. *Sushi* is a variation on sashimi, involving raw fish served in parcels of vinegared rice, which originated as a way of preserving fish. *Teppanyaki* bars offer food grilled for a number of people sitting round a large, very hot iron plate. Strips of meat, fish and vegetables are cooked on this plate before you. *Shabu shabu* is where thin strips of meat are dipped individually into a hot pan of stock to cook it. *Sukiyaki* just means dishes of beef and vegetables cooked together, while teriyaki is meat marinated in sake, *mirin* (a Japanese sweet rice wine) and soy sauce, and then grilled and served in this sauce. *Yakitori* bars specialise in barbecued meat cooked on skewers.

The most popular food in Japan is noodles (*menrui*), as can be seen in the wonderful movie *Tampopo*. In fact many of the noodles served in Japan are *ramen*, which are actually Chinese in origin, but have been adapted to Japanese tastes.

Many Japanese dishes are based on a basic stock called *dashi*, based on shavings of *bonito*, which is sold in blocks and is made from dried mackerel and giant kelp. The most elaborate style of cuisine is *kaiseki*, which evolved as an offshoot of the formal tea ceremony *chanoya*. Such a banquet consists of many small dishes, chosen to reflect a harmony of colours, tastes and textures; there are hardly any establishments in the UK which offer kaiseki.

The Japanese are great ones for ritual. Saké is served at the start of the meal, but put away when the rice arrives (sake is a rice wine, so is thought not to go well with rice). By the way, there are a couple of things to avoid when eating with chopsticks in Japanese restaurants. Do not stick your chopsticks upright in a bowl of rice after you have finished, nor use chopsticks to pick up food from someone else's chopsticks – these two actions both relate to Japanese funeral services. I was mortified when I discovered this faux pas, and was then further advised not to rest my chopsticks on an empty bowl but to return them to the special rest. I enquired why this was not done, assuming another ancient tradition, only to be told 'to stop the dishes falling over'.

Like fine French food, however, Japanese food requires top-quality ingredients and extremely labour-intensive preparation, which results in sky-high prices – the Mitsukoshi department store in Regent Street has a basement restaurant that will serve you a kaiseki banquet for a little matter of £120 *per head* for the food alone. This is a bargain compared to the top Japanese restaurants in Japan, where the bill can easily climb past £300 per head. This is all a bit hard to take unless you are on a bottomless expense account, but there are more reasonable alternatives set out below.

Arisugawa

Price (lunch):	£10-£25
Price (dinner):	£15-£50

Address	27 Percy Street, Bloomsbury, London W1
Phone:	0171 636 8913
Fax:	0171 323 4237
Reservations?	Yes
Nearest tube:	Goodge Street
Set lunch:	£15.95
Set dinner:	£20 - £38
Open lunch:	Monday - Friday 12:30 - 14:30
Open dinner:	Monday - Saturday 18:00 - 22:00 (21:30 Saturday)
Closed:	Bank Holidays
Seats:	100
Private Room?	Yes (20 people)
Credit cards:	Visa,Amex,Access, Diners
Disabled access?	No
Music played?	Yes
Non-smoking?	No
Chef:	Akira Takeuchi

The Arisugawa is an excellent place to take people unfamiliar with Japanese food, as the cooking is reliable across several styles, and it is very good value, especially at lunch. You can eat sushi, which is of high quality, or sit at the teppanyaki bar and watch your food being grilled before you. The teriyaki sauce to accompany the grilled meats is delicious, and miso soup is good here. If you investigate the more obscure areas of the menu then there are some unusual dishes for the courageous. Service is polite, and the cooking is a notch above most of its competitors, despite the relatively reasonable prices. There is a wine list, but the best bet is Japanese beer or saké.

Miyama

Price (lunch):	£25-£30
Price (dinner):	£35-£60

Address:	38 Clarges Street, Mayfair, London W1Y 7PJ
Phone:	0171 499 2443
Fax:	0171 493 1573
Reservations?	Yes
Nearest tube:	Green Park
Set lunch:	£12 to £18
Set dinner:	£32 to £40
Open lunch:	Monday - Friday 12:00- 14:30
Open dinner:	All week 18:00 - 22:30
Closed:	Christmas
Seats:	67
Private Room?	Yes (6 or 10 people)
Credit cards:	Visa,Amex,Access, Diners
Disabled access:	Yes
Music played?	Yes
Non-smoking?	No
Chef:	Fumio Miyama

This has long been one of the most reliable Japanese restaurants in London. Despite its location, tucked away between Curzon Street and Piccadilly, prices are not absurdly high for cooking of this calibre. The dining room is tastefully decorated, and there is a pleasing sense of tranquillity, assisted by polite and efficient service. There are several set menus available for those wishing to experience sushi, tempura, teriyaki and the more familiar dishes of Japanese cuisine, while the more adventurous can sample things from the main menu. As with the best Japanese restaurants, the concentration on high-quality ingredients is almost obsessional, and both the cooking and presentation are skilled. The wine list is not its strength, so stick to saké or Japanese beer.

Suntory

Price (lunch):	£25-£60
Price (dinner):	£50-£100

Address	72 St James's Street, London SW1A 1PH
Phone:	0171 409 0201
Fax:	0171 499 0208
Reservations?	Yes
Nearest tube:	Green Park or Piccadilly Circus
Set lunch:	£15 - £33.50
Set dinner:	£50 - £67
Open lunch:	Monday - Saturday 12:00 -14:00
Open dinner:	Monday - Saturday 18:00 - 23:00
Closed:	Sundays, Bank Holidays
Seats:	120
Private Room?	Yes (8 people)
Credit cards:	Visa,Amex,Access, Diners
Disabled access?	Yes (not to toilets)
Music played?	No
Non-smoking?	No
Chef:	Mr K. Kato

The Suntory is probably the best Japanese restaurant in London, but bring your biggest credit card. In the basement teppanyaki bar you don a bib and watch your food being expertly grilled on the hotplate before you. Needless to say, the meat is impeccable, and the sauces are expertly prepared. On the ground floor is the à la carte restaurant where the menu changes according to the availability of ingredients in season, and includes some very exotic dishes for the adventurous. There are also three private tatami rooms available. People may balk at the prices, but never the quality of the cooking. There is an expensive wine list, but saké or Japanese beer are a better bet (this place is, after all, owned by the Suntory corporation).

Ten Ten Tei

Price (lunch):	£10-£15
Price (dinner):	£15-£20

Address	56 Brewer Street, Soho, London W1R 3FA
Phone:	0171 437 7695
Fax:	0171 434 2352
Reservations?	Yes
Nearest tube:	Piccadilly Circus
Set lunch:	£6 to £12
Set dinner:	£12.80 - £16.80
Open lunch:	Monday -Saturday 12:00 - 15:00 (16:00 on Saturday)
Open dinner:	Monday - Saturday 17:00 - 22:30
Closed:	Bank Holidays
Seats:	55
Private Room?	No
Credit cards:	Visa,Access,Diners
Disabled access?	Yes (not to toilets)
Music played?	Yes
Non-smoking?	No
Chef:	Mr Ishibashi

A relatively recent addition to the string of Japanese restaurants in Brewer Street, in the heart of Soho. So far this has yet to be 'discovered', and seems geared towards a Japanese rather than Western clientèle. It is a simple café, and has refreshingly simple prices to match. There are a range of set menus which are easy on the wallet, and the standard of cooking is just as high as at many pricier places. Meat dishes in particular are prepared well, but sashimi is also reasonable. You should not expect fawning service, but the atmosphere is friendly enough. A rare Japanese bargain.

Wagamama

Price (lunch):	**£10-£15**
Price (dinner):	**£10-£15**

Address	4 Streatham Street
	London WC1A 1JB
Phone:	0171 323 9223
Fax:	0171 323 9224
Reservations?	No
Nearest tube:	Tottenham Court
	Road or Holborn
Open lunch:	All week
	12:00 - 14:30
	(15:00 weekends)
Open dinner:	All week
	18:00 - 23:00
	(22:00 Sundays)
Closed:	Christmas
Seats:	104
Private Room?	No
Credit cards:	None
Disabled access?	No
Music played?	No
Non-smoking?	All non-smoking
Chef:	Ayumi Meada

The ever-present queues outside testify to the success of this canteen-style formula. You do not get sushi here, but the fast-food-style noodles which will be familiar to those who have seen the movie *Tampopo*. The restaurant is in a brightly lit, simply decorated basement. You sit at long benches, and your order is taken on a little hand-held computer; minutes later your choice is delivered to your table. The menu is fairly short, and consists mainly of huge servings of noodle soups, or conventional noodle (or rice) dishes. The cooking is actually very good, and at these prices the Wagamama is great value.

Jewish

I have ambivalent views on Jewish food. Jewish people have acquired a reputation as a race of foodies, yet restaurants in Israel have a ghastly reputation. By all accounts the best food in Israel derives from the many different ethnic races which have settled there, rather than distinctly Jewish food itself. Middle Eastern Sephardic Jews serve food much as in most Middle Eastern countries, e.g. hummus, falafel and grilled meats, while the Eastern European Ashkenazi Jews prepare the style of food we see in Woody Allen films: chopped liver, chicken soup, etc. Jewish cooking has also given us beigels and gefilte fish, and you can buy kosher food in the many Jewish delis in London. There are a few Jewish restaurants, the most famous being the old-fashioned restaurant Blooms, but though eating here is an interesting experience it would be hard to get overly excited by the cooking. Sample real beigels, rather than the ghastly fast-food imitations, at the Brick Lane Beigel Bake (159 Brick Lane, 0171 729 0616) open 24 hours a day.

Blooms

Price (lunch):	**£10-£20**
Price (dinner):	**£10-£20**

Address	90 Whitechapel High Street, London E1 7RA
Phone:	0171 247 6001
Fax:	None
Reservations?	Yes
Nearest tube:	Aldgate East
Open:	Sunday - Friday 11:30 - 21:30 (3:00 on Friday)
Closed:	Christmas, Jewish holidays
Seats:	150
Private Room?	No
Credit cards:	Visa,Amex,Access, Diners
Disabled access?	Yes
Non-smoking?	No

Blooms continues serving Jewish food the traditional way, long after most of its original clientèle have moved out to more affluent areas. Potato latkes, gelfilte fish, hearty chicken soup and chopped liver are all on offer here, served with a pile of rye bread. There is a refreshing absence of pandering to modern concepts of healthy cooking; no balsamic vinegar or rocket salad on the menu here. Nobody could accuse the cooking here of being innovative, and both the decor and waiters seem from another era, but this is certainly an interesting place. Woody Allen would love it.

Korean

The staple food in Korea has long been rice, along with dried or pickled fish and pickled vegetables. The further south on the Korean peninsula, the spicier the food becomes, much as in India. The country's long coastline means there is a wide variety of seafood, while further inland there are vegetables, fruit and pulses. A dish served with every meal is *kimchi*: spicy pickled vegetables (usually cabbage) salted, and seasoned with garlic, ginger and chilli pepper. *Bulgogi* is another famous dish, strips of beef marinated in soy sauce, sesame oil, garlic and ginger. Cattle are the main live-stock, with pigs raised mainly in the north of the country. There is a definite Japanese influence to the cooking, not surprising given the history of the country, but many aspects of the cooking are unique.

It is normal for Korean dinners to be served with many side-dishes. Food is not served in separate courses as in the West; instead people pick and choose from a variety of dishes offered, whether soups, stews, beef or vegetables. Restaurant tables tend to have an inlaid well in the centre, where meat dishes are grilled. This can either be fed by gas pipes or, more simply, by hot coals brought to the table by waiters. Perhaps this love of flame-cooked food comes from the Mongol ancestry of Korean people.

Jin

| Price (lunch): | **£10-£15** |
| Price (dinner): | **£20-£30** |

Address	16 Bateman Street, Soho, London W1V 5TB
Phone:	0171 734 0908
Fax:	None
Reservations?	Yes
Nearest tube:	Tottenham Court Road
Set lunch:	No
Set dinner:	£15.50 or £19.50
Open lunch:	Monday - Saturday 12:00 - 14:30
Open dinner:	All week 18:00 - 23:00
Closed:	Christmas
Seats:	60
Private Room?	No
Credit cards:	Visa,Amex,Access, Diners
Disabled access?	No
Music played?	Yes
Non-smoking?	No
Chef:	Mr Lee

You can try all the classics of Korean cooking at the Jin in Soho. The tables are inlaid with a gas-fired grill, intended for dishes such as bulgogi. Decor is smart and the service courteous. The spicy soups are worth trying, and there are dishes such as *yache pokum* (vegetables with beef, shrimps and fish cakes cooked in sesame oil). However to have an authentic meal with lots of side dishes would soon send the bill up, since the side-dishes are not cheap. Indeed overall this is by no means a bargain, though it is interesting for those hankering after a change from Thai or Chinese.

Mexican

Mexico had a head start on most other cuisines, as the Aztec civilisation had a thriving agriculture by 7000 B.C. Making heavy use of the peppers which grow there, Mexican cuisine can be very interesting indeed, and any cuisine that can successfully use chocolate in savoury dishes (the famous molé) has to have something going for it. Sadly in most 'Mexican' restaurants in Britain we have to put up with Tex-Mex food, whereas the USA has a number of genuine Mexican restaurants serving unusual Mexican dishes without a burrito or enchilada in sight. The nearest thing we had in the UK was the late lamented Richmond Cantina, which was obviously far too authentic for the British public to cope with.

Down Mexico Way

Price (lunch):	£15-£25
Price (dinner):	£15-£25

Address	25 Swallow Street Piccadilly, London W1R 7HD
Phone:	0171 437 9895
Fax:	0171 287 1427
Reservations?	Yes
Nearest tube:	Piccadilly
Set lunch:	No
Ser dinner:	No
Open:	All week 12:00 - 24:00 (22:30 Sunday) Bar open till 3:00
Open dinner:	All week
Closed:	Christmas
Seats:	150
Private Room?	Yes (35 people)
Credit cards:	Visa,Amex,Access, Diners
Disabled access?	No (but can be arranged)
Music played?	No
Non-smoking?	No
Chef:	Frank Harkart

Hidden away in a little road behind Regent Street is a surprisingly grand dining room featuring a reasonably serious attempt at Mexican cooking. You enter through an archway with an ornate wrought iron gate, up a flight of stairs into a spacious, romantic setting. The building has some beautiful tiling, donated by the King of Spain back in the 1920s, making this one of the few Grade II listed dining rooms in London. The dining room has a fountain on one wall, and a little alcove with a love seat (which apparently used to have a curtain for discreet liaisons). The menu ventures beyond Tex-Mex, featuring for example some Mexican dishes like *huachinango y mariscos*, red snapper marinated in lime and then baked. The basics like guacamole and refried beans are here, but more care is taken with them than at most places, the beans still having a recognisable texture. A fillet steak of Argentinian beef was very tender indeed. For dessert you can try *chimichanga dulce*, a fried flour tortilla filled with banana and chocolate. Service is chirpy and effective. There is Mexican beer, including the excellent Bohemia, which is a good job since the wine list is fairly ordinary, lacking even information on vintages.

Pakistani

There are few distinctly Pakistani restaurants in the UK. The food overlaps substantially with some Indian styles, which is to be expected since the countries have only had a separate history since 1947. Punjabi cooking in Pakistan is clearly similar to Indian Punjabi cooking. Pakistan's Muslim faith allows the eating of beef, which is not allowed in Hindu India, and Pakistan is the home of basmati rice, but breads such as paratha and naan are also widely eaten.

Salloos

Price (lunch):	£25-£40
Price (dinner):	£35-£55

Address	62-64 Kinnerton Street, Knightsbridge, London SW1X 8ER
Phone:	0171 235 4444
Fax:	0171 245 6821
Reservations?	Yes
Nearest tube:	Knightsbridge or Hyde Park Corner
Set lunch:	£16
Set dinner:	£25
Open lunch:	Monday - Saturday 12:00 - 14:30
Open dinner:	Monday - Saturday 19:00 - 24:00 (last orders 23:15)
Closed:	Sundays only
Seats:	65
Private Room?	No
Credit cards:	Visa,Amex,Access, Diners
Disabled access?	No
Music played?	No
Non-smoking?	No
Chef:	Abdul Aziz

If you want to sample authentic Pakistani cooking then try Salloos, but check with your bank manager first. In a quiet street in Knightsbridge, Salloos caters strictly for the wealthy, and there is a distinct sucking sound of money leaving your wallet from the moment you walk in. Service is distinctly variable, and can appear arrogant. The cooking, however, is very good indeed. Tandoori chops are a speciality and are mouth-wateringly tender, while some of the vegetarian dishes are excellent. Pilau rice is beautifully fragrant and is no longer served in minuscule portions. Breads are very good. The spicing is subtle and accurate, though any slips are less forgivable given the astronomical prices.

Pizza

Though the pizza originated in Naples, I have classified it sepa-
rately from other Italian cuisine since many establishments spe-
cialise in pizza rather than other Italian food. In my view the best
of the pizza chains is Pizza Express, but as well as these there are
some independent places well worth a visit.

Pizzeria Bel Sit

Price (lunch):	**£10-£15**
Price (dinner):	**£10-£15**

Address	439 Woodford High Road, Woodford, Essex IG8 0XE
Phone:	0181 504 1164
Fax:	None
Reservations?	No
Nearest tube:	Woodford
Open lunch:	Tuesday - Saturday 12:00 - 14:30
Open dinner:	Monday - Saturday 18:00 - 23:00
Closed:	Christmas
Seats:	86
Private Room?	No
Credit cards:	None
Disabled access?	Yes (not to toilets)
Music played?	Yes
Non-smoking?	No
Chef:	Serafino Real

In my view, the best pizzas in London
can be obtained here, an oasis in the culi-
nary desert of East London. This serves
authentic Italian (as distinct from
American) pizza with delicious thin
crusts and excellent, fresh toppings.
Though other Italian food is on offer, it is
wise to stick to the pizza. This is a noisy,
bustling place, usually packed out with
Essex boys and girls, who must hardly
believe that food this good has turned up
on their doorstep. The rather tacky
atmosphere is exemplified by the occa-
sional interruption for someone's birth-
day, when some ice cream with sparklers
is brought out from the kitchen to loud
accompaniment from the waiters, who
seem to have an eye for the ladies. There
are usually queues (you cannot book),
but these move at a reasonable pace now
that the owners have bought the
premises next door and doubled the
capacity.

Pizzeria Castello

Price (lunch):	**£10-£15**
Price (dinner):	**£10-£15**

Address	20 Walworth Road, Elephant & Castle, London SE1 6SP
Phone:	0171 703 2556
Fax:	None
Reservations?	Yes
Nearest tube:	Elephant & Castle
Open	Monday - Friday 12:00 - 23:00 Saturday 17:00 - 23:00
Closed:	Sundays, Bank Holidays
Seats:	140
Private Room?	No
Credit cards:	Visa,Amex,Access
Disabled access?	Yes
Music played?	Yes
Non-smoking?	No
Chef:	F. Arrigoni

There are few enough decent restaurants in this part of the world, so the Castello is a place to be cherished. Nestling amongst the hideous pink shopping complex surrounding a busy round-about, people do not come here for the view. The decor leaves much to be desired, but the pizzas are superb, with good dough and generous toppings. In addition the pasta is home-made and there is very good garlic bread. Salads and desserts are best avoided. This is a busy place, and there can be long waits for tables. Service is rather frantic. The wine list is cursory, but there is Peroni beer.

Pizzeria Condotti

Price (lunch):	**£10-£15**
Price (dinner):	**£10-£15**

Address	4 Mill Street, off Regent Street, London W1R 9TE
Phone:	0171 499 1308
Fax:	None
Reservations?	Yes
Nearest tube:	Oxford Circus or Piccadilly Circus
Open:	Monday - Saturday 11:30 - 24:00
Closed:	Bank Holidays
Seats:	100
Private Room?	Yes (50 people)
Credit cards:	Visa,Amex,Access, Diners
Disabled access?	Partial (2 steps)
Music played?	No
Non-smoking?	No
Chef:	Mahmood Eskendry

Tucked away off Regent Street, this restaurant serves very good pizzas indeed. It is often quiet here, but this is caused by the sleepy location rather than the cooking. The decor is bright and modern, and service is very friendly. Pizzas have excellent dough and good quality toppings; they are very similar in style to the Pizza Express chain, which is due to an indirect connection in owner-ship. Given the number of ghastly pizza joints in this part of town, the Pizzeria Condotti deserves all the support it can get. There are reasonable salads and pleasant garlic bread as a bonus. The wine list is not serious, so drink Peroni beer instead.

Pizza on the Park

Price (lunch):	**£10-£15**
Price (dinner):	**£10-£15**

Address	11-13 Knightsbridge, London SW1 7LY
Phone:	0171 235 5550
Fax:	0171 235 6853
Reservations?	No
Nearest tube:	Hyde Park Corner (take exit 4)
Open:	09:15 - 24:00 daily
Closed:	Christmas Day
Seats:	100
Private Room?	At lunch only (up to 80 people)
Credit cards:	Visa, Amex, Access, Diners
Disabled access?	Yes
Music played?	Yes
Non-smoking?	Separate section
Chef:	Mustafa

It seems slightly odd to eat pizza in such posh surroundings. Blessed with a marvellous location just off Hyde Park Corner, Peter Boizot's establishment does Pizza Express style pizzas but with greater attention to detail. The premises are cavernous, with a large basement area where live music is played, in addition to the ground floor. The pizzas themselves are classic, with thin crusts and generous toppings. Service is also a cut above the norm, and yet prices are only a little higher than most high street places. Live jazz, often of a high standard, is played in the evenings from 9 p.m.

Polish

Poland's troubled history has led to it having had a wider range of influences than most on its cuisine. Polish dishes draw heavily on pork, cabbage and potatoes, and there are some Russian-like dishes. Specialities include *uszka*, small pastries stuffed with mushrooms, and *bigos mysliwski* (hunter's stew). Meat is often cooked in ragouts, and game is sometimes served with fruit, e.g. wild boar with stewed apples.

Wodka

Price (lunch):	**£25-£35**
Price (dinner):	**£25-£35**

Address	12 St Alban's Grove, London W8 5PN
Phone:	0171 937 6513
Fax:	0171 937 8621
Reservations?	Yes
Nearest tube:	High Street Kensington or Gloucester Road
Set lunch:	No
Set dinner:	No
Open lunch:	Sunday-Friday 12:30 - 14:30
Open dinner:	Monday - Saturday 19:00 - 23:00
Closed:	Bank Holidays
Seats:	60
Private Room?	Yes (30 people)
Credit cards:	Visa,Amex,Access, Diners
Disabled access?	No
Music played?	No
Non-smoking?	No
Chef:	Mirek Golos

Here you can eat all the blinis you like in smart surroundings. Recently refurbished, the Wodka is aiming up-market, offering Polish food which is some way away from its peasant roots. Here the emphasis is on sophistication and subtlety rather than earthy home cooking. The blinis themselves are delicious, with a variety of toppings including smoked salmon and even Beluga caviar. Wild boar and venison sausages have strong flavour, and there are dishes like stuffed cabbage as well as the chilled soups. Service is slick and the wine list quite good, but it would seem a shame not to try one or more of the extensive selection of vodkas on offer. My main caveat is that the price is rather high for this standard of cooking.

Scandinavian

The closest many people will have come to seeing Scandinavian cooking is the film *Babette's Feast*, from which one would conclude that boiled cod was the pinnacle of culinary achievement there. Well, that may not be so wide of the mark in Norway, but there are some interesting dishes elsewhere. Throughout Scandinavia a lot of fish is eaten, e.g. herring and cod, and the staple is potatoes. Norwegian cooking scores *nil points* on the culinary excellence scale, and really does involve a lot of boiled fish (with salt fish for variety). Finnish cooking makes good use of the excellent mushrooms which grow there, and many dishes are based on herring and reindeer. Even some cheese is made. Danish cooking has many pork dishes, such as loin of pork stuffed with prune and apples, but for the sweet-toothed there are the world renowned Danish pastries. Sweden invented the smorgasbord, literally 'bread and butter table'. In this a whole feast of dishes are served together: first herring in a variety of styles, then cold meats and finally hot dishes such as meatballs. In addition they have given the world the delightful *gravadlax* (salmon marinated with dill). Specialities include 'Jansson's Temptation', a potato and anchovy casserole, and *nyponsoppe*, a soup of rose hips, almonds and whipped cream. Much herring is eaten, as is reindeer, though following Chernobyl the wise reindeer shopper takes a Geiger counter as well as a cheque book.

In London virtually the only Scandinavian restaurant of note is Anna's Place, a long-established, cosy little place in Islington.

Anna's Place

Price (lunch):	£20-£30
Price (dinner):	£20-£30

Address	90 Mildmay Park, Islington, London N1 4PR
Phone:	0171 249 9379
Fax:	None
Reservations?	Yes
Nearest tube:	Highbury & Islington or Angel
Open lunch:	Tuesday - Saturday 12:00 - 14:15
Open dinner:	Tuesday - Saturday 19:15 - 24:00 (last orders 22:30)
Closed:	Christmas, August
Seats:	45 (65 in summer)
Private Room?	No
Credit cards:	None
Disabled access?	Yes (not to toilets)
Music played?	Yes
Non-smoking?	No
Chef:	Beth Daidone

The best place in London to try Scandinavian food, Anna Hegarty's establishment has for many years been serving excellent gravadlax, apple cake and other Swedish specialities. The menu changes to some extent seasonally, but marinated herrings are always present, and very good they are too. Part of the appeal is the friendly and laid-back service from Anna and her daughter, and there is a very nice, relaxed atmosphere. Prices are not bargain basement but not unreasonable given the standard of cooking. No credit cards are accepted here.

Spanish

Spanish cuisine is basically peasant cooking. Specialities include things like *cocio*, a stew, *chorizo*, a spicy sausage, and the famous *gazpacho* cold soup. Spanish cooking relies on rice as a staple (this was actually introduced by the Moors) and is noted for seafood dishes. The best known Spanish dish is *paella* from Valencia, but the most 'foodie' area is thought to be the Basque region. I'd always thought this best known for its line in lingerie, but you will also find here extensive use of red and green peppers, 'piperade', tomatoes and local fish, such as sardines, mullet and tuna. Serrano ham, from the south, is well known even outside Spain. In bars there is a tradition of serving little snacks while people drink. This style, *tapas*, has recently swept London, and tapas bars are now about as exotic as fish and chip shops in most areas. Many are truly terrible, with the best one I have come across being the Meson Don Felipe.

Spanish food in restaurants in London is, as a rule, grim, with irritating guitar music and Spanish waiters doing Manuel impressions serving some ghastly version of paella. Madrid has the fourth highest number of Michelin-starred restaurants in Europe, so presumably the best thing is to get on a plane if you want to sample the real thing.

Albero & Grana

Price (lunch):	**£30-£40**
Price (dinner):	**£30-£40**

Address	Chelsea Cloisters, 89 Sloane Avenue, South Kensington London SW3 3DX
Phone:	0171 225 1048
Fax:	0171 581 3259
Reservations?	Yes
Nearest tube:	South Kensington
Open lunch:	All week 11:30 - 15:00 (last orders 14:00)
Open dinner:	All week 18:00 - 02:00 (last orders 24:00)
Closed:	None
Seats:	50 (70 for tapas)
Private Room?	No
Credit cards:	Visa, Amex, Access, Diners
Disabled access?	No
Music played?	Yes
Non-smoking?	No
Chef:	Angel Garcia

Hailed as the first real Spanish restaurant in London, this establishment is certainly elegantly designed, with a front bar serving tapas, with a dining room behind serving grander dishes. The bar area can be quite hectic, while the service in the dining room can slow to a halt. The wine list reflects some of Spain's wonderful wines, though there are some surprising omissions. Certainly popular with the chic set, the menu is very short and can offer limited choice to those with less than exotic tastes. There are some unusual peasant dishes, and the cooking is competent enough, but the prices are very high in the dining room – the tapas bar represents better value.

Meson Don Felipe

Price (lunch):	**£15-£25**
Price (dinner):	**£15-£25**

Address	53 The Cut,
	Waterloo,
	London SE1 8LF
Phone:	0171 928 3237
Fax:	None
Reservations?	Lunchtime only
Nearest tube:	Waterloo
Open:	Monday - Saturday
	12:00 - 24:00
Closed:	Bank Holidays
Seats:	50
Private Room?	No
Credit cards:	Visa,Access
Disabled access?	Yes
Music played?	Yes
Non-smoking?	No
Chef:	Salvador Orchilles

The main problem with this place is actually getting in. It is very popular in an area almost entirely bereft of decent places to eat or drink, and this means it is very hard to get a seat. The bar is the heart of the place, with seats around it and others crammed in at the sides. As if there wasn't enough noise, a guitarist plays intermittently. Still, the tapas selection is well above average, nicely prepared (certainly compared to most tapas in the capital). The wine list has some good choices on it, e.g. some from Miguel Torres, and service is pleasant enough. The bill can quickly add up to rather more than expected, however.

There are also branches at 125 Dawes Road, SW6 7EA (0171 386 5901) and 37 Kensington Park Road, W11 2EU (0171 243 0666).

Straits Cooking (Singapore)

In Singapore you frequently see "Straits" cuisine, which is a sort of mixture of Chinese, Malay and Thai. The best exponent of this in London is the Singapore Garden, though there are a number of Singapore restaurants which cook in a similar style.

Singapore Garden

| Price (lunch): | £20-£30 |
| Price (dinner): | £20-£30 |

Address	83-83A Fairfax Road, London, NW6 4DY
Phone:	0171 328 5314
Fax:	0171 624 0656
Reservations?	Yes
Nearest tube:	Finchley Road or Swiss Cottage
Set dinner:	£16
Open lunch:	All week 12:00 - 14:45
Open dinner:	All week 18:00 - 22:45 (23:15 Fri, Sat)
Closed:	Christmas
Seats:	100
Private Room?	Yes (50 people)
Credit cards:	Visa,Amex,Access, Diners
Disabled access?	Yes (not to toilets)
Music played?	Yes
Non-smoking?	No
Chef:	Mrs S. Lim

A long-established haven of good cooking. There is a menu of daily selections, but a common theme is the competent handling of seafood; prawns here are succulent, not rubbery, and they know how to combine spicy tastes without overpowering the taste of the seafood itself. Singapore noodles are very good here, as is the Malaysian beef rendang. Chilli crab is a speciality. Service is pleasant and the atmosphere relaxed. There is also a branch in Marylebone (154-156 Gloucester Place, NW1, 0171 723 8233); the Piccadilly branch has, sadly, closed.

Thai

Thai cuisine has blossomed at a remarkable rate in London in recent years. A few years ago there were a handful of Thai restaurants in the capital; now you trip over them as you walk down residential streets. The characteristic tastes of Thai food are lime leaves, lemon grass, fish sauce, coriander, galangal, garlic and coconut milk. Classic dishes include the spicy prawn soup *tom yum gung* (spelt in as many ways as *popadom*), Thai beef salad, and *pad thai* fried noodles. In the north of Thailand there are dishes like *s uah*, a spicy sausage, *khao niew*, sticky rice, and *oo pla*, steamed fish in a banana leaf. Thai food can be very spicy indeed. Most London restaurants tone down their chilli quota somewhat but curries, being coconut-based, are usually quite mild.

Ayudhya

Price (lunch):	£25-£30
Price (dinner):	£25-£30

Address:	14 Kingston Hill, Kingston upon Thames, Surrey KT2 7NH
Phone:	0181 549 5984
	0181 546 5878
Fax:	None
Reservations?	Yes
Nearest tube:	None (Kingston BR)
Set lunch:	No
Set dinner:	No
Open lunch:	Tuesday - Sunday 12:00 - 14:30
Open dinner:	All week 18:30 - 23:00
Closed:	Most Bank Holidays
Seats:	80
Private Room?	Yes (30 people)
Credit cards:	Visa, Amex, Access, Diners
Disabled access?	Yes (not to toilets)
Music played?	Yes
Non-smoking?	Special section
Chef:	Ms Somjal Thampho

Some of the better Thai cooking in the London area is to be found in these attractive premises on Kingston Hill. Smartly decorated with lots of dark wood panelling reminiscent of a Thai house, the Ayudhya offers polite service to match. The cooking covers all the familiar territory of red and green curries and spicy soups, but also ventures into less charted waters, e.g. curried seafood mousse. There is a sure hand in the kitchen throughout the wide repertoire, with consistency a strength here. Even the wine list is far more serious than most attempts to be seen in ethnic restaurants. It has been carefully chosen to offer wines, such as fruity whites, which will complement the fiery tastes of the cooking, and while Singha beer is a sensible alternative, it is surprising how well some wines can withstand the spices. The great rush towards Thai food in recent years has spawned many inferior restaurants happy to cash in on the trend, but the Ayudhya offers the real thing.

Bahn Thai

Price (lunch):	£25-£40
Price (dinner):	£25-£40
Price (bar):	£15

Address:	21A Frith Street, Soho, London W1V 5TS
Phone:	0171 437 8504
Fax:	0171 439 0340
Reservations?	Yes
Nearest tube:	Leicester Square
Set meal:	'Small eats' menu downstairs from £4 to £8.50
Open lunch:	All week 12:00 - 14:45
Open dinner:	All week 18:00 - 23:15
Closed:	Christmas
Seats:	100
Private Room?	Yes (30 people)
Credit cards:	Visa,Amex,Access, Diners
Disabled access?	Yes
Music played?	Yes
Non-smoking?	No
Chef:	Penn Squires

The Bahn Thai is one of the longest established Thai restaurants in London, here well before the recent craze for Thai cooking. The standard Thai dishes are well executed, and there is also a good range of more exotic possibilities: for example Thai blue swimming crabs. The Bahn Thai has had its ups and downs over the last few years. The tables are a little cramped, service is not as good as it could be, and prices are a little higher than at many Thai places, but the food here is excellent and worth the extra. Overall it is perhaps the best Thai restaurant in central London. The wine list is, unusually, well thought out, though many may prefer beer with this type of food. The downstairs has now been replaced with a more casual area serving Thai snacks, such as pad thai noodles and various spicy nibbles.

Bedlington Café

Price (lunch):	n/a
Price (dinner):	£24-£35

Address:	24 Fauconberg Road, Chiswick, London W4 3JY
Phone:	0181 994 1965
Fax:	None
Reservations?	Yes (essential)
Nearest tube:	Turnham Green
Set meals:	£10 - £12
Open lunch:	All week 09:00 - 14:00
Open dinner:	All week 18:30 - 22:00
Closed:	Christmas Day
Seats:	35
Private Room?	No
Credit cards:	None
Disabled access?	Yes
Music played?	No
Non-smoking?	No
Chef:	Mrs P. Priyanu

Becoming a bit too popular for its own good now, the Bedlington nonetheless continues to produce very competent Thai food at unusually low prices. There are now two evening sittings, and it would be hard to imagine squeezing in any more tables, but once you have been shoe-horned into your seat you can enjoy the normally excellent food, which is not watered down to perceived Western tastes. The curries, e.g. green curry or jungle curry, are excellent, and all the dishes feature very fresh ingredients and lively use of spices. There is no licence, so bring your own beer, which helps keep the price down. Service can be strained at times, but is always good-humoured. In the summer there are a few outside tables to cope with the demand. At lunchtime it metamorphoses into a greasy spoon.

The Chiang Mai Restaurant

Price (lunch):	£25-£30
Price (dinner):	£25-£30

Address:	48 Frith Street, Soho, London W1V 5TE
Phone:	0171 437 7444
Fax:	0181 985 1767
Reservations?	Yes
Nearest tube:	Leicester Square or Tottenham Court Rd
Set dinner:	£18.78 - £21.78
Open lunch:	Monday - Saturday 12:00 - 15:00
Open dinner:	Monday - Sunday 18:00 - 23:00
Closed:	Bank Holidays
Seats:	80
Private Room?	Yes (20 people)
Credit cards:	Visa,Amex,Access,
Disabled access?	No
Music played?	Yes
Non-smoking?	No
Chef:	Vatcharin Bhumichitr

The Chiang Mai Restaurant is one of the oldest Thai restaurants in London owned by chef and cookery writer Vatcharin Bhumichitr. 'Vatch' has been busy with new ventures in Manchester and Chiswick (see 'Thai Bistro' entry) this left the Chiang Mai rather neglected for some time and standards slipped, but I am pleased to say that it now appears to be back on form. The dining room is just down from Ronnie Scott's jazz club, and attracts a mixed clientele. Service is polite but can be a little hurried at times. The standard Thai classics are executed well, e.g. spicy prawn soup, pad thai noodles and various red and green curries. There are also various dishes from the cooking of Northern Thailand to supplement the more familiar ones, and there is a complete vegetarian menu. As in most Thai places, forget the wine list and stick to beer.

Phuket

Price (lunch):	n/a
Price (dinner):	£20-£30

Address:	246 Battersea Park Road, Battersea, London SW11 3BP
Phone:	0171 223 5924
Fax:	None
Reservations?	Yes
Nearest tube:	None (Battersea BR)
Set dinner:	£12.50-£15 (min 2)
Open lunch:	None
Open dinner:	All week 18:00 - 23:30
Closed:	4 days Christmas
Seats:	60
Private Room?	No
Credit cards:	Visa,Amex,Access
Disabled access?	Yes (not to toilets)
Music played?	Yes
Non-smoking?	Separate section
Chef:	Ms O. Mungnatee

This little place in the foodie area of Battersea is streets ahead of many of the Thai places which have sprung up in the last few years. The narrow dining room is well designed, with tasteful use of mirrors to give an illusion of space and lots of greenery. The cooking is precise, prawns are tender, spices are in their correct proportions. Tom yung gung soup is served in a steamboat, with sensible spoons so that you can extract the soup without feeling like a competitor in the Krypton Factor. There are also some less common dishes, e.g. 'prawns in a blanket', which show a delicate touch. Service is efficient and unobtrusive and there are even some acceptable wines, though beer is probably best. The background music can be rather incongruous, with Elvis or the Everley Brothers an unlikely accompaniment to Thai cooking, but it is not too intrusive.

Sri Siam

Price (lunch):	£15-£20
Price (dinner):	£20-£30

Address:	14 Old Compton Street, Soho, London W1V 5PE
Phone:	0171 434 3544
Fax:	None
Reservations?	Yes
Nearest tube:	Leicester Square or Tottenham Court Rd
Set lunch	£9
Set dinner	£14.95
Open lunch:	Monday - Saturday 12:00 -15:00
Open dinner:	All week 18:00 - 23:15 (22:30 on Sunday)
Closed:	Christmas Eve - Boxing Day, New Year's Day
Seats:	80
Private Room?	No
Credit cards:	Visa,Amex,Access, Diners
Disabled access?	Yes (not to toilets)
Music played?	Yes
Non-smoking?	No
Chef:	Rodpadish

The Sri Siam is one of the most reliable Thai restaurants in London. Surroundings are less cramped than many rivals, with a long, tastefully decorated dining room. The curries are excellent, as is the seafood. Service is good, and the complimentary prawn crackers actually taste of prawn. Thai fish cakes are very well executed, and the presentation is very pretty, with painstakingly carved vegetables much in evidence. The Sri Siam has a full vegetarian menu in addition to the main one, one of the few Thai restaurants to do this. The main complaint may be that the cooking is not as adventurous as some, but given the questionable standards of many of the new Thai places opening reliability is still a virtue.

Also at:

Sri Siam City 85 London Wall, EC2M 7AD
(0171 628 5772)

Thai Bistro

Price (lunch):	£15-£25
Price (dinner):	£15-£25

Address:	99 Chiswick High Road, Chiswick, London W4 2ED
Phone:	0181 995 5774
Fax:	None
Reservations?	Yes
Nearest tube:	Turnham Green
Set lunch:	No
Set dinner:	No
Open lunch:	Thursday - Tuesday 12:00 - 15:00
Open dinner:	All week 18:00 - 23:00
Closed:	Bank Holidays
Seats:	50
Private Room?	No
Credit cards:	Visa, Access
Disabled access?	Yes (not to toilets)
Music played?	No
Non-smoking?	No
Chef:	Mrs Tavorn

A new venture by Vatcharin Bhumichitr (see also Chiang Mai entry) in Chiswick's busy high street. Here the arrangement is a series of benches rather than conventional table and chairs, which lends to an informal, lively atmosphere. The menu has the usual classics but also features regional dishes from around Thailand. A nice touch is that there is a separate, and very extensive, vegetarian menu. 'Vatch' appears to spend his time between here and the Chiang Mai, and some inconsistency between visits shows that his team have not yet learned to function as well when he is not there. Still, in general the cooking works well, and at its best is very good. Classic dishes like pad thai and red curry work well, though a spicy beef salad was only ordinary. Service copes with the busy periods, and is always civil. Singha beer is best with such spicy food rather than wine.

Thai Garden

Price (lunch):	£10-£15
Price (dinner):	£15-£25

Address:	249 Globe Road, London E2 0JD
Phone:	0181 981 5748
Fax:	None
Reservations?	Yes (essential)
Nearest tube:	Bethnal Green
Set lunch:	£6.50
Set dinner:	£16 - £21
Open lunch:	Monday to Friday 12:00 - 15:00
Open dinner:	Monday - Saturday 18:00 - 23:00
Closed:	Sundays & Bank Holidays
Seats:	32
Private Room?	Yes (14 people)
Credit cards:	Visa,Access
Disabled access?	Partial (1 step) - not to toilets
Music played?	Yes
Non-smoking?	Section upstairs
Chef:	Miss Thnomjid Kaeokam

Home of the Kray Twins, Bethnal Green is not normally associated with fine cuisine. However this little café is an exception, offering an excellent selection of Thai vegetarian and seafood dishes at very fair prices (no meat dishes are served). The spicy prawn soup is superb as is the oyster mushroom sate and the vegetable curries. The 'sweet and sour fish', so often a ghastly concoction of frozen cod and E numbers, is here a wonderful steamed pomfret with a rich sauce; not an additive in sight. Surroundings are basic but service is friendly and efficient.

Thailand

Price (lunch):	n/a
Price (dinner):	£25-£35

Address:	15 Lewisham Way, New Cross, London SE14 6PP
Phone:	0181 691 4040
Fax:	None
Reservations?	Yes (essential)
Nearest tube:	New Cross Gate
Set dinner:	£20
Open lunch:	None
Open dinner:	Tuesday - Saturday 18:00 - 23:00
Closed:	Sundays, Mondays, 2 days Christmas & 2 days New Year
Seats:	25
Private Room?	No
Credit cards:	Visa,Amex,Access
Disabled access?	No
Music played?	Yes
Non-smoking?	No
Chef:	Khamkong Kambungoet
N.B.	Small children not encouraged

In my view the best Thai restaurant in London, this delightful little place serves better Thai food than I have had on my visits to Thailand. The location, between a couple of Chinese take-aways, does not augur well, and the place is so tiny that initially you may assume you have accidentally stumbled into someone's living room: the crockery is kept in the cupboard under the stairs. The cook (Khamkong Kambungoet) is from northeast Thailand, and the restaurant has a number of Laotian dishes on the menu. Her ex-husband is Scottish, which accounts for the unusual feature in a Thai restaurant of having a wide range of malt whisky. It is really hard to go wrong on the menu, but do try the Laotian pork with rice balls, and don't miss the tom yum spicy prawn soup, which is superb here. Prawn rice is excellent, as are the noodles. There are two sittings for dinner, one at around 6:45, and one at around 9:15. Although in an unlikely location, this is well worth the trip.

Turkish

Turkish food has obvious similarities with many other
Mediterranean cuisines. The west of Turkey does indeed offer
cooking like that in Greece, with much use of olive oil and many
fish dishes. In the central south, borghul (cracked wheat) is the sta-
ple, as in many Arab cuisines, while in eastern Turkey there are
similarities with Iranian cuisine, with much use of yoghurt, for
example. If you want to find authentic Turkish food then try
family-run places catering for the Turkish community in the Stoke
Newington area, rather than those in central London.

Iznik

Price (lunch):	£15-£25
Price (dinner):	£15-£25

Address:	19 Highbury Park, Highbury, London N5 1QJ
Phone:	0171 354 5697
Fax:	None
Reservations?	Yes
Nearest tube:	Arsenal or Highbury & Islington
Open lunch:	All week 10:00 - 16:00
Open dinner:	All week 18:30 - 23:00
Closed:	4 days Christmas
Seats:	54
Private Room?	No
Credit cards:	None
Disabled access?	Partial (1 step)
Music played?	Yes
Non-smoking?	No
Chef:	Ahmet Poyraz

The Iznik is a world apart from the nor-
mal London examples of Mediterranean
restaurant. The unusual decor manages
to conjure up images of Turkish delight
rather than that of stag-nights and Club
18-30, with Turkish rugs and lamps and
clever lighting. The food itself offers out-
standing interpretations of familiar
dishes like dolam (vine-leaves), while
tempting the adventurous further afield
into dishes like Karniyarik (aubergines
stuffed with minced beef, served with
rice suffused with dill). The sticky
dessert baklava is wonderful here, and
service is competent and friendly. The
food here was vastly better than any-
thing I ate on a recent trip to Istanbul.

United States

Food in America is a mixed affair. It usually has the virtue of being cheap, but quantity seems to count at least as much as quality – personally I don't want to eat a tasteless 32oz steak. There is food of interest in God's own country, but none of it has found its way to London. Since only one in five Americans can place France in the correct continent, and 42% of American college students are unable to name a single Asian country, I guess this is not surprising. Still, there is some regional food of interest.

New England	This area is famous for its seafood: lobster, crab, oysters and clams, as well as maple syrup. This is where the exotic *clambake* comes from: seaweed laid over hot stones, strips of chicken on top of this, corn sweet potatoes over the chicken and shellfish on top of this. Don't try asking for this at MacDonald's. Pennsylvania features many German dishes, as movie goers will know from the film *Witness*.
South	Southerners have as many ways of cooking corn as Eskimos have words for snow; hence corn bread, grits, hush puppies (cakes made with, er, cornmeal), etc. There is also the cajun and creole cooking to be found in Louisiana, a mix of French, Spanish and Indian. This is one of the few regional cuisines to make use of spices, and includes such well–known dishes as *gumbo*, a soup/stew.
MidWest	Home to Kellogg's cornflakes, which I think says all that needs to be said about the commitment to fine cuisine here. Best to stick to a plate of ham, apple pie and blueberry pancakes.
West	In the country there are game recipes, e.g. rabbit stew and deer, but remember this is cattle country, so beef is the main meat eaten. If we stretch the bounds of geography to include Texas, then Mexican influence appears in the form of Tex-Mex food like chilli con carne (which most sources reckon is probably not strictly Mexican, but originates in Texas).
Pacific Coast	As well as offering sourdough bread and carpet bag steak (stuffed with oysters), Californian cuisine has been genuinely interesting in recent years. Here, cooks familiar with classic French techniques have created a cooking style drawing on local ingredients and regional recipes, along with a willingness to embrace oriental spices. At its most pretentious this is just an excuse for the worst excesses of nouvelle cuisine to be repeated, but at its best some really interesting and original cooking is going on here.

Not forgetting caribou sausage in Alaska and the luau in Hawaii, where a whole pig and chickens are cooked in an underground oven lined with banana leaves and corn husks. So next time you are contemplating a barbecue....

Clarke's

Price (lunch):	**£30-£40**
Price (dinner):	**£45-£60**

Address:	124 Kensington Church Street, Kensington London W8 4BH
Phone:	0171 221 9225
Fax:	0171 229 4564
Reservations?	Yes (necessary)
Nearest tube:	Notting Hill Gate
Set lunch:	£22 (two courses) £26 (three courses)
Set dinner:	£37
Open lunch:	Monday - Friday 12:30 - 14:00
Open dinner:	Monday - Friday 19:00 - 22:00
Closed:	10 days Christmas 2 weeks August
Seats:	90
Private Room?	No
Credit cards:	Visa, Access
Disabled access:	Yes (not to toilets)
Music played?	No
Non-smoking?	Separate section
Chef:	Sally Clarke & Elizabeth Payne

Going to Clarke's is an unusual dining experience, more like going to dinner at someone's house than to a restaurant. In Henry Ford style, you can have any dish as long as it is the single one on offer for each course (though vegetarians can be catered for given advance notice). There is also an unusually relaxed atmosphere, clever lighting and generous table spacing helping to offset the basement setting. The Californian influence is shown in the emphasis on chargrilling; and this is carried out to a very high standard, which in tandem with an obsession for high-quality ingredients means that the restaurant can sustain a clientèle of regulars despite the steep prices. The menu changes daily, with four courses including cheese, while the lunch offers a limited choice. The wine list is very fine, with an excellent selection of producers from many countries, and a large selection of good wines by the glass. The concern is not the cooking, which is indisputably good, but whether the high prices and no-choice format are too much of a limitation for some.

Vegetarian

Of course vegetarian food is not a cuisine of a particular country, but since many places in London cater exclusively for vegetarians, it seems best to have a separate section. It is a sign of our growing affluence that vegetarian food is regarded as somehow different from 'normal' food; after all, for the vast majority of people in Europe meat was a luxury until quite recently. Vegetarians can do well in those cultures with a distinct tradition of vegetarian cooking, especially Indian, and several of the restaurants listed under 'Indian' are vegetarian only. Similarly the Thai Garden (see page 92) does not serve meat and the Sri Siam (page 91) has a full vegetarian menu. Leith's (see page 21) and Mijanou (see page 47) have full vegetarian menus for those who are splashing out.

Sadly, most 'vegetarian' restaurants in London are a sorry set of cafés serving indifferently cooked pasta and a few pulses and salads, and in many cases charging surprisingly large amounts of money, given the very low cost of ingredients.

Blah Blah Blah

Price (lunch):	**£10-£15**
Price (dinner):	**£10-£15**

Address:	78 Goldhawk Road, Shepherd's Bush, London W12 8HA
Phone:	0181 746 1337
Fax:	None
Reservations?	Yes
Nearest tube:	Goldhawk Road
Open lunch:	Monday - Saturday 12:00 - 15:00
Open dinner:	Monday - Saturday 19:30 - 23:00
Closed:	Christmas, 18th December, 6th January
Seats:	68
Private Room?	Yes (30 people)
Credit cards:	None
Disabled access?	No
Music played?	Yes
Non-smoking?	No
Chef:	Patrick Curren

Though it strives rather too hard for its 'right on' image, Blah Blah Blah offers surprisingly good food in the admittedly basic surroundings. The house pasta with vegetables is remarkably good, as indeed have other pasta dishes been in my experience. The menu changes regularly, with specials appearing on a prominently displayed blackboard. Another bonus is that it is unlicensed, so you can save money and bring some of your own wine (there is an off-licence a few doors down, but don't expect a top-class selection). The service is rather inefficient, though friendly, and you can wait a long time even if things are quiet. Still, this is a place for other vegetarian places to aspire to.

The Gate

Price (lunch):	**£15-£20**
Price (dinner):	**£15-£20**

Address:	51 Queen Caroline Street, Hammersmith, London W6 9QL
Phone:	0181 748 6932
Fax:	0181 563 1719
Reservations?	Yes
Nearest tube:	Hammersmith
Open lunch:	Tuesday - Friday 12:00 - 15:00
Open dinner:	Monday - Saturday 18:00 - 23:00
Closed:	Bank Holidays
Seats:	45
Private Room?	No
Credit cards:	Visa,Amex,Access
Disabled access?	No
Music played?	Yes
Non-smoking?	Separate section
Chef:	Adrian Daniel

The Gate has an unexpectedly attractive setting, lurking as it does off the Hammersmith Broadway. You enter a courtyard and then go upstairs to a high-ceilinged room that was once an artist's studio. An enormous picture window lets in lots of natural light, and the dining room itself is very spacious. The food is a cut above the usual, with imaginative dishes from a variety of cooking styles, e.g. a tostada from Mexico alongside a wild mushroom ragu. If I sound surprised at this it is because my expectations were set by the almost limitless capacity to disappoint that most pure vegetarian places manage so effortlessly. The wine list is limited but at least is fairly cheap, while service can be slow. However prices are fair, and the cooking and setting set the place apart from most competitors.

Vietnamese

The best place to try Vietnamese food, other than Vietnam, is Paris, due to France's colonial links with Vietnam. By comparison, London has a more limited choice, and there are no restaurants which are outstanding. Most are either nondescript or have put more emphasis on interior design than the cooking. Vietnamese cooking has many similarities with Chinese, a legacy of history, but there are some distinctive dishes, and it borrows from Thai cooking in its use of lemon grass. The fish sauce *nuoc-nam* is used heavily in dish preparation, just as its equivalent is in Thailand, and there are specialities such as *pho*, rice noodle soup.

Mekong

Price (lunch):	£18-£25
Price (dinner):	£18-£25

Address:	46 Churon Street, Pimlico, London SW1V 2LP
Phone:	0171 834 6896
Fax:	None
Reservations?	Yes (advisable)
Nearest tube:	Victoria or Pimlico
Set lunch	£12, £14 or £16
Set dinner	£12, £14 or £16
Open lunch:	All week 12:00 - 14:30
Open dinner:	All week 18:00 - 23:30
Closed:	Christmas
Seats:	50
Private Room?	Yes (14 people)
Credit cards:	Visa, Access
Disabled access?	No
Music played?	Yes
Non-smoking?	No
Chef:	V. Tran

The Mekong has a small ground floor area and a larger basement room. The Vietnamese spring rolls are genuinely good, and are a neat illustration of how Chinese and Vietnamese cooking can differ. The beef with lemon grass is served on a sizzling griddle and is usually very pleasant (though the meat can be over-cooked), and there are other unusual dishes like spiced fish balls with French beans and garlic. The set meals are reasonable value. Surroundings are pleasant, with some tables downstairs in the original cellar.

Luxury

In this section are some places whose price would preclude them from everyday eating, but which nonetheless offer good food and fine surroundings, and would be the ideal sort of place to be taken by a rich uncle or someone with a large expense account.

Blue Elephant

Price (lunch):	**£30-£55**
Price (dinner):	**£30-£55**

Address:	4-6 Fulham Broadway, Fulham, London SW6 1AA
Phone:	0171 385 6595
Fax:	0171 386 7665
Reservations?	Yes
Nearest tube:	Fulham Broadway
Set lunch:	No
Set dinner:	£25 and £28 (min 2)
Open lunch:	Sunday - Friday 12:00 - 14:30
Open dinner:	All week 19:00 - 00:30
Closed:	24th-27th December
Seats:	250
Private Room?	Yes (150 people)
Credit cards:	Visa, Amex, Access, Diners
Disabled access:	Partial (2 steps)
Music played?	Yes
Non-smoking?	No
Chef:	Rungsan Mulijan

There is no denying the impact of the setting here, like walking into a Thai village, complete with stream, waterfall, ornamental fish and exotic plants. Service is very gracious, and you are certainly left feeling pampered. The menu sounds very enticing and does its best to make it sound as if the high prices are worthwhile. Once the fanfare is over the food, always competent, can seem rather ordinary now that we have become so familiar with Thai cuisine. The renditions of many of the classic Thai dishes are no better than at many Thai restaurants of a lower price. There is at least plenty of choice, and there are set menus like the 17-dish Royal Thai banquet. This certainly gets you a wide selection of dishes, and one which the kitchen gets lots of practice cooking, so is quite a sensible option. There is also a wine list with some fairly steep margins, but beer is the wisest thing to drink. Whatever my reservations on the value-for-money factor, this is certainly a very grand night out, good for a special occasion.

Connaught

Price (lunch):	£35-£45
Price (dinner):	£50-£120

Address:	Carlos Place,
	Mayfair,
	London W1Y 6AL
Phone:	0171 499 7070
Fax:	0171 492 3262
Reservations?	Yes
Nearest tube:	Bond Street
Set lunch:	£25 (£30 Sunday)
Set dinner:	£35
Open lunch:	All week
	12:30 - 14:30
Open dinner:	All week
	18:30 - 22:30
Closed:	Christmas
Seats:	75 (35 Grill room)
Private Room?	Yes (10, 22 people)
Credit cards:	Visa,Amex,Access,
	Diners
Disabled access:	Yes (except ladies
	toilet)
Music played?	No
Non-smoking?	No
Chef:	Michel Bourdin

This is perhaps the height of traditional hotel dining. The dining room is wonderfully grand, the waiting staff dressed up to the nines and extremely courteous. It seems timeless here, as though you had stepped back a century. Dishes are brought to the table on silver platters and unveiled in front of you. Roasts are displayed on great trolleys, and carved ceremoniously to order. The dishes can be quite plain, e.g. steak and kidney pie or bread-and-butter pudding, as well as grand and complex, and the execution is generally very correct. Michel Bourdin has been a fixture in the culinary firmament for decades now, and this certainly represent a style of dining that it is hard to imagine being done as well anywhere else. The wine list is lengthy but French-only and very expensive, which seems unnecessary in this day and age. The set lunch is quite affordable, though the selection is naturally more limited than the full à la carte in the evening.

Four Seasons

Price (lunch):	£35-£45
Price (dinner):	£70-£85

Address:	Four Seasons Hotel,
	Hamilton Place,
	Park Lane,
	London W1A 1AZ
Phone:	0171 499 0888
Fax:	0171 493 6629
Reservations?	Yes
Nearest tube:	Hyde Park Corner
Set lunch:	£25 (£28 Sunday)
Set dinner	No
Open lunch:	All week
	12:30 - 15:00
Open dinner:	All week
	19:00 - 24:00
Seats:	60
Private Room?	Yes (12-30 people)
Credit cards:	Visa,Amex,Access,
	Diners
Disabled access:	Yes
Music played?	No
Non-smoking?	No
Chef:	Jean-Christophe
	Novelli

The Four Seasons (formerly Inn on The Park) had its gastronomic reputation developed by Bruno Loubet, who has now moved on to his own venture (see Bistro Bruno, page 42). His place has been take by the capable Jean-Christophe Novelli, who continues to produce fine food. The dining room here rather lacks warmth, though it is certainly spacious and grand. The cooking is complex and uses not only rich ingredients but also offal, and there is plenty of seafood to satisfy non-carnivores. A pleasant surprise is the wine list: encyclopaedic in coverage, with a wide range of good house selections by the glass. Naturally the mark-ups are high here, but it is possible to drink well without a second mortgage. The lunch menu provides an affordable glimpse of the cooking here.

Lanesborough

Price (lunch):	£35-£45
Price (dinner):	£50-£70

Address:	The Lanesborough, 1 Lanesborough Place, London SW1X 7TA
Phone:	0171 259 5599
Fax:	0171 259 5606
Reservations?	Yes
Nearest tube:	Hyde Park Corner
Set lunch:	£19 (2 courses) £22.50 (3 courses)
Set dinner	£28.50 (3 courses)
Open lunch:	All week 12:00 - 14:30
Open dinner:	All week 18:30 - 24:00
Closed:	Never
Seats:	106
Private Room?	Yes (30-100 people)
Credit cards:	Visa,Amex,Access, Diners
Disabled access:	Yes
Music played?	Yes
Non-smoking?	No
Chef:	Paul Gayler

The Lanesborough hotel is the beautifully restored Regency building that was previously the St George's Hospital. No expense has been spared, and the gorgeous library bar here is a great place to have a pre-dinner drink. The Conservatory dining room is also very striking, with various expensive knick-knacks from different parts of the world amongst the greenery. Paul Gayler's experimental cooking style is not to everyone's taste, but there are certainly some triumphs here. One very positive feature is the emphasis on vegetarian cooking, with a complete menu of delightful dishes, sure to confound those who assume vegetarian food stops with a few beans. The cooking also explores different influences, for example a Chinese dish of crab with ginger was exquisite. An odder tendency is to offer some very ordinary dishes indeed, presumably for the benefit of elderly guests, e.g. prawn cocktail. The wine list is priced at surprisingly moderate levels, and there are lots of half bottles and wines by the glass.

Neal Street Restaurant

Price (lunch):	£45-£70
Price (dinner):	£45-£70

Address:	26 Neal Street, Covent Garden, London WC2H 9PS
Phone:	0171 836 8368
Fax:	0171 497 1361
Reservations?	Yes
Nearest tube:	Covent Garden
Set lunch:	No
Set dinner:	No
Open lunch:	Monday - Saturday 12:30 - 14:30
Open dinner:	Monday - Saturday 19:30 - 23:00
Closed:	Christmas
Seats:	65
Private Room?	No
Credit cards:	Visa,Amex,Access, Diners
Disabled access:	Partial (1 step)
Music played?	No
Non-smoking?	No
Chef:	Nick Melmoth-Combs

The long dining room makes excellent use of light and has some spectacular flower displays; as you pass by the bar there is a basket of beautiful wild mushrooms to heighten the appetite. Service varies according to which member of staff you deal with, at best charming, at worst aloof. The menu has plenty of choice, and the quality of ingredients is remarkably high. Skill in the cooking was also demonstrated in a very tender dish of squid without a hint of chewiness. A plate of grilled mushrooms was as good as you would hope in a place whose owner has written a book on mushrooms, and medallions of tender beef were served with a remarkably intense and delicious cep sauce. Mange touts were perfect, just barely cooked, while other vegetables were also fine. I would be the last one to defend the admittedly stiff charges, yet the extremely high quality of ingredients and the generally capable standard of cooking go at least some way to justifying the cost. The wine list is long, predominately Italian, with little under £20.

Le Soufflé

| Price (lunch): | £35-£45 |
| Price (dinner): | £50-£80 |

Address:	Le Soufflé, Intercontinental Hotel, 1 Hamilton Place, Mayfair, London W1V 0QY
Phone:	0171 409 3131
Fax:	0171 491 0926
Reservations?	Yes
Nearest tube:	Hyde Park Corner
Set lunch:	£27.50
Set dinner:	£37.50 - £43
Open lunch:	Tuesday - Friday and Sunday 12:30 - 15:00
Open dinner:	Tuesday - Saturday 19:00 - 22:30
Closed:	August
Seats:	80
Private Room?	No
Credit cards:	Visa,Amex,Access, Diners
Disabled access:	Yes
Music played?	Yes
Non-smoking?	Separate section
Chef:	Peter Kromberg

The Intercontinental Hotel's appearance seems rather dated now, rather rooted in the 60s. Therefore it is even more of a pleasant surprise when one enters the dining room here, which despite a lack of natural light is extremely attractively decorated. The ancillary elements of the meal were wonderful: the bread excellent, the service flawless. The tasting menu offered a selection of dishes, revealing a variable standard of execution. A duck terrine with a side terrine of foie gras and a little salad of fresh green leaves was sublime, almost perfect. Yet a fillet of turbot with langoustines was rather carelessly cooked. The cheese selection is gorgeous, with the offerings being kept in lovely condition. A soufflé itself was, dare I say it, not perfectly cooked, though the sauce was delicious. Coffee is also excellent here. The wine list has the expected pages of expensive classics, but there is also a good selection of wines by the glass.

FOOD SHOPS

Every good cook agrees on the importance of high-quality ingredi-
ents, but where do you find such things? London is blessed with a
fine range of food shops, some of the best of which are listed in the
following pages.

Bread

Harrods

Address:	Knightsbridge, London SW1X 7XL
Phone:	0171 730 1234
Fax:	0171 584 0470
Nearest tube:	Knightsbridge
Open:	
Mon, Tue, Sat	10:00-18:00
Wed-Fri	10:00-19:00
Closed:	Sundays (except 10th & 17th December), Christmas
Credit cards:	Visa,Amex,Access, Diners
Disabled access?	Yes

The Harrods bakery has a remarkable
range of breads. If you just want a crum-
pet or a plain loaf then you may do better
elsewhere (at considerably lower prices),
but Harrods does have a wide range of
interesting and exotic bread, with no
fewer than 130 different types. The wal-
nut bread is excellent. For those wanting
something different on their side plates,
there is only one Harrods.

Clarke's

Address:	122 Kensington Church Street, London W8 4BH
Phone:	0171 229 2190
Fax:	0171 229 4564
Nearest tube:	Notting Hill Gate
Open:	
Mon-Fri	08:00-20:00
Sat	09:00-16:00

Clarke's is both a bakery and a well-
known restaurant. The restaurant offers
a no-choice menu, changing daily, and is
very popular with the chic set; the cook-
ing is very good, though for around £50 a
head I prefer some choice in what I am
served. The bakery is an offshoot of the
restaurant, and serves genuinely excel-
lent bread, as well as a selection of other
deli bits and pieces. Clarke's has a symbiotic relationship with the Neal's
Yard Dairy (see under 'Cheese'). Clarke's sells cheese from Neal's
Yard Dairy, while the dairy sells bread from Clarke's.

Cullens

Various branches	
Open:	
All week	(check branches for local opening hours)

I'm a real fan of the bread here, which is
of a very high standard, and has the great
advantage of being sold from premises
open virtually all the time (until at least 9
p.m. every day of the week – they even
open on Christmas Day). Hence this is
one of the few places you can get freshly baked bread on a Sunday (the
bread is semi-baked centrally, then sent to the branches for the baking to be
completed). The range is not vast, but the 'pain rustique' rolls and the crois-
sants are delicious. Cullen's flagship shop in Holland Park now has a spe-
cialist pâtisserie shop (selling pastries by the Roux Brothers) incorporated.

Maison Blanc

Address:	102 Holland Park Avenue, Holland Park, London W11 4UA
Phone:	0171 221 2494
Fax:	0171 221 7794
Nearest tube:	Holland Park
Open:	
Monday-Friday	08:00 - 19:30
Saturday	07:30 - 19:00
Sunday	08:30 - 18:00
Closed:	25th-27th December
Credit cards:	Visa,Access
Disabled access:	Yes
Also branches at:	
27b The Quadrant, Richmond, Surrey, TW9 1DN 0181 332 7041	
11 Elystan Street, London SW3 3NT 0171 584 6913	
62 Hampstead High Street, London, NW3 1QH 0171 431 8338	

Holland Park is quite a foodie area. Within a few doors of this place are the butchers Lidgate and a good branch of Cullens. Originally based in Oxford (connected with the Manoir Aux Quat' Saisons restaurant), the Maison Blanc establishment sells bread and pâtisserie French style. If you are missing the lovely bread and pastry of France then look no further. The pâtissière here really is French; this is not one of those places where he calls himself Pierre but actually comes from Peckham.

Cheese

Harrods

Address:	Knightsbridge, London SW1X 7XL
Phone:	0171 730 1234
Fax:	0171 584 0470
Nearest tube:	Knightsbridge
Open:	
Mon, Tue, Sat	10:00-18:00
Wed-Fri	10:00-19:00
Closed:	Sundays (except 11th & 18th December), Christmas
Credit cards:	Visa,Amex,Access, Diners
Disabled access?	Yes

With over 500 varieties, Harrods has probably the widest selection of cheeses in London. The quality is rather inconsistent, and the staff are less welcoming than at some of the other places in this Guide (or perhaps I didn't look prosperous enough) but this is certainly the place for something a little different. Make sure you pick a cheese in good condition, and ask to taste before buying. There are wonderful cheeses to be had here, but also disappointing ones, so shop with care.

Jeroboams

Address:	51 Elizabeth Street, Victoria London SW1W 9PP
Phone:	0171 823 5623
Fax:	0171 823 5722
Nearest tube:	Victoria or Sloane Square
Open:	
Mon-Wed, Fri	09:00 - 18:00
Thursday	09:00 - 19:00
Saturday	09:00 - 14:00
Closed:	Bank Holidays
Credit cards:	Visa,Amex
Disabled access?	No

It is hard to believe that hidden away behind Victoria coach station is a gourmet haven. Jeroboams has a very good range of British and French farmhouse cheeses. It also branches out into French and Italian charcuterie, olive oils and a selection of up-market wine. Various types of wild rice are available, and there is a good selection of pulses, such as puy lentils and aduki beans.

Neal's Yard Dairy

Address:	17 Shorts Gardens, London WC2H 9AT
Phone:	0171 379 7646
Fax:	0171 240 2442
Nearest tube:	Covent Garden
Open:	
Mon-Sat	09:00 - 19:00
Sunday	11:00 - 17:00
Closed:	Christmas, New Year's Day
Credit cards:	Visa,Access
Disabled access:	No

Tucked away off Neal Street is this delightful shop, overflowing with interesting English cheeses, and blessed with friendly and competent staff. Buying direct from a variety of English farms, there is a genuine sense of enthusiasm here. All but two cheeses on offer are made from unpasteurised milk. Fine cheeses abound, including the wonderful Colsten Bassett Stilton. There is an excellent cheese list with details of their products, and you can pick up bread from Sally Clarke's fine bakery (see separate entry).

Paxton & Whitfield

Address:	93 Jermyn Street, London SW1Y 6JE
Phone:	0171 930 0259
Fax:	0171 321 0621
Nearest tube:	Piccadilly Circus
Open:	
Mon-Sat	09:00 - 17:30
Closed:	Bank Holidays
Credit cards:	None
Disabled access:	Yes

To walk along Jermyn Street is to travel back in time to a street of fine old English shops catering to the upper crust. This is where an English gentleman – shopkeepers in this street have a limited acquaintance with the ideas of Colette Dowling and Andrea Dworkin – can purchase the essentials: shoes (New & Lingwood), briefcases (Fosters), shirts (Turnbull & Asser), soap (Czech & Speake), or pop in for a tie at Simpsons or tea at Fortnum & Mason. Fortunately one no longer has to be one of the aristocracy to sample the delights of the street. One of these is the establishment of Paxton & Whitfield, founded 1797, specialising in English cheeses. The range is not as wide as some shops, but the quality is very good. For those forced to spend a spell in the provinces or the colonies, there is a mail order service; the postman will love you.

The Real Cheese Shop

Address:	96a High Street, Wimbledon London SW19 5EG
Phone:	0181 947 0564
Fax:	No
Nearest tube:	Wimbledon
Open:	
Tues - Sat:	09:00 - 17:00
Credit Cards:	None
Disabled access?	Yes (1 step)

An excellent cheese shop specialising in British farmhouse cheeses. There are fine cheddars and the superb Colsten Bassett Stilton, and in total no fewer than 169 different cheeses stocked, the vast majority unpasteurised and from the UK. The service and advice are particularly friendly and knowledgeable.

Villandry

Address:	89 Marylebone High Street, Marylebone, London W1M 3DE
Phone:	0171 487 3816
Fax:	0171 486 1370
Nearest tube:	Baker Street or Bond Street
Open:	
Mon-Sat	08:30 - 19:00
Closed:	Bank Holidays, one week at Christmas
Credit cards:	Visa,Access
Disabled access:	Yes

Villandry stocks cheese from the great cheese maker Philippe Olivier of Boulogne-Sur-Mer, whose cheeses grace the tables of most of the top restaurants in London and Paris. Villandry imports a selection of his cheeses weekly. English cheeses are from Neal's Yard (see entry) so this is serious stuff. There is also bread from Sally Clarke's (see entry) and a range of other deli products. You can eat these along with freshly prepared dishes at lunchtime at one of a few tables in the back of the shop; the cooking here is in fact very good.

Chocolate

Charbonnel et Walker

Address:	28 Old Bond Street, London W1X 4BT
Phone:	0171 491 0939
Fax:	0171 495 6279
Nearest tube:	Green Park or Bond Street
Open:	
Mon-Wed + Friday	09:00 - 17:30
Thursday	09:00 - 1800
Saturday	10:00 - 16:00
Closed:	Bank Holidays
Credit cards:	Visa,Amex,Diners
Disabled access?	1 inch step

A rather aristocratic shop which sells very fine chocolates, provided you can put up with the plummy accents of the staff. Prices are very high, but the chocolates (mostly hand made) are genuinely good. All sorts of speciality and novelty chocolates can be obtained. Lovers of marzipan swoon at the various marzipan-based offerings, while the usual truffles and creams are also present in abundance. Ideal shop for that £380 Easter egg (I kid you not), but also for a very good mixed half pound.

Sara Jayne

Address:	(mail order only) 517 Old York Road, Wandsworth, London SW18 1TF
Phone:	0181 874 8500
Fax:	0181 874 8575

Though there are no retail premises, Sara Jayne's truffles are a delight, and well worth ringing up to sample. They make ideal gifts, and truffle connoisseurs assure me they are very fine indeed. Sara's culinary background is impeccable (she runs the Académie Culinaire).

Prestat

Address:	14 Prince's Arcade, (between Piccadilly and Jermyn Street), London SW1Y 6DS
Phone:	0171 629 4838
Fax:	None
Nearest tube:	Piccadilly Circus or Green Park
Open:	
Mon-Fri	09:30-17:30
Saturday	10:00-17:00
Closed:	Sundays
Credit cards:	Visa, Access, Amex, Diners
Disabled access?	Yes

Tucked away in a little arcade, Prestat is perhaps *the* shop for truffles. The premises are quite small and a little gloomy, but the service is good though the prices are a little high. Prestat offer a full range of chocolates, but truffles are the thing here, either pre-packed or a selection of your own.

Coffee & Tea

Algerian Coffee Stores Ltd

Address:	52 Old Compton Street, Soho, London W1V 6PB
Phone:	0171 437 2480
Fax:	0171 437 5470
Nearest tube:	Leicester Square or Piccadilly Circus
Open:	Monday - Saturday 09:00 - 19:00
Closed:	Bank Holidays
Credit cards:	Visa,Amex,Access, Diners
Disabled access?	No

Established over a hundred years ago, this shop specialises in tea and coffee from guess which North African country. Also a wide range of coffees from other countries, and a large stock of teas. The shop is quite cramped but the staff are friendly and helpful.

H.R. Higgins

Address:	79 Duke Street, Mayfair, London W1M 6AS
Phone:	0171 629 3913
Fax:	None
Nearest tube:	Bond Street
Open:	
Mon-Wed	08:45-17:30
Thu-Fri	08:45-18:00
Sat	10:00-17:00
Closed:	Bank Holidays
Credit cards:	Visa,Amex,Access
Disabled access?	Yes (not to tasting room)

Not the cheapest place to buy your coffee, but then this is where the Queen pops down to stock up. Coffees from Tanzania, Costa Rica, Colombia, India and Ethiopia, and teas from Ceylon, Sri Lanka and Taiwan. These are of a very high quality, and you can buy little quarter-pound bags to taste. The downstairs tasting room is now, happily, re-opened, and there is a mail-order service.

Monmouth Coffee Company

Address:	27 Monmouth Street, Covent Garden, London WC2H 9DD
Phone:	0171 836 5272
Fax:	none
Nearest tube:	Covent Garden or Tottenham Court Road
Open:	
Mon-Sat	09:00 - 18:30
Sun	11:00 - 17:00
Closed:	Christmas Day, Boxing Day, New Year's Day
Credit cards:	Visa,Access
Disabled access:	Yes (not to sampling room)

A delightful shop, where you are encouraged to sit down and try one of the coffees from Kenya, Colombia, Costa Rica, and even Papua New Guinea. There is a limited range here, but this means that they are bought in bulk, and prices are very low indeed. Coffee is roasted on the premises, rather than in some anonymous warehouse, so it is particularly fresh. Friendly staff.

Whittards

Address:	Whiteleys, Queensway, London W2 45B
Phone:	0171 243 0350
Nearest tube:	Bayswater or Queensway
Open:	
all week	10:00-20:00
Credit Cards:	Visa,Amex,Access, Diners
Disabled access:	Yes

At the time of writing there are 13 other branches. Ring the head office on 0171 924 1888 for a full list.

Whittards has a dazzling selection of speciality teas from India, China, Japan, Taiwan and Sri Lanka. Whittards has been selling tea since 1886, and has numerous branches dotted around London. They also sell coffee, but can be less knowledgeable about coffee than tea. As well as the consumables you can purchase a wide range of teapots and related accessories.

Cookery Equipment

Books For Cooks

Address:	4 Blenheim Crescent, Ladbroke Grove, London W11 1NN
Phone:	0171 221 1992/8102
Fax:	0171 221 1517
Nearest tube:	Ladbroke Grove, or Notting Hill Gate
Open:	Monday - Saturday 09:30-18:00
Closed:	Christmas
Credit cards:	Visa,Amex,Access, Diners
Disabled access?	No

What more crucial item of kitchen equipment can there be than a recipe book? Whatever it is you are looking for, however obscure, if you can't find it here then you might as well give up. The indexing system is not immediately apparent, but this just gives you an excuse to browse. If you are in a hurry then ask Clarissa Dickson-Wright, who has an encyclopaedic knowledge of all printed matter related to food. If all this browsing leaves you peckish you can have lunch at one of the tables at the back of the shop.

David Mellor

Address:	4 Sloane Square, Chelsea, London SW1W 8EE
Phone:	0171 730 4259
Fax:	0171 730 7240
Nearest tube:	Sloane Square
Open:	
Mon-Sat	09:30-17:30
Closed:	Bank Holidays
Credit cards:	Visa,Access
Disabled access?	No

Not the cheapest place in town, but this shop stocks an excellent range of high-quality cooking equipment. All those little essentials that the cookery books mention two-thirds the way through the recipe can be found here in the cavernous basement. There is just a small selection at ground level, including a classy choice of kitchen knives. There was a branch in Shad Thames, but this has now closed.

Divertimenti

Address:	45-47 Wigmore Street, Marylebone, London W1H 9LE
Phone:	0171 935 0689
Fax:	0171 224 0058
Nearest tube:	Bond Street
Open:	
Mon-Fri	09:30-18:00
Sat	10:00-18:00
Closed:	Bank Holidays
Credit cards:	Visa,Amex,Access, Diners
Disabled access?	Yes
(also at 139-141 Fulham Road, London SW3 6SD, 0171 581 8065)	

Just the shop for that unusual pastry cutter that you just can't seem to find anywhere. With an excellent selection of equipment, this shop supplies to both the public and to trade, so the staff don't look down their noses when you want to spend less than a thousand pounds. Raymond Blanc (the chef at Le Manoir Aux Quat' Saisons) shops here. Apparently he was in one day when a customer fiddling with a piece of equipment turned to him and said 'Do you know how this works?' The shop assistants hid behind the counter waiting for the reaction, but he explained the mystery without batting an eyelid. Trying this sort of thing with chefs of the more temperamental variety, however, is not compatible with a long and healthy life.

Pages

Address:	121 Shaftesbury Avenue, London WC2H 8AD
Phone:	0171 379 6334
Fax:	0171 240 9467
Nearest tube:	Leicester Square
Open:	
Mon-Sat	09:00-18:00
Closed:	Bank Holidays
Credit cards:	Visa,Amex,Access, Diners
Disabled access?	Yes

Though strictly speaking aimed at the trade (hence the 'No VAT included' signs), Pages offers plenty of good-quality equipment for the amateur chef. The range of equipment is vast, and the staff are always happy to help, even if this is your first saucepan.

Delicatessens/Emporia

I Camisa

Address:	61 Old Compton Street, London W1V 5PN
Phone:	0171 437 7610
Fax:	None
Nearest tube:	Piccadilly Circus or Leicester Square
Open:	
Mon-Sat	09:00-18:00
Disabled access?	Yes

There are not too many shops in London where you have to queue to get in on a weekday afternoon, but you do here. I Camisa is the quintessential Italian deli, selling very high quality hams, cheese, olive oil, pasta and just about anything else you can think of. The olives stuffed with anchovies, chillies and garlic are lovely. It is one of the few places you can get arborio rice (the best rice for risotto). The premises are tiny and always packed, so it is not an easy place in which to browse, but the staff are helpful. Around Christmas time they sell fresh white truffles.

Carluccio's

Address:	28a Neal Street, Covent Garden, London WC2H 9PS
Phone:	0171 240 1487
Nearest tube:	Covent Garden
Open:	
Mon	12:00-19:00
Tue-Sat	10:00 - 19:00

Antonio Carluccio is the owner of the Neal Street Restaurant (next door to this shop). In between TV appearances and writing books (such as the excellent *A Passion For Mushrooms*) he found time to open this interesting deli. Here you can buy the delicious wild mushrooms for which Carluccio is well known, as well as a range of Italian delicacies: fresh pasta, of course, and white truffles in the autumn/winter.

Fortnum & Mason

Address:	181 Piccadilly, London W1A 1ER
Phone:	0171 734 8040
Fax:	0171 437 3278
Nearest tube:	Piccadilly Circus or Green Park
Open:	
Mon-Sat	09:30-18:00
Closed:	Bank Holidays
Credit cards:	Visa,Amex,Access, Diners
Disabled access:	Yes

Just the place to stock up on provisions before going off for a spell in distant lands, Fortnums has been an institution since 1707. You can get just about any delicacy here, and it is a good place to buy presents for foodies. The packs of tea and jars of jams are great, the fresh food counters surprisingly limited. Fun to browse.

Fratelli Camisa

Address:	1A Berwick Street, Market, Soho London W1V 3LG
Phone:	0171 437 7120
Fax:	0171 287 1953
Nearest tube:	Leicester Square
Open:	
Mon - Sat	08:30 - 18:00
Disabled access?	Yes

In the heart of Soho in the excellent Berwick Street market, perhaps the best place for fresh fruit and veg in London, is this long established Italian deli. They have a fine range of salami and olive oils. They specialise in freshly made pasta and offer a range of home-made sauces, for example their fragrant truffle sauce.

Harvey Nichols

Address	109- 125 Knightsbridge, London SW1X 7RJ
Phone:	0171 235 5000
Fax:	0171 235 8560
Nearest tube:	Knightsbridge
Open:	
Mon - Fri	10:00 - 19:00
Wed	10:00 - 20:00
Sat	10:00 - 18:00
Credit cards:	Visa,Amex,Access, Diners
Disabled access:	Yes

Famous for its designer clothes, Harvey Nichols has now opened a superb food market on its top floor. Beautifully designed, there is a wonderful range of delicious things, from marmalades to breads, meats to cheeses and excellent fresh vegetables. There are many own-label items. There is an airy, usually packed café, a bar and a restaurant attached to the food market (see page 17).

The House of Albert Roux

Address:	229 Ebury Street, Victoria, London SW1W 8UT
Phone:	0171 730 4175/3037
Fax:	0171 823 5043
Nearest tube:	Victoria or Sloane Square
Open:	07:00 - 21:30
Closed:	Christmas, Easter, August
Credit cards:	Visa,Amex,Access, Diners
Disabled access:	Yes

This is the ideal place for that little French delicacy. Interestingly, though the poultry and charcuterie are imported from France, beef and lamb are British. All but the most chauvinistic French chefs acknowledge that the best British beef, lamb and game is at least as good as that which is obtainable in France (though a veil is best cast politely over our chicken). The shop sells fine pastries, patés, ready-made dishes, breads and vegetables. French cheeses in prime condition and superb foie gras are also sold here.

Justin de Blank

Address	42 Elizabeth Street, Victoria, London SW1X 9BW
Phone:	0171 730 3721
Nearest tube:	Victoria
Open:	
Mon-Fri	09:00-19:00
Sat	09:00-15:00

General purpose deli, offering very high-quality fruit and veg as well as the usual deli offerings. They specialise in providing meals for dinner parties, for those Pimlico inhabitants who desperately need to impress but can't quite find the time to cook for themselves.

Mortimer & Bennett

Address:	33 Turnham Green Terrace, Chiswick, London W4 1RG
Phone:	0181 995 4145
Fax:	081 742 3068
Nearest tube:	Turnham Green
Open:	
Mon-Fri	08:30 - 19:00
Saturday	08:30 - 17:30
Closed:	Sundays
Credit cards:	Visa,Access
Disabled access:	Yes
Also at:	14 Cucumber Alley, Shorts Gardens, Covent Garden WC2H 9AW, 0171 240 6277

An excellent deli, with Di Bennett making an enthusiastic and knowledgeable owner. This shop has bread courtesy of Sally Clarke (see entry) and also other sources (herb bread from Canada, of all places – well, it is frozen) various cheeses and other delicacies, and also offers a good selection of wild mushrooms changing with the season, mostly from the New Forest, with some from France. There are some excellent olive oils and also fine hams and salamis.

Salumeria Napoli

Address:	69 Northcote Road, Wandsworth London SW11 1NP
Phone:	0171 228 2445
Fax:	None
Nearest tube:	None near (Clapham Junction BR)
Open:	
Mon - Sat	09:00 - 18:00
Disabled access?	Yes

This friendly Italian delicatessen offers an excellent range of the things you might expect, with a particularly fine range of olive oils and a good selection of Italian cheeses. Fresh pasta here is very good, and the fresh pesto made here is described by an expert foodie friend as the best he has tried anywhere.

Fish

Blagden's

Address:	65 Paddington Street, Marylebone London W1M 3RR
Phone:	0171 935 8321
Fax:	None
Nearest tube:	Baker Street:
Open:	
Mon - Fri	07:30-17:00
Sat	07:30-13:00
Credit cards:	None
Disabled access?	Yes

A lovely old-fashioned fishmongers. The counters groan with very fine fish, their eyes gleaming, exuding freshness. The range is good, and anything can be ordered. They also keep game, so you can order a grouse or pheasant (in season) as well as picking up some sole or bream.

Covent Garden Fishmongers

Address:	37 Turnham Green Terrace, Chiswick London W4 1RG
Phone:	0181 995 9273
Fax:	0181 742 3899
Nearest tube:	Turnham Green
Open:	
Tue-Sat	08:30 - 17:30 (17:00 on Thursday and Saturday)
Closed:	Sundays & Mondays
Credit cards:	None
Disabled access?	Yes

Chiswick is fortunate in having two good fish shops, but this one probably has the edge. Phil Diamond has written a book on fish, and is very happy to provide advice on preparation and cooking. He has appeared on the BBC Food and Drink programme. He keeps an extremely wide range of seafood, so tilapia and parrot fish sit beside the haddock and cod, and quality is high.

Steve Hatt

Address:	88 Essex Road, Islington London N1
Phone:	0171 226 3963
Fax:	None
Nearest tube:	Angel
Open:	
Tue-Sat	07:30-17:00
Thu	07:30-13:00

When living in East London I made the pilgrimage to Steve Hatt's, since my local fishmonger greeted a request for anything beyond frozen cod with the sort of incredulity generally restricted to British Rail staff when asked for a refund. There is an excellent choice, fish are smoked on the premises, and you can even get cheap pieces of smoked salmon, which are ideal for making paté.

Harrods

Address:	Knightsbridge, London SW1X 7XL
Phone:	0171 730 1234
Fax:	0171 584 0470
Nearest tube:	Knightsbridge
Open:	
Mon, Tue, Sat	10:00-18:00
Wed-Fri	10:00-19:00
Closed:	Sundays (except 10th & 17th December), Christmas
Credit cards:	Visa, Amex, Access, Diners
Disabled access?	Yes

I love going to Harrods just to wander around the food halls to take in the sights and smells, even if there is the occupational hazard of being trampled by elderly ladies in mink coats. Some things at Harrods are a rip-off, and it is hardly the place to stack up on tins of tomatoes, but the fish department is outstanding and charges no more than most high street fishmongers. The range here is unparalleled, with every fish you have ever heard of, and many you have not, stocked as standard. There is a marvellous display of fish in the corner. The buyer here is excellent, and the quality of the fish is very high.

Jarvis

Address:	56 Coombe Road, Norbiton, Kingston, KT2 7AF
Phone:	0181 546 0989
Fax (office):	0171 635 9760
Nearest tube:	Norbiton BR
Open:	
Monday - Saturday (ring for hours - due to change as we went to press)	
Credit Cards:	Visa, Amex, Access, Diners
Disabled access?	Yes

Jarvis is renowned for the queues of Japanese customers, a recommendation in itself. They smoke their own fish and have an exceptionally wide range. Jarvis has recently been acquired by Cutty Catering Ltd, which supplies fish to some of the top restaurants in London, but there are no plans to change a winning formula.

Nicholson's

Address:	46 Devonshire Road, Chiswick London W4
Phone:	0181 647 3922
Fax:	None
Nearest tube:	Turnham Green
Open:	
Mon-Fri	08:00-18:00
Sat	08:00-17:00

Not too many fish shops stock a range of over fifty French cheeses, but this one does, and very nice they are too; the Brie de Meaux in particular is superb. John Nicholson is not your stereotype fishmonger: an enthusiastic man who from his plummy accent sounds as if he ought to have a law degree (he has). The fish is good, and a wide range is stocked.

Richards

Address:	21 Brewer Street, Soho, London W1R 3FL
Phone:	0171 437 1358
Fax:	None
Nearest tube:	Piccadilly Circus or Leicester Square
Open:	
Tues-Thur	08:00 - 17:00
Fri	08:00 - 17:30
Sat	08:00 - 15:00
Closed:	Sundays, Mondays, Christmas & New Year, Good Friday and Tuesdays after Bank Holiday
Credit cards:	None
Disabled access?	Yes

Probably the best fishmonger in London, this long-established fixture of Soho is everything you could ever want from a fish shop. The produce is very fresh and of extremely high quality; if something is less than excellent they don't try to palm it off on you, they just don't buy it in the first place. A wide range of fish can be obtained without prior notice, but virtually anything can be procured if you order in advance. Lots of Japanese people shop here, and they know a thing or two about fresh fish (important if you plan to eat it raw).

Meat

R. Allen

Address:	117 Mount Street, Mayfair, London W1Y 6HX
Phone:	0171 499 5831
Nearest tube:	Bond Street
Open:	
Mon-Thu	04:00-16:00
Fri	04:00-17:00
Sat	05:00-12:30

Running successfully for a little matter of 200 years, Allen's serves high-quality meat at fairly high prices. They hang their own meat, and supply a lot of restaurants. If you are an early bird then you can pop down at 4 a.m. most days.

John Best

Address:	66 Northcote Road, London SW11 6QL
Phone:	0171 228 2965
Fax:	None
Nearest tube:	None near (Clapham Junction BR)
Open:	
Mon - Sat:	08:00 - 17:30
Credit Cards:	None
Disabled access?	Partial (1 step)

The Northcote Road has several fine food shops. This long-established family butcher has particularly helpful staff and an excellent range of meats. There is prime Scottish beef, pork from Wiltshire and English and New Zealand lamb. Chickens are free range and there is a selection of game; if there is something unusual you need they will get it for you.

Lidgate

Address:	110 Holland Park Avenue, London W11 4UA
Phone:	0171 727 8423
Fax:	0171 229 7160
Nearest tube:	Holland Park
Open:	
Monday-Friday	07:00 - 18:00
Saturday	07:00 - 17:00
Closed:	Sundays, Bank Holidays, 25-27 December
Credit cards:	None
Disabled access?	Yes

A long established (1850) family butcher, serving top quality meat and game, as well as pies and sausage rolls made on the premises. David Lidgate is founding chairman of the Q Guild (the 'Q' stands for Quality), a society of butchers aimed at raising meat standards. If you are lucky enough to have a butcher near you who is a member of the Q Guild, you are assured of very high-quality meat. Lidgate uses organic produce of the finest quality. As well as a vast range of meats, home-made sausages and meat pies, there are farmhouse cheeses from England and France and free-range eggs. You can barely get in the shop for the display of awards which Lidgate has won, and the meat is so beautifully displayed it is like a work of art.

Slater & Cooke & Bisney & Jones

Address:	68 Brewer Street, Soho, London W1R 3FB
Phone:	0171 437 2026
Nearest tube:	Leicester Square or Piccadilly Circus
Open:	
Mon-Thu	07:30-17:00
Fri	07:30-17:30
Sat	07:30-14:30

Brewer Street really is a foodie's paradise. The meat here is of the highest quality and is very reasonably priced. Sausages are made on the premises. Prices are fair and you can get virtually any style of meat, cut in any way you like.

Oriental Food

Loon Fung Supermarket

Address:	42 Gerrard Street, Soho, London W1D 7LP
Phone:	0171 437 7332
Fax:	None
Nearest tube:	Leicester Square
Open:	
All week	10:00-20:30

A stalwart of Chinese supermarkets for many years, situated in the heart of Chinatown. You can buy just about any authentic Chinese ingredient here, from shark's fin to pig's trotter to many parts of animals that it is really best not to think about too much. Service is the Cantonese norm, i.e. rude and unpleasant unless you speak the language, so it helps if you know what you are looking for. For soy sauce try to find the Fo Hsan Superfine brand, which is generally reckoned to be the best. The next-door shop sells cooking utensils and crockery.

Sri Thai

Address:	56 Shepherds Bush Road, Shepherds Bush, London W6 7PH
Phone:	0171 602 0621
Fax:	Same
Nearest tube:	Shepherds Bush
Open:	
All week:	09:00 - 20:30
Credit Cards:	None
Disabled access?	Partial (1 step)

The boom in Thai restaurants and cooking has seen a number of Thai shops appear. The Sri Thai has absolutely everything you need for authentic Thai cooking, from the basics like lemon grass and galangal to holy basil. The premises are a little cramped but the service is courteous. Ingredients are imported weekly from Thailand, so everything is very fresh.

Tawan Oriental Supermarket

Address:	18-20 Chepstow Road, Bayswater, London W2
Phone:	0171 221 6316
Nearest tube:	Bayswater
Open:	
All week	09:30-20:30
Also at:	
179 Wandsworth High Street, SW11	
0181 874 7742	

If you want to experiment with Thai or south-east Asian cooking then you will need certain ingredients in order to give it an authentic taste, e.g. lemon grass, galangal, fish sauce. At this establishment you will find all these things and more, with the more exotic ingredients flown in twice a week. They also sell things like coconut milk and various exotic frozen seafood. You can buy Asian cookery equipment, such as steamers, here.

Pâtisserie

Pâtisserie Valerie

Address:	44 Old Compton Street, Soho, London W1V 5PB
Phone:	0171 437 3466
Fax:	0171 935 6543
Nearest tube:	Leicester Square or Piccadilly Circus
Open:	
Mon-Fri	08:00-20:00
Sat	08:00-19:00
Sun	10:00-18:00
Closed:	Bank Holidays
Credit cards:	None
Disabled access?	Yes

A small, crowded café which serves delicious pastries baked on the premises, and also sandwiches and savoury snacks. It is popular with the luvvies of Soho, the main problem being the ever-present queue. There is also a branch in Knightsbridge.

See also entries under 'Bread Shops' earlier for Cullens and Maison Blanc, which also do very good pâtisserie.

Miscellaneous

Alara Wholefoods

Address:	58-60 Marchmont Street, London WC1 2NX
Phone:	0171 837 1172
Fax:	0171 833 8089
Nearest tube:	Russell Square
Open:	
Mon - Thu	09:00 - 18:00
Friday	09:00 - 18:30
Saturday	10:00 - 18:00
Disabled access?	Yes

As well as an enormous range of packaged wholefood offerings, Alara's has excellent muesli and exotic things like the aromatic Afghan Hunza apricots. There is a wholesale business as well, and this explains why prices are very low indeed. This is also a good place to stock up on herbs and spices. Alara have just started a 'fax for lunch' service, where on sending a fax to the number listed here a menu of wholefood delicacies will be faxed back and your selection delivered to you, whether your taste be sandwiches, salads or tofu.

Konditor & Cook

Address:	21 Cornwall Road, Waterloo London SE1 8TW
Phone:	0171 261 0456
Fax:	0171 261 9021
Nearest tube:	Waterloo
Open:	
Monday - Friday	8:00-18:00
Disabled access?	Yes

A charming little shop in the barren culinary wastelands of Waterloo. There are two sections: at the front are various cakes and pastries and some bread (partly from Clarke's, some made on the premises), while in a room at the back are refrigerated sandwiches (made fresh daily) and other savouries. A vegetarian pasty was genuinely good, with light flaky pastry and excellent ingredients. An egg sandwich was also fine, made with free-range eggs and having just the right seasoning. The cakes are scrummy.

Marine Ices

Address:	8 Haverstock Hill,
	London NW3 2BL
Phone:	0171 485 3132
Fax:	Same
Nearest tube:	Chalk Farm
Open:	
Mon - Sat:	10:30 - 23:00
Credit Cards:	None
Disabled access?	Yes

An established fixture of North London, Marine Ices really does make some of the very best ice cream around. Everything is made fresh on the premises, and the chocolate ice cream is just one of the many delights. Sugar cones are used - another nice touch. This is as good as ice cream in Italy.

Where Can I find?

While it is nice to browse food halls and markets, sometimes it is far from obvious where to find some things at all. Below are some suggestions for a few of those harder-to-find items: of course the places below may not be the only options, but they are at least a starting point if you are having problems.

Foie Gras   House of Albert Roux (see page 111)

Fresh Olives   Fresh Olives Direct,
                         Mail order; phone 01865 201 046 for catalogue.

Tortillas   Mexicolore,
                         28 Warriner Gardens, Battersea,
                         London SW11 4EB
                         Phone: 0171 622 9577
                         Fax: 0171 498 3643

Truffles   White: I Camisa (see page 110) or Carluccio's
                         (see page 110).
                         Black: House of Albert Roux (see page 111), or
                         Harrods (see page 103).

Wild Mushrooms   Carluccio's (see page 110), Mortimer & Bennett
                         (see page 111), Harvey Nichols (see page 111)
                         Harrods (see page 103).

Single Malt Whiskies   Milroys,
                         3 Greek Street, Soho,
                         London W1V 6NX
                         Phone 0171 437 0893

Luxuries: Truffles and Foie Gras

If you are tempted to treat yourself and indulge in a truffle, or some foie gras, then here are a few tips.

Truffles are the most expensive food in the world, famed for their remarkable fragrance. They are used in up-market French cuisine to flavour various foods. As well as being used in elaborate haute cuisine, one well-known thing to do with a truffle is to place it in a basket of eggs overnight. The eggs will absorb the scent of the truffle, adding an unusual touch to your breakfast. Truffles, unlike mushrooms, have defied attempts to cultivate them, so a mystique has grown up around them. Pigs and (more frequently now) dogs are used to hunt them down in their natural habitat, frequently near oak trees.

If you want to sample this famous food, however, there is a catch. The first thing to note is that there are two different types of truffle: black truffles, the best of which come from Périgord in France, and white truffles, the best of which come from Piedmont in Italy. Both are in fact wonderful, and even the chauvinistic French have a sneaking suspicion that the white truffles are actually rather nice, if not quite as good as their own black variety, of course. From the point of view of the unbiased gourmet both are lovely. The main problem is that what is passed off in expensive department stores in jars as 'truffles' are actually a pale imitation of the real thing. Truffles are in season around December and January, and do not keep well. Spurred on by greed, and relying on the ignorance of the general public, manufacturers have taken to preserving and bottling them, in little (very expensive) jars. The only slight drawback is that these truffles lose all their scent and have as much aroma and taste as a piece of cardboard. The only way to actually try truffles properly is to buy one around December/January from a specialist shop. Truffles cannot be successfully preserved, so resist any temptation to try anything other than a real one.

The situation is similar with foie gras, which to my mind is about the only delicacy really worth the money (caviar tastes to me rather like, er, fish eggs). Again it is remarkably easy to get ripped off. Be very careful when ordering foie gras that you are getting the real thing and not pâté de foie gras, which is often someone's attempt at making the real stuff into a pâté, using hardly any of the genuine article and charging you an outrageous price. Probably the best place to buy foie gras is the House of Albert Roux (see page 111).

THE WINE GAME

Beating The System

Wine buying is a minefield. There is a mass of incomprehensible jargon, quality often bears little relation to price, wines frequently become unavailable just after you have discovered you like them, and the wine trade has so many charlatans and wide-boys that estate agents look competent and trustworthy by comparison. How do you find your way through? This section attempts to demystify things and help you improve your chances of finding decent, affordable wine. There are masses of expensive pitfalls and I have fallen into almost all of them. This section is intended to help you avoid doing likewise.

The first thing to say is that if you are still at the stage of being fond of Liebfraumilch and Blue Nun, which is how most of us are introduced to wine, then you should seriously consider stopping right there. If you like wine like this, costing about £3, then think carefully about whether you want to embark down the path into better wines, for it is a slippery slope. Soon the £5 wines will taste good, but not quite as good as the odd £8 bottle you have tried. Then the occasional £12 bottle will taste really wonderful, and so it will continue. Worse, there is no way back. It is rather like going from black and white television to colour; you were, after all, perfectly happy with black and white once, but once you get used to colour it would be unimaginable to go back (unless you are Woody Allen).

The Ultra Cheap Wine Trap

If those people over the Channel can buy wine for under £1, why can't we? Apart from requiring an unusually advanced form of masochistic streak to actually drink the wine they sell at £1 a bottle, there is a good reason why we don't get wines at this price. With the joie de vivre for which the British are famed, and a beady eye on the size of the national health budget for liver conditions, the British government treats wine as just another sin to be taxed. Consider the following table:

Wine costs in pence

Retail Price	299	399	499	599	999
VAT 17.5%	52	70	87	105	175
Excise fixed	98	98	98	98	98
Distribution fixed	20	20	20	20	20
Shipping fixed	15	15	15	15	15
Retailer profit, say 15%	45	60	75	90	150
Winemaker profit, say 10%	30	40	50	60	100
Money available for wine	39	96	154	211	441

Excise duty on a bottle of wine is, at the time of writing, £1.02 per bottle in Britain (plus an extra 10p if the wine comes from outside the EC). Adding to this shipping costs (about 15p a bottle from France), distribution cost (about 20p a bottle), and VAT at 17.5%, we can quickly see why there are no £1 bottles of wine in the UK. Most of these costs are essentially fixed, whatever the contents of the bottle, as are the cost of the bottle and cork, so you can see that below a certain threshold almost no money is being spent on production of the wine itself. By paying, say, £3.99 rather than £2.99 you are, at least in principle, getting a wine that has had more than twice as much spent on it.

Though there are some very good wines at around the £4 mark you can see, from the above fixed costs, that producing good wine for much less than £3 is going to be tricky. Yet more than 65% of sales of wine in supermarkets are of bottles under £3.00.

Storing Wine

According to one survey, over 80% of wines bought from an off-licence are drunk within a few hours of purchase. This fact brings us to two important things to consider when buying wine: storing it, and the ageing process.

If you do not have anywhere to store wine properly then you should join the 80% and drink your wine quickly. Few people have a proper cellar, and yet wine will deteriorate within weeks if kept poorly. I have been to more than one dinner party where someone has produced a bottle of something special they have been keeping for ten years, only for it to taste like a grue-some version of the salad dressing.

The ideal conditions for storing wine are horizontally (so the cork does not dry out) in a dark room at a constant 10C (55 F). The key word here is con-stant. The actual temperature does not matter too much within reason; wine kept at more than 10C will mature more quickly than usual, that at less than 10C more slowly. However if you keep wine in conditions where the temperature fluctuates rapidly then you are asking for trouble. The worst conceivable place in which to keep wine? A centrally heated house, and I bet none of you live in one of those. This causes a certain dilemma for those of us who do not have cellars which maintain a nice constant temperature. For such unfortunates the best thing to do is to either buy a specialist wine fridge (which is expensive), or pay a reputable wine merchant to store the wine for you. As well as costing money, the latter does rather take the spon-taneity out of wine drinking. There is nothing like filling in half a dozen forms and driving a few miles to instil a sense of discipline into your laying-down strategy.

If neither wine fridges nor professional cellaring appeals, store your wine in the place where the temperature is most constant, maybe a garage. Laying down wine in inappropriate conditions is a sure-fire but expensive way of producing vinegar.

Wine Ageing

The next pitfall when buying wine is to remember that a great deal of red wine (and some white) above the Liebfraumilch level is actually sold at an age when it is not ready to drink (yet remember that 80% of people drink their wines within hours of buying it, and of those who don't, less than 100% have cellars). It is as if car manufacturers sold you their products years in advance of being ready, with delicate components needing careful storage, and made you pay for warehousing. When you next read a gush-ing review of a wine in a newspaper or magazine, bear in mind that they may be assessing potential, not necessarily how it tastes now.

The New & Old World

For years good wine has been associated with France, with a few adventurous souls discovering some treats in Germany, Spain or Italy, but in the last decade we have been fortunate enough to see the rise of wines from California, Australia and others to challenge the old order. Much has been written about this trend, but the key thing from the consumer viewpoint has been the appearance of approachable, consistent, fruity wine at fair prices. Certainly among the better growers like Penfolds, it is quite hard to go wrong with Australian wine. This is true especially when compared to buying French wine, which is full of traps for the unwary. If you want wine between £4 and £10 a bottle then buying something from Australia is a relatively safe bet.

There are several reasons for this. The climate helps, and the fact that the wine makers were not hidebound by tradition or restrictive laws and so felt free to experiment, in particular to take advantage of modern technology. The invention of the cool fermentation process has also enabled wine makers in hot climates to make better wine (hot climate wines have other hazards though – one South African wine maker had most of his crop one year eaten by baboons). This, and the more consistent climate, has meant that vintage variation is much less significant than in Europe, which again adds consistency for the buyer. The success of New World wine makers has delivered a healthy jolt to French wine makers. Australia has excellent reds and whites in the classic grape varieties, New Zealand produces fabulous Sauvignon Blanc and is increasingly improving its Chardonnay (though few New Zealand reds are reliable yet). California seems to be pricing itself out of the market to some extent; I think the success of Californian wines in the early 1980s has gone to their heads, and many producers decided to charge French-style prices.

Shopping Around

One problem with buying wine is that it is not a commodity like sugar or baked beans, which are available at all shops. Most wines can only be obtained from a limited number of merchants, sometimes only one. This makes assessing value for money quite difficult, since it is not easy to compare prices for the more unusual wines. However, it is worth persevering since there are some quite shocking differences in mark-up. One extreme example I encountered recently was that of the great dessert wine Tokay Aszu Essencia (see later). At the time of my searching, the 1963 sold for a little matter of £160 a bottle in Berry Brothers, while the 1957 (a better year) could be obtained for £65 from Oddbins Fine Wines. Similarly, the Tokay Aszu 5 Puttonyos 1983 was £14.75 a bottle in Fortnum & Masons, yet £6.4 from Wines of Westhorpe. This kind of difference is more than just loose change.

Of course, for most wines the differences are not so extreme, and sometimes you will not be able to find several merchants with the same wine to compare. However, the above examples illustrate that, especially if purchasing several bottles, it is worth going to some trouble to get different quotes. A useful book in this regard is the annual Webster's Guide, edited by O Clarke, which provides a supplier index as well as just a list of wines.

Are Expensive Wines Worth the Money?

The more time you spend trying wines, the more your taste will inevitably slide towards the better ones, and there will always be the temptation to try that special wine. I wasted a lot of money by not realising that wine prices are dictated by the law of supply and demand, which may bear little or no relationship to actual quality. For example, during the boom years of the 1980s, rich Americans and Japanese, guided by the writings of expert wine critic Robert Parker, bought large quantities of the top Burgundies and clarets, pushing the prices up to ludicrous levels. I had the good fortune to taste the top wine of Burgundy, the Romanée Conti (the 1972; not even a great year, selling for a little matter of £750 a bottle). While undoubtedly a lovely wine, there was absolutely no way this sort of price could be justified by the quality of the wine; there are several other wines I have had at a twentieth of the price which to me seemed equally delightful.

One indication that famous (expensive) wine is frequently over-hyped is what happens when the wines are tasted blind. In a famous tasting in 1976, a set of French wine judges compared some Californian Cabernet Sauvignons against top French first growth clarets; the Californian wines won. There are other examples of similar upsets when wine experts were not aware of the contents of the bottles in advance. Marketing counts as much as quality in many cases. For example, most of the famous champagne houses produce a 'grande marque' champagne at around twice the price of their usual brands. Yet twice the price does not equal twice the quality, and at one champagne tasting I attended, the Dom Perignon (the up-market marque of Moët & Chandon) was felt by most present to be significantly less attractive than other champagnes half its price. Certainly Louis Roederer Cristal and Bollinger RD do taste quite special, but in most cases the grand marques appeal on the basis of exclusivity, not taste. Just to prove that such tactics are not the sole preserve of the French, Vega Sicilia, the most prestigious Spanish bodega, produce a very expensive, but divine wine called Unico at around £50 a bottle. I went to a tasting where several vintages of this were compared with their rare Reserve Especial. Despite costing twice as much as the Unico, it seemed to me virtually indistinguishable from it.

Buying that special wine, therefore, may well end in tears if you go simply for a famous French name. In my own view, some of the top wines from Germany, Spain and Australia are at least as appealing as some of the much more famous and expensive French wines that I have tasted.

It is also worth noting, when considering more expensive purchases, that really top growers make good wine in bad years. Generally a bad vintage (such as 1984 in Bordeaux) will drive the price of all 1984 wines down, yet the really classy growers will still make good wine in such years. This is often one source of (relative) bargains.

Who Can Be Trusted?

The motto of the wine trade might well be: 'Never give a sucker an even break', and this is not a recent development. In 1966 Nicholas Tomalin of the Sunday Times revealed that a large wine retailer, the Société des Vins de France, offered three main varieties of wine: a Beaujolais, a Nuits-Saint-George and a Chateauneuf du Pape. Nothing wrong with that, other than the fact that all three were in fact different blends of the same two generic table wines, bearing no relation to the claimed areas. This was mere deception, but things can be worse. In 1985 it was revealed that certain Austrian wine-makers were adding diethylene glycol, a chemical used in anti-freeze which can cause liver and kidney failure in humans, to their wine. This only emerged when one of the producers was greedy enough to claim VAT refunds on the diethylene glycol he had used. In 1986 a bottle of Italian wine claiming to be made from the Barbera grape caused the deaths of the three people who had consumed it, due to illegal addition of methanol to the wine; again this had been going on for years, but on this occasion a particular batch of the wine had too much methanol added. Of course these are exceptions but it demonstrates that extremely cheap wines can sometimes be so for reasons other than the ultra-efficiency of the grower. As revealed by Andrew Barr in his excellent book Wine Snobbery, some wine sold as Frascati is produced (according to the label) from vineyards which, rather than nestling in some attractive valley, have in fact been under several tons of concrete for years. Where the wine actually comes from is anyone's guess.

Given the above, you might think that the safest thing to do is buy a copy of Decanter and read the reviews of the professional wine journalists. Nope. Specialist wine magazines rely primarily on advertising for their revenue, and many wine journalists have a habit of accepting more than a hint of hospitality from wine growers, ranging from free samples to expenses-paid trips to the vineyards. It stretches credibility to think that journalists who have just had a free plane ticket and been wined and dined by a company are likely to have their critical faculties at their most acute. One honourable exception to this is the respected wine critic Robert Parker, whose Wine Buyer's Guide is a classic work of reference, and who refuses to accept any free wine or inducements. Unfortunately few journalists are successful enough to be able to afford his high principles.

Tastings
To my mind, the only way to select that which you like is not to rely on some article in a wine magazine, but to taste it yourself. Since buying whole bottles without trying them is an expensive and usually infuriating experience, the best way is to go to organised tastings. There are plenty of these around, of varying quality and seriousness, and they represent a relatively cheap way of trying wines out before committing yourself to a purchase. Some stockists which organise regular tastings are listed later.

Golden Rules
The above points can be summarised as follows. They are just common sense, but should help you increase your enjoyment of wine.

- Be careful when storing wine
- Check your wines are ready to drink
- Shop around for prices, especially for expensive wines
- Trust no one – just your own taste
- Buy from good stockists
- Go to tastings rather than rely on articles in magazines

A Personal Wine Selection

While taste in wine is inevitably a personal thing, you may not have time to go to endless wine tastings, and so below are some wines which I have found over years of serious drinking to be particularly good in their own category and price range. Most of the wines listed are over £5 a bottle, which shows just how far down the slippery slope my own wine habits have gone, but I think they all represent good value within their class. Of course you may not like all of them, but some will hopefully be to your taste. Note that prices listed were correct at the time of writing but of course things can change. There are many other guides to more modest wines available.

White Wines

Wine: *Cloudy Bay Sauvignon Blanc*
Country: New Zealand   **Region:**   South Island
Price: About £9.50 for the 1993   **From:**   Fine Wines of New Zealand, others

Notes: Cloudy Bay is the most prestigious producer of New Zealand. It shot to fame from a standing start in 1985, when it was established, under the leadership of oenologist Kevin Judd and managing director David Hohnen. Blessed with perfect conditions in the Marlborough area, Cloudy Bay is a high-tech vineyard. Grapes are picked at different stages of the harvest, some very late, and the juice blended later. Fermentation is in stainless steel vats, soil humidity monitored, hygiene strictly observed. The result is a wine with intense fruit and a sharp, clean taste, which came first in a Wine Magazine tasting of top Sauvignon Blancs with the very first vintage produced. Demand outstripped supply, and though production in 1990 was a respectable 40,000 cases a year from 45 hectares (110 acres) of vines, most Cloudy Bay is still sold out within weeks of arriving in the UK (around November). In 1990 the French champagne maker Veuve Clicquot bought a 70% stake in Cloudy Bay, and aims to increase production; it is to be hoped that the quality does not suffer, and there is certainly no sign of this so far.

Wine: *Maximin Grünhauser Abstberg Riesling Spätlese – von Schubert*
Country: Germany   **Region:**   Ruwer
Price: £13.22 for the 1989 **From:**   O.W. Loeb

Notes: From one of the largest, and also most prestigious estates in the Ruwer valley (30 hectares, still tiny by Australian standards), this Spätlese is an example of the best of German wine making. 1988, 1989 and 1990 were a rare trio of excellent vintages in this area, and this is one of the finest wines from it, a rich fruity wine yet with good acidity.

Wine: *Braunberger Juffer-Sonnenuhr Spätlese – Willi Haag*
Country: Germany   **Region:**   Mosel
Price: £9.20 for the 1990   **From:**   O.W. Loeb
Notes: German wines are a great bargain at the moment. In 1900 the best German wines sold for more than the top clarets but now, with their brand image destroyed by wine lakes of Liebfraumilch, the top growers are unable to charge high prices. This means that at the top end of the market there are

some wonderful wines at fair prices. Willi Haag is a very small producer (5 hectares, just 5,000 cases a year) established back in 1605, but his wines are held in high regard, sufficiently so that 30% are exported. This Riesling is a wonderful example of its type.

Wine:	*Montana Sauvignon Blanc*		
Country:	New Zealand	**Region:**	South Island
Price:	£4.99 for the 1992	**From:**	Oddbins, others

Notes   By far the largest producer in New Zealand, Montana makes nearly half of all New Zealand wine and controls over half of its vines. It was built up during the 1950s by Ivan Yukich, who in 1973 decided to try and move up-market and plant wines in the Marlborough area. This proved very successful, and Montana, more than any other grower, has symbolised the renaissance of the New Zealand wine industry. Montana Sauvignon Blanc is a classic of its type and, unlike many successful wines, has actually improved in quality since it achieved success.

Wine:	*Petaluma Chardonnay*		
Country:	Australia	**Region:**	Southern Australia
Price:	£9.99 for the 1992	**From:**	Oddbins, others

Notes: Brian Croser is the archetypal high-tech wine maker. After studying wine-making in California, in 1978 he set up a successful wine consultancy in his home country Australia. Croser is a firm believer in making use of technology in the wine-making process. The Chardonnay juice is shielded from air by a layer of inert gas, and ferments in stainless steel vats, followed by a year in Vosges oak barrels. The result is a Chardonnay delicate compared to many other Australian wines, with plenty of fruit and a complexity more reminiscent of France than Australia.

Wine:	*Mas de Daumas Gassac*		
Country:	France	**Region:**	Southern France
Price:	£15.99 for the 1993	**From:**	Oddbins, others

Notes: Aimé Guibert started this vineyard in the Midi, a featureless area of France long known only for wine destined straight for the European wine lake. He bought some land in 1971 and had no background in growing wine, but a friend of his was Henri Enjalbert, professor of oenology at the University of Bordeaux. On a visit to his friend, Enjalbert noticed the soil on Guibert's land was perfect for wine growing, and persuaded him to plant vines. The initial wine produced in 1978 was from red grapes, and this is now established as one of France's best red wines (see later). More recently he has been producing a white wine, made mainly from the local grape Viognier, and this is also remarkable stuff. Full of fruit and yet well balanced, it has similarities to the famous Condrieu wine of the Rhône, but many wine critics believe it to be already superior to this. Unfortunately success has driven up prices, but even now this is still a reasonable price for wine of this quality.

Wine:	*Rosemount Show Reserve Chardonnay*		
Country:	Australia	**Region:**	Hunter Valley
Price:	£7.99 for the 1990	**From:**	Oddbins, others

Notes: Rosemount was established by Bob Oatley, a successful coffee and cocoa plantation owner. In 1977, he bought up a huge 500-acre vineyard of Chardonnay from Penfolds, and another nearby vineyard (Roxburgh) from a struggling wine company. With good management and careful attention to all aspects of the wine-making progress, a Chardonnay blend from these two vineyards, the Rosemount Show Reserve, was an immediate success in 1980, scooping gold medals everywhere. Full of fruit, this is a classic example of New World Chardonnay.

Wine:	*I Sistri*		
Country:	Italy	**Region:**	Tuscany
Price:	£10.49 for the 1991	**From:**	Wine Cellars

Notes: Italy is undergoing a renaissance in wine making at present. For years tradition and restrictive legislation have resulted in a string of heavy wines at the top end, and often undrinkable ones at the low end. Now a series of more enlightened wine-makers are producing fresh and delicious wines, often out of the confines of the DOCG (the equivalent of the French Appellation Controllée) regulations. This Chardonnay, from the Felsina Berardenga winery under winemaker Giuseppe Muzzocolin, is a lovely oak-aged Chardonnay, with a fresh taste and lots of character.

Wine:	*Santa Carlina Sauvignon Blanc*		
Country:	Chile	**Region:**	
Price:	£3.99 for the 1993	**From:**	Oddbins

Notes: Chile is one of the trendy areas in wine making, with a long tradition in viticulture, and very good conditions. There are some lovely cabernet sauvignons at fair prices, and now some very attractive whites also. This is an example of this, with plenty of attractive fruit and good acidity.

Red Wines

Wine:	*Mas de Daumas Gassac*		
Country:	France	**Region:**	Southern France
Price:	£9.99 for the 1992	**From:**	Oddbins

Notes: The story of how Mas de Daumas Gassac was started is related above. This was the wine that caused all the excitement. Half of the 25 hectares of vines here are Cabernet Sauvignon, the other red grapes being Merlot, Syrah and Malbec. The red wine is a blend of 75% Cabernet Sauvignon with the other red grape varieties, and the result is an extraordinarily intense wine: a dark, thick liquid which is quite unlike traditional clarets and yet completely delicious. Oddbins Fine Wines have back-vintages of this wine, but since his wines seem to get better with each vintage, these are only a good idea if, like me, you have run out and are too impatient to wait for the new wine to age. These wines will age well, so the 1991 needs to be laid down for several years. The 1982 is now drinking well, while the 1986 is beginning to be ready.

Wine:	*Penfolds Bin 2 Shiraz Mourvèdre*		
Country:	Australia	**Region:**	South East Australia
Price:	£4.69 for the 1992	**From:**	Oddbins

Notes: Penfolds are one of Australia's largest producers (1.8 million cases a year). Established in 1844, they came into the forefront of the New World wine revolution under the tutelage of Max Schubert. Inspired by some trips to Europe, he produced in 1951 the first Grange Hermitage, made from the Shiraz grape (known in France as Syrah) but using techniques he had seen in France. He had produced this wine on his own initiative, and when it was presented to Penfolds commercial directors it was still full of tannin, and they didn't like it. It had to wait for nine years for a sympathetic board member to taste one of the early 1951 wines, which was just opening out. He was given another chance, and in 1962 Grange won numerous gold medals. It is now established as the best wine of Australia and one of the great wines of the world. Penfolds now produce a wide range of wines, and they have a remarkably high consistency throughout the range. The Bin 2 is at the bottom end of their product line, but is still fruity and immediate; excellent value.

Wine:	*Penfolds Bin 389 Cabernet Shiraz*		
Country:	Australia	**Region:**	South Australia
Price:	£6.99 for the 1989	**From:**	Oddbins

Notes: In the middle of the Penfolds range, this is a classic Australian blend of Cabernet Sauvignon and Shiraz, full of fruit and eminently quaffable.

Wine:	*Penfolds Bin 707 Cabernet Sauvignon*		
Country:	Australia	**Region:**	South Australia
Price:	£14.99 for the 1991	**From:**	Oddbins

Notes: One down from the Grange in the Penfolds stable, this wine is outstanding, full of balanced acidity and fruit, dark and complex. This wine needs ageing, so don't open the 1989 for another couple of years at least. It will keep for much longer, at least 10 years (the more prestigious Grange will last more than 20 years).

Wine:	*Torres Gran Coronas*		
Country:	Spain	**Region:**	Penedes
Price:	£7.99 for the 1990	**From:**	Moreno Wines, Sainsburys

Notes: If you are French, Miguel Torres is one of the top wine makers in the world outside France. If you are not French, you can just leave off the 'outside France'. Miguel Torres senior built up the family wine-making business from the 1930s, with his son Miguel taking over in the 1960s after having studied wine making in Burgundy. Torres now sells 1.4 million cases of wine a year, and they have vineyards in California and Chile as well as Spain. The Gran Coronas is a quite stunning wine for its price, smooth and elegant, made without the over-exposure to oak which plagues most Spanish wine.

Wine: *Torres Gran Coronas Black Label*
Country: Spain   **Region:** Penedes
Price: About £22.50 for the 1985   **From:**   Moreno Wines

Notes: Miguel Torres junior produced his first 'black label' wine in 1970, using mainly Cabernet Sauvignon but with some local grapes also. At a 1979 Gault Millau blind tasting, the Gran Coronas Black label beat the Château Latour 1970 and Château La Mission Haut Brion 1961, two of the great wines of France, and Spanish wine making had arrived. The Torres Black Label is a remarkable wine, one of the greatest wines of Spain, but why believe me when you can try it for yourself? The 1985 is certainly drinking now, but will improve. This is a serious wine, with even the 1976 still delicious. I have tried many Black Label vintages, and even in 'difficult' years it is excellent.

Wine: *Rioja Alta 904 Gran Reserva*
Country: Spain   **Region:** Rioja
Price: About £16.25 for the 1983   **From:**   Moreno Wines

Notes: Another beautiful Spanish wine from one of Spain's most respected producers. In 1904 Rioja Alta became a limited company, hence the name of the wine. It is made from local grapes: 80% Tempranillo, the other 20% being Graciano, Mazuelo and Viura. The wine is kept for a year in tank, then six years in oak and at least three years in bottle before release. At the many Moreno wine tastings I have selflessly attended in the interests of research, the 904 frequently appears and scores incredibly high marks, often as high as wines twice its price. Velvety smooth, it is extremely approachable and a real bargain.

Wine: *Wolf Blass President's Selection Cabernet Sauvignon*
Country: Australia   **Region:** South Australia
Price: £9.49 for the 1989   **From:**   Oddbins

Notes: Wolf Blass has won more gold medals than any other Australian wine maker, and his range of red wines is quite superb. This fine wine is a lovely example of New World Cabernet Sauvignon, bursting with fruit.

Wine: *Wolf Blass Black Label*
Country: Australia **Region:** South East Australia
Price: £15.99 for the 1989 **From:** Oddbins

Notes: The top wine of Wolf Blass, this is a deep, complex wine that is just beginning to drink now but will improve for several years. To see what a mature Black Label tastes like you can go to Oddbins Fine Wines and buy a back vintage for £19.99. Tremendous stuff.

Sparkling Wines

Until very recently champagne had a cosy monopoly on fizzy wine of quality, and each year saw rising prices, arranged by a cartel of big producers with large marketing budgets. This led to extreme greed on the part of the producers, with quality forgotten in the rush to sell more bottles. The recession has caused this to come to an end, together with the rise of New World sparkling wines, some of which are every bit as good as most champagne, yet are half the price. The more astute champagne growers have seen the writing on the wall, so while publicly denigrating the upstart New World wines, they have been busily investing in the more promising areas.

Wine: *Deutz Marlborough Cuvée*
Country: New Zealand **Region:** South Island
Price: £8.56 **From:** Oddbins

Notes: A joint venture between Montana and Deutz, a French champagne house, Deutz Marlborough Cuvée is in the vanguard of the New World sparkling wines that are so upsetting the producers of champagne.

Wine: *Mumm Cuvée Napa (non vintage)*
Country: California **Region:** Napa Valley
Price: £8.56 **From:** Oddbins

Notes: It seems odd that Mumm, who make some fairly ordinary champagne, own the vineyards which produce one of the very best New World sparkling wines. If only the same care and attention went into their champagne production.

Wine: *Seaview Pinot Noir Chardonnay*
Country: Australia **Region:** South Australia
Price: £6.42 for the 1990 **From:** Oddbins

Notes: Owned by a brewery, the Seaview vineyards nonetheless produce excellent, good-quality sparkling wines. Great value.

Wine: *Louis Roederer Brut Premier*
Country: France **Region:** Champagne
Price: £17.99 **From:** Oddbins, Wine Rack, others

Notes: My favourite champagne house, Roederer is one of the really top champagnes which can still surpass the New World wines, though at a price. Established back in 1760, the tsars of Russia recognised Roederer's quality when they commissioned 'Cristal' for the imperial family. This is still Roederer's top brand, selling for over £50 a bottle, and is stunning, not just a piece of marketing. Their standard brut champagne, a mixture of Pinot Noir and Chardonnay, is a high-quality product, with a lovely nose and great texture.

Dessert Wines

Dessert wines are my personal favourite of all wines, though they are not generally very popular. The unique taste of most dessert wines is due to them being made from grapes affected with botrytis ('noble rot'), which occurs in certain climatic conditions. Such grapes have to be carefully selected, which means yields are very low and hence prices for good dessert wines are inevitably high. Long the preserve of France, the New World is also producing good quality dessert wines now, though unfamiliarity can cause problems. One Californian wine maker suffered from this when his vineyards were paid a visit by federal inspectors. Seeing the rotting grapes which were going to go into his dessert wine, they ordered him to destroy the lot since they were clearly, well, rotting.

Wine:	*Brown Bros Orange Muscat*		
Country:	Australia	**Region:**	Victoria
Price:	£4.98 for half bottle of 1992	**From:**	Adnams

Notes: An excellent dessert wine from a respected Australian grower. Brown Brothers have established a good reputation, applying technology to traditional methods, not being afraid to break some rules and experiment. It is a lovely dessert wine.

Wine:	*Domaine de Coyeux Muscat Beaumes de Venise*		
Country:	France	**Region:**	Rhône
Price:	£5.08 for half bottle of 1990	**From:**	Adnams, Wine Rack

Notes: A nice alternative to the great Sauternes wines. Muscat Beaumes de Venise is a sweet wine produced not by botrytis-affected grapes, but by fortifying the wine, rather like sherry. The good producers of Muscat Beaumes de Venise, such as Coyeaux (Durban is another), use the high-quality, but low-yielding variety Muscat à Petits Grains. This produces a very refreshing wine, quite different to a Sauternes, but very pleasant and quite cheap. If you are unwilling to pay the high prices which good Sauternes commands, then you are better off buying a good-quality Muscat Beaumes de Venise than a low-quality Sauternes.

Wine:	*Chateau de Fargues*		
Country:	France	**Region:**	Sauternes
Price:	£26 for half bottle of 1983	**From:**	O. W. Loeb

Notes: One of the better kept secrets of the wine trade, this vineyard is owned and operated by the same people who produce the famous Chateau d'Yquem. Chateau d'Yquem is acknowl-

to be the finest dessert wine in the world, and a bottle of a recent vintage will set you back over £100 (older ones much more). The Chateau de Fargues costs less than half this, and yet has the same remarkable taste as the d'Yquem. Certainly, the d'Yquem has more balance and subtlety, but the de Farques is still lovely. If you want to try some of the greatest dessert wine in the world, a half bottle of this will set you back under £30 (1983 is the best of recent vintages).

Wine:	*Tokaji Azsu 5 Puttonyos*		
Country:	Hungary	**Region:**	Tokaji-Hegyalja
Price:	£6.24	**From:**	Wines of Westhorpe (also from Fortnum & Mason, at twice the price)

Notes: Hungary? No, this is not a typo. Though Hungarian wines generally evoke the same feelings as Norwegian cuisine, Hungary has long been home to one of the truly great dessert wines of the world. In the vineyards at the side of the river Bodrog, the fog sweeps down the valley and causes perfect conditions for the development of botrytis. This remarkable wine has been produced since the 17th Century. The fame of the 'azsu' (botrytis affected) wine was such that from Peter the Great's time until 1789, the tsars of Russia leased some Tokaji vineyards and assigned a garrison to protect them, while Louis XIV described it as the 'wine of kings, king of wines'. The aszu grapes are carried from the vineyards in baskets called puttony. After pulping, these grapes are then added to unfermented wine made from Furmint, a local grape. The more puttons of grape mush are added, the sweeter the wine. For a 5 Puttonyos wine, 125 litres of aszu mush is added to a 136 litre cask (called a gönc). Due to the way it is made, Tokaji tastes almost like a cross between a sherry and a wine, a flavour that is unique. In very good vintages Aszu Essencia is made; this wine has more aszu paste than the usual wine, and the grapes for it are individually selected. This wine sells for upwards of £60 a bottle. Pure Essencia is a juice which forms at the bottom of the putton (a 25-litre putton yields a quarter pint of Essencia). This intense juice is used to add richness to the other wines, but is sold separately, fetching upwards of £600 a bottle at auction.

Of course the best thing to do is to go to lots of tastings and develop your own list of favourites.

WINE SHOPS

England is immensely fortunate in the variety of wine available for sale in its shops. Perhaps this is partly because we have no feelings of chauvinistic pride when it comes to buying wine. If you try to buy a non-French wine in France you are greeted either by disbelief, utter contempt, the sort of look that implies you have been released a tad early into the 'care in the community' scheme, or a mixture of all three. Fortunately, given that almost all English wine tastes like something that should be sent off to a medical lab for tests, we have no such misdirected pride, and can drink wines from wherever we choose. The shops below represent some particularly good examples.

Adnams

Address:	The Cellar and Kitchen Store, Victoria Street, Southwold, Suffolk, IP18 6JW
Phone:	01502 724222
Fax:	01502 724805
Nearest BR:	Darsham
Open:	Monday - Saturday 10:00 - 18:30
Closed:	Bank Holidays
Credit cards:	Visa,Access
Disabled access?	Yes

OK, OK, I know it isn't actually in London, but they do deliver to London, and is so good that you should know about it anyway. Simon Loftus produces superb, entertaining catalogues and has an impeccable range of wine, with lots of interesting examples for those with jaded palates.

Berry Bros & Rudd

Address:	3 St James's Street, Piccadilly, London SW1A 1EG
Phone:	0171 396 9600/9669
Fax:	0171 396 9611
Nearest tube:	Green Park
Open:	
Mon-Fri	09:30-17:00

An amazing shop, worth going just to see the premises even if you don't buy any wine. The place hasn't changed in over 200 years, and some of the staff look as if they remember it when it opened. The wines are actually tucked away in the cellars, so there is no wine on display. Berry Bros, as might be expected, have traditional tastes, so are best at French wines, but also have a good stock of German wines and ports. Despite their terribly plummy accents, the staff's advice is competent and honest. I remember my first visit here: being advised to buy a port half the price of the one I had in mind, a phenomenon not common at most high street off-licences. Ludicrously, they are not open on Saturdays, except during December when they realise that it is sometimes necessary to give the butler a day off.

Fine Wines Of New Zealand

No retail premises	
Phone:	0171 482 0093
Fax:	0171 267 8400

Margaret Harvey is (at the time of writing) one of only 23 female Masters of Wine in the world (there are 140 odd male ones), and runs a wine importing agency specialising in wines from her country of origin. A small but constantly updated list of the finest New Zealand wines available, mainly from small producers who don't produce large enough quantities for the big chains. For real expertise in New World wines, this is the place to ring.

Fortnum & Mason

Address:	181 Piccadilly, London W1A 1ER
Phone:	0171 734 8040
Fax:	0171 437 3278
Nearest tube:	Piccadilly Circus or Green Park
Open:	
Mon-Sat	09:30-18:00
Closed:	Bank Holidays
Credit cards:	Visa,Amex,Access Diner
Disabled access?	Yes

Though expensive, Fortnum's stocks certain wines which are hard to get elsewhere (for example, Cloudy Bay from New Zealand around November/ December time). An excellent range of champagnes in particular, though if you can find what you want at Majestic or Oddbins you will find things cheaper. A great place in which to browse.

The Grape Shop

Address:	135 Northcote Road Wandsworth London SW11 6DX
Phone:	0171 924 3638
Fax:	0171 924 3670
Nearest tube:	None (Clapham Junction BR)
Open:	
Mon - Thu:	10:00 - 14:00
	17:00 - 21:30
Fri, Sat:	10:00 - 21:30
Sunday	12:00 - 15:00
	19:00 - 21:00
Disabled access?	Yes

An excellent wine merchant in the busy Northcote Road, the Grape Shop is crammed to overflowing with wine. The range is wide and carefully chosen, with a good selection of Australian and Italian wines, and a fine list of champagnes and ports, as well as New World sparklers, e.g. the excellent Deutz Marlborough Cuvée. The service is knowledgeable and helpful.

Lay & Wheeler

Address:	The Wine Market, Gosbecks Road, Colchester, Essex CO2 9JT
Phone:	01206 764446
Fax:	01206 560002
Nearest BR:	Colchester
Open:	
Mon-Sat	08:00 - 20:00
Closed:	Bank Holidays
Credit cards:	Visa,Amex,Access
Disabled access?	Yes

Another gem of a shop that is too good to miss out, even though it is not in London. Ring up to be added to their distribution list, and you will receive as fine a wine catalogue as exists anywhere in the country. Their list of wines is comprehensive and intelligently chosen, and has, for example, a good selection of German wines, wines that are poorly treated by most London wine merchants. Lay & Wheeler will deliver to London (ring for details).

Lea & Sandeman

Address:	301 Fulham Road, London SW10 9QH
Phone:	0171 376 4767
Fax:	0171 351 0275
Nearest tube:	South Kensington or Brompton Road
Open:	
Monday-Friday:	09:00 - 20:30
Saturday:	10:00 - 20:30
Closed:	Bank Holidays
Credit cards:	Visa,Amex,Access
Disabled access?	Yes

Lea & Sandeman have a general range of wines, but have a particularly good selection of sherries, ports and madeiras. There is another branch at 211 Kensington Church Street, London W8 7LX (0171 221 1982).

O. W. Loeb

No retail premises	
Phone:	0171 482 0093
Fax:	0171 928 1855

Loeb's are a traditional wine merchant who have easily the best list of German wines in the UK. They are really a shipper, so have no retail premises, but will send you their excellent list if you give them a ring. They offer trustworthy advice.

Majestic

various branches	

Generally the cheapest place to buy wine, mainly because you have to buy a minimum of 12 bottles at a time. So if they sell your favourite wine here, you are unlikely to find it anywhere else for less.

Moreno Wines

Address	11 Marylands Road, London W9 2DU
Phone:	0171 286 0678
Fax:	0171 724 3813
Nearest tube:	Paddington
Open:	
Mon-Sat	09:00-21:00
Sun	09:00-12:00
Also at:	
2 Norfolk Place, Paddington, W2,	
0171 706 3055	

A pair of delightful shops which sell mostly Spanish wine, with a touch of Chilean for variety. Such gems as the Gran Coronas Torres, Rioja Alta 904 Reserva and more illustrious bottles such as those from Vega Sicilia may be found here, as well as plenty of good-value reds (sampling Spanish white wines is generally a disappointing or expensive experience, or both, so stick to the reds unless you are a fan of heavy oak-ageing).

Oddbins

Various branches	
Head office:	
Address:	31-33 Weir Road, Durnsford Industrial Estate, Wimbledon, London SW19 8UG
Phone	0181 944 4400
Fax	0181 944 4411

Consistently the best of the chains, Oddbins combines an excellent and diverse list with (generally) helpful and knowledgeable staff. They have an excellent range of New World wines. The only irritation with Oddbins is that their buying power means that they can get now rather arrogant and refuse to stock your favourite wine if they can't get the price they are after. This may be justified by saying 'Oh, that wine wasn't good this year' even when this is patently untrue. This gripe aside, the staff are normally to be trusted and the wines are excellent value.

Oddbins Fine Wines

Address:	41a Farringdon St, London EC4 4AN
Phone:	0171 329 6989
Nearest tube:	Farringdon or Chancery Lane
Open:	varies by branch

This is Oddbins first attempt at moving into the higher end of the market, and the very best of luck to them. The range is good and margins are significantly lower than at some of the more established up-market merchants. Their entry will inject some long overdue competition into the fine-wine market, which is plagued by upper-class twits and ludicrously high profit margins. There is now an alternative branch in Notting Hill (141 Notting Hill Gate, London W11 3LB 0171 229 4082).

La Réserve

Address:	56 Walton Street, Knightsbridge London SW3 1RB
Phone:	0171 589 2020
Fax:	0171 581 0250
Nearest tube:	Knightsbridge, South Kensington or Sloane Square
Open:	
Mon-Sat	9:30 - 21:00
Closed:	Bank Holidays
Credit cards:	Visa,Amex,Access
Disabled access?	Yes (not to cellar)

This up-market establishment, catering to the denizens of Knightsbridge, is not the place to look for bargains as margins here are quite high. However they do have a particularly fine range of dessert wines. As a nice additional touch, the shop contains 'The Cellar', where for a rather excessive £10 you can sit down and sample cheeses by Philippe Olivier and pâtés by the Roux Brothers, and you can purchase one of the wines on sale in the shop to try with the food. They run very professional tastings, some offering you the chance to sample rare and expensive wines that would normally be unobtainable, unaffordable, or both.

Howard Ripley

No retail premises	
Address:	35 Eversley Crescent, London N21 1EL
Phone:	0181 360 9804
Fax:	0181 360 9804

A specialist importer of wines from Burgundy, Howard Ripley offers a remarkably wide coverage of the quality wine of this region, so much so as to win 'Burgundy Merchant of the Year' from Wine Magazine for the last two years running. Howard is charming and knowledgeable; ring for a catalogue.

La Vigneronne

Address:	105 Old Brompton Road, South Kensington, London SW7 3LE
Phone:	0171 589 6113
Fax:	0171 581 2983
Nearest tube:	South Kensington
Open:	
Mon-Fri	10:00 - 21:00
Sat	10:00 - 19:00
Closed:	Bank Holidays
Credit cards:	Visa,Amex,Access, Diner
Disabled access?	No

Master of Wine Liz Berry and her husband Mike run this friendly little shop on the busy Old Brompton Road. There is a wide range, from the modest to the greats, and in particular there is a very fine selection of wines from Alsace. Probably the most comprehensive range of wine tastings in London are run by Vigneronne at nearby Imperial College; these are expertly tutored and are excellent value, covering modest regional French wines up to the great classics.

Wine Cellars

Address:	153-155 Wandsworth High Street, Wandsworth, London SW18 4JB
Phone:	0177 871 3979/3970
Fax:	0181 874 8380
Nearest tube:	East Putney, or (BR) Wandsworth Town
Open:	
Mon-Fri	11:30 - 20:30
Saturday	10:00 - 20:30
Closed:	Bank Holidays
Credit cards:	Visa,Access
Disabled access?	Yes

Specialists in Italian wine, Wine Cellars have an excellent range of wines from the new, exciting producers who are lifting Italian winemaking out of the doldrums at present. There is a good general selection, and you can even buy olive oil. They run regular wine tastings in a room above the shop; these are relaxed and informative.

Bibliography

Larousse Gastronomique, Mandarin 1988, 0-74930316-6

Barr, Andrew, *Wine Snobbery*, Faber & Faber 1988, 0-571-15060-8

Bhumichitr, Vatcharin, *The Taste Of Thailand*, Pavilion Books 1991, 185145-183-8

Broadbent, Michael, *Michael Broadbent's Pocket Guide to Wine Tasting*, Mitchell Beazley 1992, 0-85533-690-0

Brock, Stephen, *Liquid Gold*, Constable 1987, 0-09-466920-1

Clarke, Oz, *New Classic Wines*, Mitchell Beazley 1991, 0-85533-911-X

Encyclopedia Britannica, The, 15th edition, 0-85229-529-4

Grigson, Jane (editor), *The World Atlas of Food*, Spring Books 1988, 0-600-55929-7

Howe, Robin, *Regional Italian Cookery*, International Wine & Food Society 1972, 0-7153-5182-6

Isuji, Shizuo, *Japanese Cooking: A Simple Art*, Kodansha 1980, 0-87011-399-2

Jackson, Michael, *Michael Jackson's Beer Companion*, Mitchell Beazley 1993, 1-85732-181-2

Jaffrey, Madhur, *A Taste of India*, Pavilion 1985, 0-85145-198-6

Little, Alistair, *Keep It Simple*, Conran Octopus 1993, 1-85029-531-X

Millon, Marc and Kim, *Flavours of Korea*, André Deutsche 1991, 0-233-98635-9

Owen, Sri, *Indonesian Food and Cookery*, Prosper Books 1976, 0-907325-29-7

Richie, Donald, *A Taste of Japan*, Kodansha 1982, 4-7700-1707-3

Roden, Claudia, *A New Book Of Middle Eastern Food*, Penguin 1986, 0-14-04588-X

So, Yan-Kit, *Classic Cuisine of China*, MacMillan 1992, 0-333 57671 3

Wells, Patricia, *Cuisine Actuelle*, MacMillan 1993, 0-333-57595-6

FEEDBACK FORM

Restaurant/Shop Report

To: Andy Hayler
           c/o Boxtree
           Broadwall House
           21 Broadwall
           London
           SE1 9PL

Restaurant/Shop Name:
Restaurant/Shop Address:

Price Of Meal (per person):

Your Name & Address: *(this is optional, but enables us to acknowledge your comments)*

Your Comments:

RESTAURANTS WITH A NON-SMOKING SECTION

Restaurant	Page	Restaurant	Page
Aubergine	41	Odette's	24
Brilliant	56	Orso	68
Chetna's	56	Osteria Antica Bologna	69
Chez Moi	44	P'tit Normande	49
Chutney Mary	57	Pizza on the Park	82
Clarke's	103	Pizzeria Bel Sit	80
Del Buongustaio	67	Quercia d'Oro	69
Downstairs at 190	16	Rani (Monday & Saturday)	62
Four Seasons	100	Regent	70
The Gate	97	Sabras	62
Iznik	93	Le Soufflé	102
Kensington Place	20	Thai Garden	92
Leith's	21	Two Brothers	39
Mijanou	47	Vegetarian Cottage	34
Museum Street Café	22	Wagamama	75
Noughts & Crosses	23		

RESTAURANTS WITH A ROOM FOR PRIVATE PARTIES

Restaurant	Number Accommodated	Page
L'Altro	45	67
Arisugawa	20	73
Associés	37	41
Atlantic Bar & Grill	150	13
Blah Blah Blah	30	96
Blue Elephant	150	99
Bombay Brasserie	80-100	55
Boyds	40	14
Brilliant	40	56
Capital	24	43
Chez Max	15	43
Chez Nico at Ninety	20	44
Chiang Mai	25	90
Connaught	10 or 22	100
dell'Ugo	14-60	16
Diwana Bhel Poori	36	58
Downstairs at 190	25	16
Dragon's Nest	40	32
L'Escargot	34 or 50	44
Florians	24	68
Four Seasons	12-30	100
Fulham Road	12	18
Fung Shing	30	32
Gay Hussar	12	10
Granita	55	18
Harbour City	40 or 50	36

Restaurant	Number Accommodated	Page
Imperial City	18	33
Ivy	60	20
Kalamaras	26	52
Lanesborough	30-100	101
Launceston Place	12 or 30	21
Le Gavroche	8-20	46
Leith's	40 or 55	21
Les Saveurs	10	50
Madhu's Brilliant	60	60
Maymyo	22	29
Mekong	14	98
Melati	40	64
Mijanou	20	47
Miyama	6 or 10	73
Namaste	35	61
New Loon Fung	30	36
New World	300	37
Nosh Brothers	70	23
Noughts & Crosses	25	23
Odette's	8 or 30	24
Pied à Terre	40	49
Pont de la Tour	22	25
Quercia d'Oro	60	69
Ragam	20	61
Rani	23-60	62
Regent	60-300	70
Royal China	15	37
Rules	18-46	27
Singapore Garden	50	87
Shree Krishna	60	63
Suntory	8	74
Thai Garden	14	92
Vegetarian Cottage	30	34
Wodka	30	83

Entries By Area

Area	Postcode	Name	Type	Page
Central				
Belgravia	SW1	Lanesborough	Restaurant	101
Bloomsbury	W1	Arisugawa	Restaurant	73
Bloomsbury	W1	Museum Street Café	Restaurant	22
Bloomsbury	W1	Pied à Terre	Restaurant	49
Covent Garden	W1	Pages	Cookery Equipment	109
Covent Garden	WC2	Calabash	Restaurant	8
Covent Garden	WC2	Carluccio's	Delicatessen	110
Covent Garden	WC2	Ivy	Restaurant	20
Covent Garden	WC2	Monmouth Coffee Co.	Coffee Shop	108
Covent Garden	WC2	Mortimer & Bennett	Delicatessen	114
Covent Garden	WC2	Neal Street Restaurant	Restaurant	101
Covent Garden	WC2	Neals Yard Dairy	Cheese	105
Covent Garden	WC2	Orso	Restaurant	68
Covent Garden	WC2	Quercia d'Oro	Restaurant	69
Covent Garden	WC2	Rules	Restaurant	27

Soho	W1	Melati	Restaurant	64
Soho	W1	Milroys	Whisky	118
Soho	W1	New Loon Fung	Restaurant	36
Soho	W1	New World	Restaurant	37
Soho	W1	Patisserie Valerie	Patisserie	117
Soho	W1	Poons	Restaurant	34
Soho	W1	Richard's	Fish Shop	114
Soho	W1	Slater & Cooke & Bisney & Jones	Butcher	115
Soho	W1	Sri Siam	Restaurant	91
Soho	W1	Ten Ten Tei	Restaurant	74
Victoria	SW1	House of Albert Roux	Delicatessen	111
Victoria	SW1	Jeroboams	Cheese	104
Victoria	SW1	Justin de Blank	Delicatessen	111
Victoria	SW1	Mekong	Restaurant	98
Victoria	SW1	Simply Nico	Restaurant	98

West

Bayswater	W2	Bombay Palace	Restaurant	55
Bayswater	W2	Kalamaras	Restaurant	52
Bayswater	W2	Tawan Oriental Supermarket	Food Shop	116
Bayswater	W2	Royal China	Restaurant	37
Bayswater	W2	Whittards	Tea Shop	108
Chelsea	SW3	Albero & Grana	Restaurant	85
Chelsea	SW10	Aubergine	Restaurant	41
Chelsea	SW3	Canteen	Restaurant	42
Chelsea	SW3	Divertimenti	Cookery Equipment	110
Chelsea	SW1	David Mellor	Cookery Equipment	109
Chelsea	SW3	La Tante Claire	Restaurant	51
Chelsea	SW3	Turner's	Restaurant	51
Chiswick	W4	Bedlington Café	Restaurant	89
Chiswick	W4	Covent Garden Fishmongers	Fish Shop	112
Chiswick	W4	Mortimer & Bennett	Delicatessen	111
Chiswick	W4	Nicholson's	Fish Shop	113
Chiswick	W4	Thai Bistro	Restaurant	91
Ealing	W5	Noughts & Crosses	Restaurant	23
Fulham	SW6	Blue Elephant	Restaurant	99
Fulham	SW10	Chez Max	Restaurant	43
Fulham	SW10	Chutney Mary	Restaurant	57
Fulham	SW3	Fulham Road	Restaurant	18
Fulham	SW10	Nosh Brothers	Restaurant	23
Fulham	SW6	Tandoori Lane	Restaurant	62
Gloucester Road	SW7	Bombay Brasserie	Restaurant	55
Hammersmith	W6	River Café	Restaurant	70
Hammersmith	W6	The Gate	Restaurant	97
Holland Park	W11	Chez Moi	Restaurant	44
Holland Park	W11	Lidgate	Butcher	115
Holland Park	W11	Maison Blanc	Bakery	104
Kensington	W8	Clarke's Bakery	Bakery	103
Kensington	W8	Clarke's	Restaurant	95
Kensington	W8	Kensington Place	Restaurant	20
Kensington	W8	Launceston Place	Restaurant	21
Kensington	W8	Wodka	Restaurant	82-83
Kingston	KT2	Ayudha	Restaurant	83
Kingston	KT2	Jarvis	Fish	113
Kingston	KT2	Petit Max	Restaurant	48

South

East

City	EC1	Stephen Bull's Bistro & Bar	Restaurant	28
City	EC2	Sri Siam City	Restaurant	90
Farringdon	EC1	Eagle	Restaurant	17
Farringdon	EC4	Oddbins Fine Wines	Wine	136
Farringdon	EC1	Quality Chop House	Restaurant	26
Leytonstone	E11	Plantation Inn	Restaurant	30
London Bridge	SE1	Pont de la Tour	Restaurant	25
London Bridge	SE1	Butlers Wharf Chop House	Restaurant	15
Whitechapel	E1	Blooms	Restaurant	76
Whitechapel	E1	Lahore Kebab House	Restaurant	60
Whitechapel	E1	Namaste	Restaurant	61
Woodford	Essex	Pizzeria Bel Sit	Restaurant	80

North

Belsize Park	NW3	Vegetarian Cottage	Restaurant	34
Camden	NW1	Belgo	Restaurant	11
Crouch End	N8	Associés	Restaurant	41
Crouch End	N8	Florians	Restaurant	68
Euston	NW1	Diwana Bhel Poori	Restaurant	58
Euston	NW1	Viniron	Oriental Food Shop	116
Finchley	N3	Rani	Restaurant	62
Finchley	N3	Two Brothers	Restaurant	39
Haverstock Hill	NW3	Marine Ices	Icecreams	118
Highbury	N5	Bodali	Restaurant	54
Highbury	N5	Iznik	Restaurant	93
Islington	N1	Anna's Place	Restaurant	84
Islington	N1	Granita	Restaurant	18
Islington	N1	Steve Hatt	Fish Shop	112
Kilburn	NW6	Singapore Garden	Restaurant	87
Muswell Hill	N10	Toff's	Fish'n'chips	39
Primrose Hill	NW1	Odette's	Restaurant	24
Willesden	NW10	Sabras	Restaurant	62
Wembley	Middlesex	Chetna's	Restaurant	56
Wembley	Middlesex	Curry Craze	Restaurant	57
Wembley	Middlesex	Geetanjali	Restaurant	58

INDEX

Central London

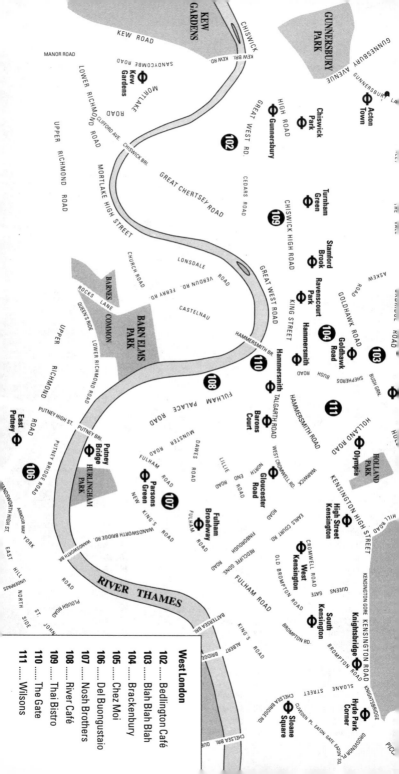

KEW GARDENS

KEW ROAD

CHISWICK

KEW BRI

MANOR ROAD

LOWER RICHMOND ROAD

SANDYCOMBE ROAD

Kew Gardens Φ MORTLAKE

CLIFFORD AVE.

UPPER RICHMOND ROAD

MORTLAKE HIGH STREET

GREAT CHERTSEY ROAD

GUNNERSBURY PARK

GUNNERSBURY AVENUE

GUNNERSBURY LA.

Acton Town Φ

HIGH ROAD

Gunnersbury Φ

Chiswick Park Φ

GREAT WEST RD.

102

CEDARS ROAD

CHISWICK BRI

Turnham Green Φ

CHISWICK HIGH ROAD

109

LONSDALE ROAD

CHURCH ROAD

VERDUN RD.

FERRY RD.

CASTELNAU

GREAT WEST ROAD

Stamford Brook Φ

Ravenscourt Park Φ

KING STREET

Hammersmith Φ

GOLDHAWK ROAD

Goldhawk Road Φ

104

ASKEW ROAD

103

BUSH GRN.

BARNES COMMON

ROCKS LANE

QUEEN'S RIDE

BARN ELMS PARK

LOWER RICHMOND ROAD

HAMMERSMITH BR.

Hammersmith **110** Φ

SHEPHERDS BUSH ROAD

111

HAMMERSMITH ROAD

HOLLAND ROAD

HOLLAND PARK

UPPER RICHMOND ROAD

PUTNEY HIGH ST.

PUTNEY BRI.

108 Φ FULHAM PALACE ROAD

TALGARTH ROAD

Barons Court Φ

WEST CROMWELL RD.

WARWICK ROAD

Olympia Φ

KENSINGTON HIGH STREET

East Putney Φ

PUTNEY BRIDGE ROAD

Putney Bridge Φ

HURLINGHAM PARK

NEW KING'S ROAD

DAWES ROAD

MUNSTER ROAD

FULHAM ROAD

Parsons Green Φ

107

LILLIE ROAD

NORTH END ROAD

Gloucester Road Φ

Fulham Broadway Φ

FINBOROUGH ROAD

EARLS COURT RD.

West Kensington Φ

CROMWELL ROAD

High Street Kensington Φ

KENSINGTON GORE KENSINGTON ROAD

HILL ROAD

106

WANDSWORTH HIGH ST.

ARNDUR WAY

YORK ROAD

EAST HILL

NORTH SIDE

ST. JOHN'S

PLOUGH ROAD

WANDSWORTH BRIDGE RD.

KING'S ROAD

RECLIFFE GDNS.

OLD BROMPTON ROAD

South Kensington Φ

QUEENS GATE

BROMPTON RD.

KENSINGTON GORE

Knightsbridge Φ

Hyde Park Corner Φ

SLOANE STREET

KNIGHTSBRIDGE

PIC

RIVER THAMES

BATTERSEA BRI.

ALBERT BRIDGE

KING'S ROAD

CHELSEA BRIDGE RD.

EATON GATE EATON SQ.

GROSVENOR PL. EATON

Sloane Square Φ

CHELSEA BRI.

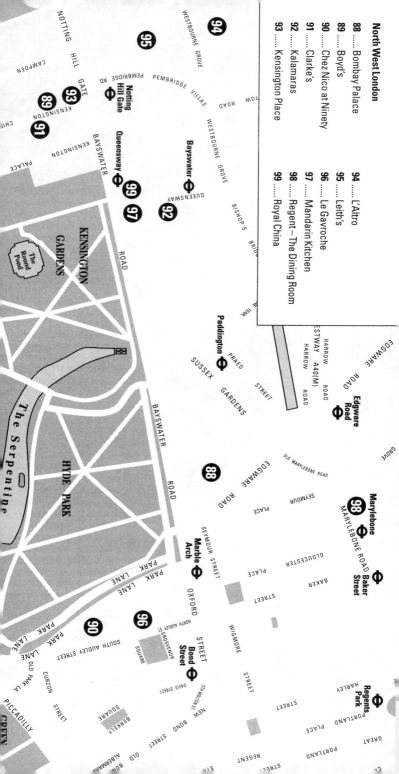

North West London

88 ...... Bombay Palace
89 ...... Boyd's
90 ...... Chez Nico at Ninety
91 ...... Clarke's
92 ...... Kalamaras
93 ...... Kensington Place

94 ...... L'Altro
95 ...... Leith's
96 ...... Le Gavroche
97 ...... Mandarin Kitchen
98 ...... Regent – The Dining Room
99 ...... Royal China

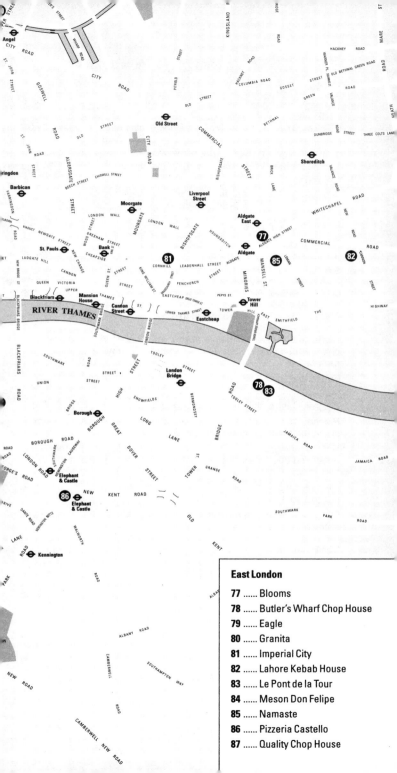

HOW TO ORDER TITLES FROM BOXTREE

REFERENCE:
1-85283-920-1 London Transport Capital Guide   £6.99 pb

QUIZ:
0-7522-0814-4 Trekmaster Quiz Book (David MacCandless) £4.99 pb

COOKERY:
1-85283-952-X Robert Carrier's Gourmet Vegetarian   £9.99 pb
1-85283-998-8 Wagamama: Way of the Noodle   £10.00 pb

HUMOUR:
0-7522-0854-3 Dilbert: Always Postpone Meetings with
              Time Wasting Morons (Scott Adams)   £4.99 pb
0-7522-0849-7 Dilbert: Shave the Whales (Scott Adams)   £4.99 pb
0-7522-0943-4 Beavis and Butthead: This Book Sucks   £6.99 pb

FILM TIE-IN:
0-7522-0886-1 Solitaire For 2   £5.99 pb

STREET FICTION:
0-7522-0925-6 Backstreets: Big Up   £3.99 pb
0-7522-0925-6 Backstreets: Slackness   £3.99 pb
0-7522-0925-6 Backstreets: Herbsman   £4.99 pb
0-7522-0925-6 Backstreets: Junglist   £4.99 pb

*All these books are available at your local bookshop or can be ordered
direct from the publisher. Just tick the titles you want and fill in the
form below.*

Prices and availability subject to change without notice.

Boxtree Cash Sales, P.O. Box 11, Falmouth, Cornwall TR10 9EN

Please send a cheque or postal order for the value of the book and
add the following for postage and packing:

U.K. including B.F.P.O. – £1.00 for one book plus 50p for the second
book, and 30p for each additional book ordered up to a £3.00
maximum.

Overseas including Eire – £2.00 for the first book plus £1.00 for the
second book, and 50p for each additional book ordered.

OR please debit this amount from my Access/Visa Card (delete as
appropriate).

Card Number | | | | | | | | | | | | | | | | |

Amount £ ....

Expiry Date ....

Signed ....

Name ....

Address ....

....

....